Masculinities without Men?

Sexuality Studies Series
Becki Ross, General Editor

This series focuses on original, provocative, scholarly research examining from a range of perspectives the complexity of human sexual practice, identity, community, and desire. Books in the series explore how sexuality interacts with other aspects of society, such as law, education, feminism, racial diversity, the family, policing, sport, government, religion, mass media, medicine, and employment. The series provides a broad public venue for nurturing debate, cultivating talent, and expanding knowledge of human sexual expression, past and present.

Jean Bobby Noble

Masculinities without Men? Female Masculinity in Twentieth-Century Fictions

UBC Press · Vancouver · Toronto

09 08 07 06 05 5 4 3 2

Printed in Canada on acid-free paper

National Library of Canada Cataloguing in Publication

Noble, Jean Bobby
Masculinities without men? : female masculinity in twentieth-century fictions / Jean Bobby Noble.

(Sexuality studies, ISSN 1706-9947)
Includes bibliographical references and index.
ISBN 0-7748-0996-5 (bound).–ISBN 0-7748-0997-3 (pbk.)

1. Gender identity in literature. 2. Lesbianism in literature. 3. Masculinity in literature. 4. Literature, Modern–History and criticism. I. Title. II. Series.

PN56.G45N62 2003 809'.93353 C2003-905045-9

Canadä

UBC Press gratefully acknowledges the financial support for our publishing program of the Government of Canada through the Book Publishing Industry Development Program (BPIDP), and of the Canada Council for the Arts, and the British Columbia Arts Council.

This book has been published with the help of a grant from the Canadian Federation for the Humanities and Social Sciences, using funds provided by the Social Sciences and Humanities Research Council of Canada.

Printed and bound in Canada by Friesens
Set in Stone by Brenda and Neil West, BN Typographics West
Copy editor: Joanne Richardson
Proofreader: Jillian Shoichet

UBC Press
The University of British Columbia
2029 West Mall
Vancouver, BC V6T 1Z2
604-822-5959 / Fax: 604-822-6083
E-mail: info@ubcpress.ca
www.ubcpress.ca

Contents

Acknowledgments

It is by now commonplace to say that a work is the product of many minds, hearts, and conversations. This was true of the project which launched this current work and it remains true of this final book version. For believing in the project I thank Jean Wilson at UBC Press. For brilliance in completing the project with me, extraordinary thanks are due also to Darcy Cullen. Irreplaceable friends provided conversation, love, respect, patience, and above all, space for me to actualize this as both an intellectual and a personal process: Anna Camilleri, Dunja Baus, Anju and Mai at the Toronto Women's Bookstore, Fleen, Chuck, Trish Salah, Christy Carlson, Susanna Luhmann, Ummni Khan, and the Khan family – all of you walked this with me and I can never fully tell you how much your company means to me. Thanks also to Christian Powell for caring for my dog, Keema. In addition, I want to send out love and respect to the many drag kings, ftm trany boyz, queer grrls and other gender queers in the Toronto scene; you've kept me grounded in what counts and I can only hope that my work here honours the courage and audacity it takes to be who you are.

The Leggett-Noble-Epp clan (my family: Helen, Mark, but especially Julie and Nelson, and Ted and Gina, who between them have the coolest kids ever – Christopher, Jason, Zachery, Sydney, and Billy) share in the joy of this like no other family ever could. I love you all. I owe an extensive intellectual debt to Bob Wallace, who supervised the original thesis project but who has since become an invaluable friend. Bob, I want to be just like you when I grow up. Thanks also to the students, staff, and faculty of the Women's Studies program at Queen's University; special thanks to Janice Helland for taking a chance on me.

Two research assistants – Sarah Trimble and Lisa Foad – went above and beyond the call of duty proofing and indexing the manuscript. Your dedication to detail and to the project continues to inspire me, as does your intelligence and great promise. Thank you for your friendship. Of course, the final errors of this text remain my own. This work began, a very long time ago, under the supervision of the late Dr. Kathleen Martindale and it stands as a testimony to her memory.

Finally, it is to brazen-femme-diva OmiSoore H. Dryden that I dedicate this work. Your fierce love and resolute desire re-make me on a daily basis. Without you I would not be half of what I am today; nor would I have had half the fun. It is the time we've spent in quiet paradox that has made these noisy words possible. I remain, devoted and in your service, always.

Introduction: The New Men of 1998

> Many of these guys have been in what would be called lesbian relationships for years.
>
> — Gerald Hannon, "Dicking over Genitals"

> I'm a lesbian man.
>
> — Holly Devor, *FTM: Female-to Male Transsexuals in Society*

Field Hockey in No Man's Land

The end of the twentieth century will be remembered as an interesting time for masculinity. Poet Robert Bly (1990) might concur with Michael S. Kimmel and Michael Kaufman (1995) when they argue that masculinity suffers from internal existential crises caused by all the wrong influences. Bly accuses women of feminizing America's sons while Kimmel and Kaufman argue that those same sons are suffering under the influence of too much of the wrong kind of men. To the horror of Bly, Kimmel and Kaufman suggest that America needs "more Ironing Johns, not more Iron Johns" (27). Still reeling from its socialization failures, masculinity then faces its constitutive absences and ambivalences as articulated by psychoanalysts. Sigmund Freud and Jacques Lacan cite different crises as constitutive of male subjectivity. Freud suggests castration anxiety whereas Lacan argues that lack, acquisition of language, and entry into the symbolic order mark the subject's coming of age. And just when masculinity's internal crises and vacuity become ironically visible, Franz Fanon (1967), Cornel West (1993), Stuart Hall (1997, Kobena Mercer (1994), and Richard Dyer (1988) de-emphasize semblance (gender) and reiterate racial difference. Masculinity, it seems, is not what it used to be. Moreover, and most productive (or perhaps most disturbing, depending upon your point of view) are the assertions of Eve Kosofsky Sedgwick (1995) and other contemporary gender scholars that, sometimes, masculinity has absolutely nothing to do with men whatsoever. My axiomatic starting point in this book borrows its argument from Judith Halberstam (1998a), who contends that the best place to find masculinity is actually the least obvious; that is, not with men at all. Masculinity, she argues, cannot and should not be reduced to the supposedly self-evident male body and its effects (1). Thus, when we want to theorize the constitutive features of masculinity, they are, as Halberstam suggests, best and most accurately discernible the further they travel from what is read as *the* white male body. Hence, *Masculinities without Men?* positions itself as much in masculinity studies as it does in the study of sexual subjectivities.

For reasons that I elaborate below, my study of masculinities in the twentieth century marks its own discursive origins in the period just following the First World War. Canadian-Lebanese novelist Ann-Marie MacDonald (1996) thematizes the discursive changes initiated by both modernity and the First World War in her first novel, *Fall on Your Knees*. MacDonald uses the phrase "No Man's Land" as a trope that is particularly productive for my purposes, suggesting that entry into No Man's Land necessitates suspending one's status as a human being. Once such suspensions have occurred, what steps into the lacunae is instead the rapid proliferation of subjects who seemingly look alike, dress alike, and equally face obliteration. Achieving a foothold on the other side, as it were, may restore humanity but like any journey, what's significant is not the end point but the effects of the process. For the characters in her novel, and indeed, for the subjects under consideration in this book, the journey through a No Man's Land of gender is key.

If gender is the process whereby individual subjects are constituted as subjects of a pre-existing social category, then, as Gayle Rubin (1984) suggests, the sex/gender system – or those sets of arrangements that perform this task – functions best by cloaking its operations and implying that its effects are those of nature. Recent scholarship in the field of gender studies exposes the technologies that construct gender as an unchanging biological essence with self-evident links to physicality, identity, and authority. Conservative ideas about gender dictate that people with male bodies naturally possess both a man's identity and a man's right to wield power. Thus, as Gail Bederman (1995, 7) argues, the ideological process of gender works through a complex political technology made up of institutions, ideas, and daily practices, which, when combined, produce a set of truths about who an individual is or can be based upon his or her body. I share with Rubin, Bederman, and other scholars a belief that this complex political technology was thrown into a crisis during the late twentieth century. In other words, it has now become a site where anatomy, identity, and authority no longer function as synonyms for each other. Thus, no man is automatically granted the status of manhood.

That ontological centre, where a man was considered a man based on the supposedly natural link between those three things, no longer holds. It has been replaced by No Man's Land, where ontological status is suspended. No Man's Land is a stretch of contestatory and discursively productive ground that no man can venture into and remain a coherently ontological subject, where a thousand versions of himself, both like and unlike him, fight for the supposedly singularly "authentic" position on that field. I use the word "productive" to evoke not only a Marxist sense of industrial manufacturing but also the process of externalization by which something is made or allowed to appear. As Calvin Thomas (1996, 34) argues, "production thus discloses ... linguistic and representational processes ... the restricted economy of sexual, textual, and political representation that hails men as masculine subjects in history."

One of the subjects of masculinity repeatedly misread but persistently entrenched within that field is female masculinity. Female masculinity references a range of subject positions – drag king, butch, female-to-male (FTM) transman (both operative and non-operative), trans-gendered man, stone butch – simultaneously constituted by irreducible contradictions between (de)constructions of "bodies" *misread in a certain way* as female and yet masculine. No one of these practices is reducible to the other as exemplary of female masculinity. While the histories of each of these practices are no more reducible to each other than are their constitutive or component parts, the "character" of female masculinity vis-à-vis its most common manifestation – stone butchness – began to undergo changes in and around 1989 with the publication of Joan Nestle's (1987) *A Restricted Country*. Nestle's work reassembled butch-femme sexual cultures of the 1950s and, despite opposition, shed light on these, at that time, long forgotten practices. Sally Munt (1998), Lynda Hart (1994), Judith Halberstam (1998a and 1998b), and others acknowledge that the phrase "butch-femme" references homosexual (differences in sexual orientation) but in terms that are hetero-gendered (differences in gender identifications) and that centre erotic practices that emerged in post-Second World War, urban working-class lesbian communities in the United States. These practices were driven underground after a harsh condemnation by lesbian-feminism in the 1970s but reappeared in the early 1980s after the acrimonious sex wars. In these skirmishes lesbian-feminism, challenging the homophobia of mainstream feminism and attempting to redress the structural inequities between women, argued that butch-femme reproduced dominant/submissive power imbalances thought inherent in heterosexuality. Lesbian-feminism sought to recentre lesbianism as quintessentially feminist by privileging a lesbian subject position – the woman-identified woman – that disavowed all manifestations of masculinity and femininity.

Cultural work in the mid-1980s began to reconceptualize butch-femme, arguing that what was being dismissed was an important erotic system as well as pre-Stonewall lesbian working-class erotic history. Nestle's *A Restricted Country* restores butch-femme as embodied resistance to the sex/gender system by establishing butch-femme as lesbian gender identities that eroticize gender, not power, differences. If sex is biology and gender the culturally constructed subjectivities of masculinity and femininity mapped onto biology, then, as Nestle (1987), Rubin (1984), Feinberg (1993, 1998), and Butler (1990) argue, boys could be girls, and girls could be boys, regardless of biology. Butch or masculine women challenge the "naturalness" and biological essentialism of the sex/gender system while lesbian and bisexual femmes trouble the necessary alignment of gender (femininity) with the overdetermined object choice (male-embodied masculinity). Butch-femme, then, is no longer an imitation of gender but a parody of heterosexuality that deconstructs the operations of the sex/gender system and, subsequently, all gender identities, as performative effects.

More recently, debates around butch-femme have widened to overlap with those of trans-gender, trans-sexuality, gender performativity, and drag "kinging," thus necessitating a similar shift in language from "butch" (referencing particular forms of lesbian masculinity) to "female masculinity" (or particular types of gender expression that bring together both ends of that phrase) (Halberstam 1998a). At stake in many of these debates are the ways in which female masculinity has erroneously become coterminous with ontological "lesbianism" (not all female masculinities are lesbian; not all lesbians are masculine; not all lesbians are female). When pressure is placed on the fault line between masculinities, what is exposed in the fissure are the limitations of heteronormative (read: binaristic) configurations of gender, embodiment, and identities. All too frequently, lesbian configurations of identity that strive towards stability and certainty have assumed a kind of concordance between body shape and gender category – a concordance that, as I show in Radclyffe Hall's *The Well of Loneliness,* Leslie Feinberg's *Stone Butch Blues,* and Rose Tremain's *Sacred Country*, have reproduced the limitations and, sometimes, the violence of a naturalized biological essentialism.

Thus, as part of a larger agenda that attempts to rethink the strategic use of gender essentialisms, *Masculinities without Men?* hypothesizes four axioms of "gender studies" (Sedgwick 1995). First, sometimes masculinity has nothing to do with men. Similarly, female masculinity and/or butch identity in women is largely, but not exclusively, lesbian. Second, masculinity and femininity are in many respects orthogonal to each other (i.e., they are not at opposite ends of the same axis but, rather, constitute different social and psychic axes). Gender-queering masculinity (drag kings, butch and stone butch masculinities, tomboys, girlfags, intersexed by design, he-she's, boydykes, etc.) is a torsional queering, or performance, of heteronormative masculinity, while transitive identities (those such as FTM trans-sexuality that are not necessarily queer but that are marked by subjectivity/somatic incongruities) linger in and around the critical limitations of heteronormative masculinities. Third, because some people are more gendered than others, masculinity and femininity are "threshold effects" where quantitative increments in somatic signifiers of gender along one axis can suddenly appear as qualitative differences on the other. For my purposes here, this penultimate axiom is crucial. Figuratively, this means that it is sometimes necessary to cross over the threshold of one thing (butchness and queerness), or to flip its switches from on to off, in order to register on an entirely different scale (FTM trans-sexual). In terms of race, however, the opposite is true. It is necessary to invert that which is normally hypervisible (people of colour) in order to see what white people are not supposed to see (whiteness). Finally, in masculinity/femininity, a dynamic of self-recognition mediates between bodies and gender performance. Influenced by the interrogation of gender on the part of second wave feminism, contemporary studies in masculinity have intensified masculinity as a heteronormative and anxious imperative, shifting the terms from straightforward descriptions of maleness to a critical exploration of "masculinity" as a complex set of meanings. This field of inquiry suggests that masculinity (and, by implication, female masculinity) is a category that alters across time, region, social class, and ethnicity.

Recalling the axioms that masculinity is not always about men, and that female masculinity is a torsional performance of masculinity, I argue that contemporary masculinity has shifted from the singular to the plural – a series of subjectivities inflected by and articulated through a variety of positions, discourses, institutions, and apparatuses. Similarly, female masculinity has proliferated and mutated from the indeterminate subject of Hall's *The Well of Loneliness* (Chapter 2), who vacillates continuously between the axes of masculinity and femininity, to the complexly transgendered and partially trans-sexed subjects that I discuss in Chapter 3 (Jess in *Stone Butch Blues* and Martin in *Sacred Country*). In other words, I argue that contemporary fictions of female masculinity are ambivalently enabled by the historical but, more important, discursive "event" (both publication and banning) of Hall's novel, signalling its productive success but also its epistemological and discursive limitations. These contemporary gender-variant fictions are grafted from a representational history articulated by Radclyffe Hall through Stephen Gordon. Thus, they inadvertently repeat what Hall did when she created Stephen; that is, they graft discursive but also self-articulating practices from past knowledges and representational practices (including those already and equally bound by discourses of race and nation) in order to present what is imagined as new in a world of *borrowed and always already inhabited language*.

In *The Well of Loneliness* Stephen Gordon finds two texts with which to rewrite himself: sexology and the Bible. Each complements his father's legacy to him – British aristocratic masculinity. Armed with the alibis that each provides, Stephen is enabled into language and into subjectivity, with the alibis functioning as the condition of both possibility and limitation.

In other words, the "revolutionary" ardour for Stephen and for the late twentieth-century gender-variant subjects that follow in his footsteps is dressed in borrowed clothing. Stephen's alibi of essence still flourishes in the discourses of female and trans-sexual masculinities at the close of the twentieth century, which suggests that each is bound by the very thing it cites. These "men" are making their own history; they are not making it under circumstances chosen by themselves but, rather, under circumstances directly encountered, given, and transmitted from the past (Marx 1977, 300). That past and those circuits of transmission are inevitably but irreducibly grafted from and bound with and by *The Well of Loneliness*.

The increasing visibility and politicization of gender-variant identities – intersexual individuals; non-operative, pre-operative, and post-operative FTM and MTF trans-sexuals; trans-gendered people – that exist outside of a supposedly referential epistemology and linguistic systems function as touchstones for what can be (somewhat reductively) identified as the condition of postmodernity. As Susan Stryker (1998, 147) notes in her introduction to "The Transgender Issue" of *GLQ:*

> That a signifier does not point to its signified in any direct manner has been something of a first principle in linguistic theory for most of the twentieth century; only more recently, however, has it become socially significant that the signifier "gender" does not reference a signified "sex" in quite the direct way assumed by the idea of a "sex/gender system." ... As such, these phenomena become sources of cultural anxiety and semiotic elaboration ... [and] provide a site for grappling with the problematic relation between the principles of performativity and a materiality that, while inescapable, defies stable representation.

Nowhere is this poststructuralist crisis of language and representation more evident than in the smallest but most resonant discursive traces that mark identity: gendered pronouns. As Stryker notes above, when "gender" no longer references "sex," then the pronouns "he" and "she" can no longer reference a discernibly gendered body. In *Masculinities without Men?* I use pronouns strategically to reference precise rearticulations of counter-discursive subjectivities and practices. If subjects are in dialogue with discourse and speak it as often as they are spoken by it, then the processes of "self-articulation," which, as I have already noted, are also the object of this book, are themselves metadiscursive. For example, the verb "to articulate" can, according to the *Oxford English Dictionary*, mean one of two things simultaneously: (1) to divide into words, pronounce, distinctly utter and (2) (as a transitive verb) to connect or mark with or by joints, or with flexibly connected sections. In other words, to articulate means to be able to express oneself fluently and coherently *and* to be the site where component parts join, as in a knee or hip joint that brings constitutive elements of the same entity together. To articulate that joint means to bring its segmented or constitutive components together to enable functionality or, conversely, to perform its dysfunctionality. When joints bend in ways they are not supposed to, they are often deemed "grotesque." As I argue in Chapter 3, the grotesque bodies of these subjects of masculinity profoundly disturb a phallic economy, the stock from which they are produced.

But the term "articulation" also references a set of theoretical problematics that emerged out of the work of Stuart Hall and his rereading of Ernesto Laclau. Laclau (1977) developed his notion of articulation in reference to Plato's allegory of the cave. Recall that, in Plato's allegory, since childhood men have had their backs to the entrance of a cave and cannot see the outside world. On the wall of the cave are projected shadows of other men, and, by linking the voices of these men to the shadows, the inhabitants conclude that the first derive from the second. One of the men leaves the cave, escapes, and perceives the true origin of the voices. As he leaves the cave the sun blinds him. As he becomes accustomed to it, the vision he gains helps him to understand and unthink the falsehood in which he has been living. Laclau argues that common sense discourse is presented as a system of misleading articulations in which concepts do not appear linked by inherent logical relations but are bound together simply by connotative or evocative links that "custom and opinion" have established between them (7). As a critique, a theory of articulation similarly seeks to break the links between concepts that are the residue of opinion and custom. Accordingly, then, knowledge presupposes a kind of rupture, a disarticulation of ideas that enables us subsequently to construct newly grafted articulations.

As a theory and a method, articulation can be understood as a way of understanding a social formation without falling into the traps of reductionism, where all formations are reduced to a mechanical relation between base and superstructure, and of biological essentialism (Slack 1996, 112). As Jennifer Slack writes, "articulation is a way of thinking the structures of what we know as a play of correspondences, non-correspondences and contradictions, as fragments in the constitution of what we take to be unities" (112). Stuart Hall uses the specific trope of the articulated lorry, or British truck, where the front cab and back trailer can, but need not necessarily, be connected to one another. The result is that the two parts are connected to each other but, because of that linkage, can also be broken apart (Hall 1996a). Thus, an articulation is the form of connection that can make a unity of two different or contradictory elements under certain conditions; but it also is a linkage that is not necessary, determined, absolute, or essential for all time (141). According to Hall, given that the unity of a discourse is really the articulation of different distinct elements that do not have a necessary "belongingness" but that can be "languaged" together, the question to ask of an articulation is: Under what conditions can the connection be forged, made, or disarticulated (141)?

Hall draws on the example of the Rastafarians in Jamaica to show how distinct elements become languaged together. According to him, new cultural (trans-)formations are manifested when what he calls "lines of tendential force" articulate a political group (e.g., Rastafarians) to political, economic, and ideological structures (e.g., the Bible). Hall suggests that Rastafarians have had to transform biblical language, develop it, inflect it, clarify it, and engage it in order to transform it and themselves into a certain kind of consciousness because that consciousness is already bound with the community's historical relation to biblical discourses (143). "In the case of the Rastafarians," Hall argues, "[they] borrowed from a text – the Bible – that did not belong to them; they had to turn the text upside-down, to get a meaning which fit their experience. But in turning the text upside-down they remade themselves; they positioned themselves differently as new political subjects; they reconstructed themselves as blacks in the new world: they became what they are ... This is a cultural transformation" (143). In other words, this particular formation is the product not of an unbroken line of continuity from the past; rather, it is a transformation through a regrafting and a reorganization of the elements of a cultural practice – elements organized together in a new discursive formation.

To articulate the selves at the heart of the texts presented here is to read how they similarly join, attach, detach, dis(as)semble, or disjoin(t) discursive and epistemological elements not only to function within those economies but also to foreground and trouble their articular machineries. These subjects also reorganize elements of existing social formations to make them, and themselves, new. They cite authoritative sex/gender discourses, which, for Radclyffe Hall, include biblical and sexological texts, to enable resistant counter-citational articulations. In other words, to create "something new," an identity or a gender supposedly not thinkable inside the sex/gender system, the authors under study often evoke an identity that is thinkable in order to resignify what that gender looks like and, indeed, how it dysfunctions outside the limitations of bodies as the current episteme "articulates" them. They performatively cite authorities at the same time as their self-articulation is enabled by them to effect dysfunctional counter-citational practices in, around, and through the category of female masculinity. This is a social category that, I argue, is inciting riotous destabilizations, performing as a category in/as crisis. That said, the particular formations of gender articulations manifest in *The Well of Loneliness* are also languaged by and with white supremacy. As Stuart Hall (1996a, 143) notes, these formations are made up of elements "which do not in themselves have any necessary political connotations." In the case of white supremacy, the imperative is that whiteness qua race does not have political connotations as it is hinged with discourses of gender to form a new discursive formation. Chapter 2 seeks to disarticulate that formation.

As I argue in detail in Chapter 1, by 1928 the sites of homosexuality and femininity became the objects of intensification via the supposedly neutral disciplinary powers of regulation, policing, and punishment when Radclyffe Hall's *The Well of Loneliness* was seized and banned. The effect was not the eradication or repression of a female homosexual subject but, rather, its epistemological realization. Many other early twentieth-century texts featured lesbian, gender-inverted, or otherwise sexually "deviant" subjects. Indeed, one of the important thematics to emerge out of the early twentieth-century modernist literary cultures of which Radclyffe Hall was a part was not only the interrogation of masculinity but, more precisely, the representations of both masculinity and femininity as modern(ist) subjects in crisis.

Regardless of whether or not one argues that a crisis in identity begins or follows modernism, there can be little argument that modernism, if not ambivalently, responds to, contests, or attempts to work through the crises of modernity. In other words, one of the irrefutable conditions of the modern world is its own paradoxically unimaginable and profound transition and destabilization due to industrialization, capitalist market relations, urbanization, sustained war, and so forth. A modernist aesthetic self-consciously (and perhaps paradoxically) experiences – indeed, hails – the end of time and history. Thematically, modernist texts began to re-imagine and reconfigure themselves in their own thematics, which were often preoccupied with identity, voice and silence, subjectivity, and (especially the fracturing of) consciousness vis-à-vis spatiality and the city. Stylistically, modernist writers often deployed a method that was anti-representational, anti-realist, obsessed with both the end of literary time and a formal poetics of the "New." In short, modernism is a wholly unresolved (and irresolvable) contradictory (anti-)tradition of rupture; it is a ruptured tradition turned against itself, aggressively rejecting the supposed authorities (moral, formal, social, literary) of its own literary and historical past. Finally, it is that which, by interrogating form over (sometimes as) content, paradoxically both affirms and denies art. In other words, that spasm of rebellion that is/was modernism compelled a contestatory imperative to break from the past in order to rupture tradition (clustered around the complexities of form, the representation of inward states of consciousness), foregrounding (rather than disavowing) the often nihilistic disorder behind the ordered surface of life and reality, consciousness itself freeing art from the burdens of the dull habit of formal and literary convention.

Male writers like F. Scott Fitzgerald, T.S. Eliot, Ernest Hemingway, Tennessee Williams, William Faulkner, and D.H. Lawrence, to mention only a few, stage this crisis in white masculinity in a variety of textually nonconventional ways. For instance, Hemingway's early novels, *The Sun Also Rises* (1970) and *A Farewell to Arms* (1969), aggressively perform, to excess, masculinity as a profound woundedness. But femininity was similarly imploding in fictions of the early twentieth century, showing the productive impossible complexities of femininity, narrative, and voice (impossibilities with which Virginia Woolf and Gertrude Stein must also come to terms). Zora Neale Hurston's (1978) *Their Eyes Were Watching God;* Nella Larsen's (1986) *Passing;* Rosamond Lehmann's (1927) *Dusty Answer;* Clemence Dane's (1936) *Regiment of Women;* Compton Mackenzie's (1928) *Extraordinary Women;* Virginia Woolf's (1942) *Orlando;* Djuna Barnes's (1979, 1928) *Nightwood* and *Ladies Almanac* are examples. As are such dramas as Sholem Asch's (1972) *The God of Vengeance* and Edouard Bourdet's (1926) *The Captive*. All of these works interrogate the supposed self-evidence of femininity as well as the relationships between sex, gender, sexuality, desire, and representation.

In many ways, what seem now to be recognizable as "lesbian" texts of the early twentieth century were exploring the paradoxes at the heart of any imperative towards self-representation. Lillian Hellman's (1942) *The Children's Hour,* for example, metatextually performs this paradox by staging the dangers of even negative representations of female same-sex desire: even though its main characters, Martha and Karen, are accused, in the terms of the play, of something horrible, Martha comes to terms, as it were, with the "new meanings" that inevitably follow Mary's accusations: "Every word will have a new meaning" (66). Martha recognizes herself in those new meanings. In other words, the world of the play actually produces a negative representation into which Martha reads herself: "There's something in you and you don't know it ... and [then] there you are, seeing it for the first time" (71). While these "meanings" are not positive in the sense of challenging negative stereotypes, they are *productive;* that is, while there are no laws per se against female same-sex desire, there are interdictions that accord it the status of the "not permitted," the "unspeakable," and the "unintelligible." The irony, of course, is that to render it non-permitted, unspeakable, or unintelligible is to continually "speak," or, for my purposes here, "represent," it. "It" becomes the thing strictly forbidden but continuously produced in order for the interdiction(s) to function. Two other early non-canonical modernist plays – *The God of Vengeance* and *The Captive,* as well as Hall's *The Well of Loneliness* – all function in such paradoxical ways: all were subject to legal interdiction (the strictly forbidden or non-permitted) while creating or opening up subject positions that produce desire (the thing continuously demanded) as their effect. Unlike novels that are usually read in private, *The God of Vengeance* and *The Captive* also contributed to the production of social space and the socio-political context of reception that, like *Salomé* in the Pemberton Billing trial (which I discuss in Chapter 1), always already taint their viewing audience.

Asch's *The God of Vengeance* was the first play with a lesbian theme produced on the American stage. While formally conservative, it challenges negative representations by presenting its themes in morally ambiguous ways. Yankel, patriarch and protagonist of the play, runs a brothel in the basement of his home. Upstairs, he purchases a Torah Scroll to help appease what he perceives to be the vengeful God of the Old Testament in order to keep his daughter, Rivkele, pure for marriage. Not only does the play actually stage physical intimacy between women – Act I ends with Rivkele and her lover, Manke (a young prostitute from her father's brothel), alone on stage passionately kissing and touching, a direct (and pleasurable) challenge to the "not permitted" interdiction; and later in Act II Manke and Rivkele "pretend" to be bride and groom on their wedding night – but it also stages a failure in "truth." In the end Yankel's religious faith is permanently shattered by his own inconsistencies and contradictions. Thus, one of the play's thematics involves a tension between "Old" World moral authorities (religion) and "new" modern values, especially those of capitalist market relations – at one point, one of the prostitutes challenges the way sexuality is burdened with an excess of moral significance: "You think we are any different from the girls who go in[to] business?" (95). But, perhaps most important, when Yankel discovers that Rivkele spent the night with her lover (he does not know her lover is a woman), he demands to know whether or not she is still a virgin. At the emotional climax of the play, Rivkele answers him with a desperate "I don't know" (111). Here the play poses a direct challenge to the "unintelligible" interdiction. While lesbianism is indeed unintelligible within terms of the sex/gender system as the play defines it, it also sends that system into a conceptual crisis, revealing its limitations and demanding of the play's audience that it, too, question the categories of supposedly self-evident sexual "truth." Even though, in the end, Rivkele's father banishes her to the brothel, the questions the play raises cannot be contained by the less-than-positive images, especially of Manke. Finally, the play itself was brought to the attention of the courts, and all the actors were arrested, charged, and convicted (by a jury) of producing a play deemed "obscene" and "immoral." The arrest and conviction made front-page news in most of the important New York daily newspapers as it was the first time that an American jury had found performers guilty of presenting immoral public entertainment. The "event" of *The God of Vengeance* enabled the proliferation of the very identities that legal interdiction attempted to contain.

Bourdet's *The Captive* was the second play to put female same-sex desire on the American stage. Here, our main character is Irène, a young woman (apparently motherless) who refuses to travel with her family and is presumed to be preoccupied with a lover. In a desperate bid to remain in Paris she gives her father the name of a young man – Jacques – who was a suitor but is now pursuing an affair with Françoise. We subsequently discover that her lover is, in fact, a woman: Mme D'Aiguines. The fascinating thing about Bourdet's play is that our seductive "villainess," Mme D'Aiguines, never appears on stage. She is the wife of a friend of Jacques, M. D'Aiguines, and she is either discussed on stage by her husband and Jacques as a powerful seductress or is represented on stage by a bouquet of violets (curiously, this play was so popular that after its well-publicized encounter with the American courts the sale of violets dropped in New York City flower stores to a small but very telling amount). Moreover, heterosexuality comes under the microscope in this play and, like religious and sexual truth in Asch's play, is troubled as a source of moral authority. The attachments between these "kinds" of woman is likened to a secret alliance of two beings who understand each other because they are of the same ontological species. Even more interestingly, "these women" are likened to a kind of country where men become the stranger and enemy. After Jacques and Irène have lived together in an "empty" marriage, Jacques courts his previous mistress and tells her that, after living in a marriage with a woman who does not return his passion, he has learned something about himself. He tells Françoise that he longs to come home to the "people of his homeland," to the people who speak his language: "It's tiresome to talk when one isn't understood. One wearies of it ... I've come back to my own people" (237).

Thus, sexual difference is represented as a kind of ethnic, linguistic, or national difference, an "other," a crisis in representation that I return to more thoroughly in Chapters 2 and 3. Moreover, the fact that Mme D'Aiguines functions as an erotically powerful absent presence facilitates a kind of pleasurable erotic transference by women in the audience, enabling them to fill in their own details, as it were. In the end, not only does Irène leave Jacques to be with her lover, but Jacques leaves his marriage to be with Françoise. While *The Captive* does portray Mme D'Aiguines negatively and Irène as a "prisoner" of her unnatural desires, the gap left by failing-to-materialize Mme D'Aiguines manipulates the "not permitted" interdiction by refusing to embody her as an object of erotic contemplation. Once again, this play suffered under the gaze of the censors and the police who staged a rather sensational "night-stick" raid on the production. One historian unknowingly articulates the ironic effect of such actions: the play "revealed to thousands of innocents the fact that the world contained such a phenomenon as homosexuality" (Curtin 1987, 44).

While these and many other texts explored lesbian and gender-variant subjects, Hall's novel began to accrue currency as "the" lesbian novel of the period due, in part, to its construction of Stephen as the prototypical invert. *The Well of Loneliness*, vis-à-vis its symbiotic relationship with nineteenth-century sexology and its alibi of essence, provides a game of truth, or what Michel Foucault (1991, 16) calls "an ensemble of rules [or procedures] for the production of truth" about the sexual self. Its protagonist, Stephen Gordon, recognizes or constitutes himself as a cross-gendered or masculine subject. At the same time, though, I argue that both sexology and *The Well of Loneliness* produce a resistant subject, for the non-masculinized "feminine" and lesbian subject recognizes/constitutes herself as a discursive and epistemological impossibility. Both of these subjects emerge as strategies of resistance to the production/invention of rigidly gendered codifications of desire in nineteenth-century sexology. Thus, two paradoxically gendered subjects emerge: the first produced by realization (female masculinity) and the second by resistance (femme, refuted as an epistemological impossibility).

One final note: These debates in No Man's Land over butchness, drag kinging, intersexuality, and trans-sexual and trans-gender identities have profoundly important implications for a subject that haunts this work (and its subjects) but remains, perhaps dangerously so, bracketed. That subject is, of course, lesbian-identified, heterogendered, or bisexual femmes. In many ways female masculinity is as guilty as is heteronormative masculinity of constructing or producing itself in relation to the thing it is compelled not to be – that is, feminine. Thus, I assume the following premise: masculinity's disavowed Other (in this case, the lesbian femme subject) remains an epistemological impossibility in sexological discourse but emerges as a problematic yet productive subject in later twentieth-century lesbian and queer discourse. What continues to be bound in the sex/gender system where same-sex desire is represented as gender inversion is queer femininity. Given that queer, or ironically performed, femininity might be the thing that pushes the limits on binding and bound gender discourses, it also remains in a discursive bind. If Judith Butler (1993, 16) is correct in suggesting that it is "important to think about how and to what end bodies are constructed ... [and which] bodies are not constructed and, further, to ask after how bodies which fail to materialize provide the necessary outside, if not the necessary support, for the bodies which, in materializing the norm, qualify as bodies that matter," then queer femininity in a female body has emerged as resistant but contradictory in relation to queer and queering discourses that have orthogonally privileged cross-gendered bodies and subjects (essentialism, sexology, queer theory). Femme is at once the subject of "nature" (Biddy Martin [1996, 73] argues that she is all too often still (mis)read as a non-performative subject of nature, as "a capitulation, a swamp, something maternal, ensnared and ensnaring"), the subject of an epistemological impossibility (neither feminism nor queer theory have adequately conceptualized her), and the subject of the technologies of white femininity in this moment of late capitalism.

While Radclyffe Hall's *The Well of Loneliness* can be seen as the most productive novel of lesbian identity in the early twentieth century, it, too, raises interesting questions about femme subjectivity that its noisy dialogism can neither contain nor account for. Although a realist text and not at all formally experimental, it, as I have suggested already, deploys an alibi of essence (vis-à-vis sexology) in order to open up new gendered and desiring subjectivities. While Hall writes the stereotypical butch, or invert, in Stephen Gordon, the most troubling and problematic image in the text is that of Mary, the supposedly "non-inverted" woman who becomes Stephen's lover. Despite the negative representations of Mary/femme subjectivity in this novel, Mary persists. Joan Nestle (1987) has argued that, in order to read for femme, one must read between the (textual) lines; by reading between the at times limited portrayal of Mary in Hall's text, one can find a resistant femme subject and a portrait of femme desire and agency. We encounter a femme gaze that pleasurably reads butch as the object of its desire: Mary and Stephen are standing in front of a mirror in their home and, while Stephen grooms herself, Mary watches her, desiring both the strong thin masculine lines as well as the curve of her breasts, "slight and compact, of a certain beauty" (Hall 1928, 321).

Moreover, in earlier scenes we see that, despite the myth in sexology of the invert as sexual aggressor, it is Mary who initiates the consummation of their relationship: Mary lays her hand upon Stephen's knee, imprisons Stephen's fingers in her own, asks Stephen to kiss her goodnight, then tells Stephen she wanted this kiss more than anything in the world (297). Subsequently, the transcripts of the judge's decision to ban the text and the text itself reveal the pleasurable moments between Mary and Stephen: "and that night they were not divided" (313) and "[as] they look[ed] straight into the eyes of a love that was changed – a love made perfect, discarnate ... they drew together" (324). At another point in the novel, Stephen is called home by her mother but is told she cannot bring her lover with her. Mary writes to Stephen in a moment filled with longing and "only one ache": "that letter was full of many things which a less privileged pen had best left unwritten – loyalty, faith, consolation, devotion; all this and much more she wrote to Stephen" (338). That letter, as a moment of enabling self-articulation, is a profound (and articulate) silence where femme desire is supposedly unimaginable but exists nonetheless.[1]

All of these subjects – gender-queers, femme-butch, FTM, MTF, invert, nellie, queen, third sex, hermaphrodite, tomboy, sissy, drag king, female impersonator, cross-dresser, and so on – represent a series of somatically signified yet productive contradictions. My questions are less "What do these contradictions really mean?" or "Who owns them and are they good or bad?" and more "What do they reveal?" "What do they allow (or, conversely, what do they not allow) discursive economies to do?" There are pivotal moments in the twentieth century in which gendered subject positions have been invested with, and articulated to, an important currency within economies of sexuality. *Masculinities without Men?* does not purport to be, as Foucault (1977b, 31) wrote, a history of those past investments in terms of the present; rather, it purports to be a history of present investments.

The Men of 1998

Four recent, albeit very different, community events demonstrate the degree to which the subject of female masculinity remains unstable and contingent regardless of how economies outside of No Man's Land attempt to invest it. While all four of these events occur outside academic institutions and the narratives of theory told inside them, nevertheless they remain intelligible outside of those institutional practices. I include them here as examples of community and so-called "non-academic" events whose subjects rearticulate complex theoretical questions that seem to be the terrain of academic discourse alone. These events skirmish across the field of No Man's Land to re-language and rearticulate elements of social formations in ever-increasing proliferations. I raise them here as examples of the dynamic and contingent nature of cultural and political articulations occurring outside of academe.

"Dicking over Genitals" is an article by Toronto academic and notorious sex-trade worker Gerald Hannon, and it is published in *NOW Magazine*, a free weekly arts magazine produced and distributed in Toronto. Hannon (1998, 18) reports on "Crossing Borders," the twelfth annual convention organized by the US-based International Foundation for Gender Education and hosted in Toronto by Xpressions, the "fastest-growing transgender club in Canada." The convention in downtown Toronto brought together several hundred transvestites, trans-sexuals,[2] cross-dressers (along with their friends, spouses, parents, and significant others) to share information, experience, and advice on living in and with differently embodied gender identities. Hannon describes the convention as a cacophonous mix of individuals. For example, in attendance was Virginia Prince, self-described as a "man for 50 years" but a "woman for 35," someone who has done "everything except go to bed with a guy" and who runs a cross-dressing and transvestite organization called the "Society for the Second Self," which serves primarily heterosexual men and which does not allow gays or trans-sexuals to join. The convention also welcomed Miqqi Alicia, a.k.a. York University philosophy professor Dr. Michael Gilbert, who characterizes her-self and the convention attendees as "the walking deconstruction of the bi-polar gender dichotomy" (21). But the convention also attracted younger people, like two MTFs (male-to-female trans-sexuals) named Siobhan and Tina, "local girls who got engaged to each other the previous Saturday," as well as, for the first time, a large FTM (female-to-male trans-sexual) contingent (21).

Black-and-white photographs of convention participants accompany Hannon's musings about gender, nature, and "the meaning of sexual liberation"; a quick glance at these images by an unsuspecting reader would seemingly reveal next to nothing other than banal and unremarkable-looking white men and women (18). To quote Hannon: "These gals dress rather conservatively ... most of these guys are straight ... [but] it was still a bit like hanging out with a gaggle of kinky Kiwanis" (21). Two things betray this particular statement and, indeed, the article, as perversely ironic: *NOW Magazine*'s choice of Hannon as reporter, and Hannon's choice of the adverb "still." Anyone who has read a Toronto newspaper or watched local news coverage in the two years preceding this article might recognize Hannon's name from the controversy surrounding his termination as professor of journalism at Toronto's Ryerson University.

While Hannon was an employee of Ryerson, he continued to work as a gay sex-trade worker; when he outed himself (as a sex-trade worker) Ryerson fired him. Hannon himself notes the irony of his own reading position: "I've been a gay activist for some 25 years, live in the [gay] ghetto, have done party drag myself ... but what I was seeing was not drag as I had come to understand it ... I spent a lot of time rather dizzily discombobulated. I met a 19-year-old woman who had cut off her own balls. I kept reading for a vocabulary that isn't there yet (though I did discover I was a 'bio-boy'). I wanted the shock of the new. I got it" (18). Clearly, Hannon was commissioned by *NOW Magazine* because of his visibility as a gay activist and sex-trade worker; he was to write a story on what would inevitably be read as a queer event. However, the primary tension that runs throughout Hannon's article and his construction of his own erotic responses to the trans-sexual men he meets at the convention is one of mildly annoying disappointment and disorientation. Sexuality, as Hannon discovers, was not at all the point. From Virginia Prince to the cute "guy," "early 20s, lanky, crew cut, tight white T, jeans," many of the subjects highlighted in Hannon's piece perform post-heterosexual identities, motivating Hannon to conclude: "this past weekend left me wondering whether sexual liberation isn't in fact a subset of a much more powerful phenomenon that's getting called 'gender agnosticism.' This past weekend left me wondering whether the torch hasn't been passed from our [i.e., gay activists'] hands" (21).

Hannon's choice of the term "agnosticism" shows both the parodic and epistemological aesthetics of a queer reading practice that does not quite fit coupled with the temporal anxiety signalled by his use of the term "still" in the simile I cited earlier ("it was still a bit like hanging out with a gaggle of kinky Kiwanis"). Despite the best efforts of feminist, gay, lesbian, and queer scholars to pry sexuality apart from gender, the two terms remain caught in an analytically illicit embrace, an ironic proximity overdetermined by crises in knowledge, constructions of time and space, and, indeed, the very language we used to talk about, well, "it" ("You begin to see the vocabulary problems" [Hannon, 18]). "It" is characterized in any number of ways, as this book suggests; how we even begin to articulate "it" overdetermines exactly how "it" might even be knowable at all.

One of the primary ways that "it" is described as thinkable is through historical and temporal relations of proximity. Hannon's own semantic choices foreground these discursive relations of time: phrases such as "it was still like," "what began as," "the torch hasn't passed from our hands," "the shock of the new" suggest that he is conceptualizing the "new" as emergent in the trans-gender movement rather than in a gay, lesbian, bisexual, or even queer movement that began in a supposedly knowable past and is now "mired in the gloomy swamp of spousal rights and pension plans" (21). At the same time, a gay and lesbian history continues to function as the frame of reference for Hannon and the conference attendees he interviewed. His interviewees would concur: "These," claims one transgender activist interviewed by Hannon, "are our Stonewall years ... This is our first generation of activists," at once evoking and deferring the epistemological, discursive, temporal, and conventionally "historical" frames of reference that make "it" intelligible. The recitation of a gay and lesbian frame of reference is fascinating, given that many of the biologically born men in the "Crossing Borders" convention dress in women's clothes but are accompanied by their female wives and spouses; it is also curious that many of the biologically born women at the convention are transitioning into male bodies through hormone treatment and surgical interventions, identifying throughout the process as heterosexual men; it is curious again that many biologically born men are similarly transitioning into female bodies to complete their sense of themselves as heterosexual women.

"Crossing Borders," the title of the convention, works against the most frequent misreading of the terms trans-sexual and trans-gender, which reads the suffix as suggesting "transcendence." Hannon's conceptualizations of the relationships between gay and lesbian discourse and trans-sexual discourse similarly work against reading the suffix as meaning "transcendence." Despite the at times acrimonious debates over how this term functions, I use the terms "trans-sexual" and "trans-gender" to suggest movement *across* gender difference, bodies, and discourses rather than *beyond* them. Bodies may be reconstructed, but gender is neither transcended nor rendered insignificant. All of the characters in the novels that I discuss find a home in a gender; it just happens to be a gender that differs in meaning from how and what "gender" is conventionally authorized to mean in relation to "sex." Such contingent precision similarly raises the question: what exactly is being crossed? A gay and lesbian liberationist politics, as Hannon suggests? A queer practice? Compulsory engendering and heterosexuality? "Crossing" suggests contrariness, a binary opposition, especially in its definitions of "passing from side to side," "intersecting," "placing crosswise." To cross from one point in a binary opposition to another is not exactly the most productive trope for my purposes here.

This process of evoking a subject only to disavow it betrays an ontological anxiety that underwrites identity politics as they are performed in Hannon's reading of this event and in the twentieth-century prose texts that are the objects of my study. To frame this point differently, the definitional crisis over the ontological discreteness of subjects produces a pattern where a fiction of origins is posited that centres a supposedly new subject in relation to an old one, hence continually (re)producing the new from within the old as if it were somehow always already outside of it. That new subject emerges in and through as well as against the old subject (the more conventionally defined gay and lesbian movements that contested essentialist alignments between bodies and genders and desires, or, conversely the "post-gay-and-lesbian" queer subject who celebrates those interventions). In many ways, the suffix "trans" suggests that somehow it is precisely this gay and lesbian past that is being trans-(c)ended.

Such a notion of transcendence or closure, however, suggests that moving beyond, past, or rising above such discursive histories is even possible. What might fit better is the trope of "grafting" that Laura Doan elucidates in her readings of the deconstructive strategies in Jeanette Winterson's novels. Grafting is a replication process "whereby a plant, perhaps tender or uncertain, is fused into a hardier member of its strain, and so the two take advantage of each other and produce a third kind, without seed or parent" (Doan 1994, 152). The literal process of grafting is an organic reproductive process, where a new shoot might be inserted into a slit of stock from which it receives enough nourishment to generate a new entity, produced by but not reducible to either of the two constitutive elements. As a figurative trope, to graft means to insert something into, on, upon, or together; to insert or fix in or on so as to produce a vital or indissoluble union; to sew together; to attach on to make a "new" thing out of the two. As Doan suggests, this is a much more useful conceptual trope, one that allows us to acknowledge the dependence of the new thing on the other two as it is made out of them but is not reducible to either. As Doan puts it:

> The transnatural practice of grafting does not circumvent, eliminate, or destroy the original ... biological matter that produces a hybrid, and as a result the process that makes an "other" ultimately registers the inceptive binarism as excess, as redundancy. The hybrid presupposes a biological precursor (as opposed to spontaneous regeneration), but cultural (in this case, scientific) intervention bears the responsibility for the act of creation. By becoming "something else" in a complex interplay of independence from and dependence on its biological precursors, the hybrid denatures dominant oppositional paradigms that set one against the other and subsequently accommodates more options. (152)

I use the trope of grafting to signify two processes: The first is that identified by Doan, although I use it as a way of thinking the relation between the manifestation of "trans-gendered" (read: "differently gendered") bodies as effects of the sex/gender system in crisis and transition. The process of grafting, not as an artificial, scientific reproductive mechanism but, rather, as a process of self-making and reproduction outside of (beyond) a heteronormative model, spawns a third hybrid sex. But this is not androgyny, a mix or blending of both (read: "natural") genders. As Doan puts it, "the notion of hybridity resonates with doing violence to nature, which results ... in the scientific equivalent of freaks, mongrels, half-breeds and cross-breeds" (153). This is a strategy of naturally denaturalizing biological essentialisms with a "sexual politics of heterogeneity and a vision of hybridized gender constructions outside an either/or proposition" in order to naturalize "cultural oddities, monstrosities, abnormalities, and [what appear to be] conformities" (154). The trope of grafting thus allows me to argue that gender differences and distinctions are still produced in these spaces but are deployed in trans-sexual and trans-gender discourses to entirely different ends.

The notion of grafting as opposed to crossing also allows me to think the imbrications and radical dependencies that these identities – gay, lesbian, bisexual as well as trans-sexual and trans-gender – have on/with each other both historically (the invert + the lesbian + the trans-sexual) and in the current moment when the differences between them often appear as the effect of productive and performative speech acts. "I am a boy" or "I am not a lesbian" have particular effects that may not be immediate but that emerge over time. One of these productive effects is the materialization or externalization of a body not visible; in the case of the subjects in the fictions I discuss, this is a boy's body. Because these speech-acts are particularly productive I refer to them as "onto-performative" speech acts. The differential process that produces the fantasy of positivity occurs through practices of self-articulation and oppositionality. Thus, my concern is not only the way in which the texts under discussion contest the alignment of bodies, identities, and power but also (indeed, perhaps moreso) the ways they contest discursive practices and force a crisis by grafting articulations onto each other.

An article that appears in April 1998 in *Girlfriends Magazine* clearly depicts this process of grafting new articulations out of older ones through a relation of proximity and oppositionality. If Hannon's argument that resemblance marks the relations between the trans-gendered and ironically heterosexual performances of "Crossing Borders" participants and the mandatory heteronormativity of a Kiwanis convention, then Athena Douris's article, "The Well of Genderlessness: Who Decides If We're Lesbian or Transsexual?," suggests, rather, that dissemblance marks relations within two members of the first group. If Hannon compares two seemingly unlike things (heterosexual men of the Kiwanis and the many different kinds of heterosexual and heterogendered "men" at "Crossing Borders"), then Douris compares two seemingly like things (FTM trans-sexuals and butch lesbians) to complicate these relations even further. Douris reports on a talk given by a developmental child psychologist and a male-to-female trans-sexual, Shoshanna Gillick, to a group of lesbian and gay journalists and scholars on the topic of gender identity disorder (GID). Gender identity disorder is the label used in the American Psychiatric Association's fourth *Diagnostic and Statistical Manual of Mental Disorders* (*DSM IV*) to name and diagnose gender identity confusions. As it now stands, children or adults have GID if they exhibit both a strong and persistent cross-gender identification and discomfort with either their biological sex or the gender role deemed appropriate to their biological sex. Girls, for instance, are well on their way to a diagnosis of GID when they insist on "wearing only stereotypical masculine clothing," "exhibit a preference for cross-sex roles in make-believe play," demonstrate a "marked aversion toward normative feminine clothing," and/or assert that "she does not want to grow breasts or menstruate" (*DSM IV*, quoted in Douris 1998, 18).

Gillick's research tries to complicate such confusing and supposedly self-evident certainties in the *DSM IV* by arguing that none of the criteria for GID in girls seems indicative of a psychological disorder. For instance, she argues that between 50 percent and 75 percent of GID children are actually misdiagnosed. Gillick insists that long-term studies show that up to 75 percent of GID-diagnosed children never have sex changes and, instead, grow up to be gay, lesbian, or bisexual (18). In other words, what appears to be a clearly definable gender identity disorder (GID) according to the *DSM IV*, potentially "correctable" by sex-reassignment surgery, might, in fact, be the early signs of a masculine or butch sexual identification in girls otherwise not "uncomfortable" with their biological sex. Simply put, and despite the resemblances, one (trans-sexual) man's gender identification is not necessarily another (lesbian) butch's sexual orientation. Again, in No Man's Land, sexuality is not necessarily the only stake.

What is at stake both in Douris's article and in the *DSM IV* diagnosis is, in fact, evoked in the article's title. "The Well of Genderlessness" cites Radclyffe Hall's 1928 novel *The Well of Loneliness*, a text that both camps that Douris discusses in her article have claimed almost exclusively as a narrative of origins. Stephen Gordon, the main character of Hall's novel, functions as a contestatory site similar to that described by Douris. As I discuss in Chapter 2, Stephen understands himself best as an "invert," the term used by late nineteenth-century sexology to describe/produce a phenomenon similar to that named by GID – that is, a discomfort, or lack of "fit," between gender identity and biological sex. Some definitions of lesbianism and, recently, FTM trans-sexuality trace discursive histories back to the late nineteenth- and early twentieth-century construction/invention of inversion and, curiously, back to *The Well of Loneliness*. What interests me here is not the truthfulness or accuracy of any of these terms but, rather, the different and numerous ways they function to legitimate different claims to power and truth. The repudiation of these identities flags the discursive limitations of each, suggesting that these subjects are thinkable through the contestation of limits, boundaries, and exclusions.

For instance, much of the lesbian criticism of Hall's novel has dismissed Stephen's masculinity in order to articulate a lesbian-feminist subject not (obviously) bound by gender difference but, rather, by object choice: girls instead of boys. Recent trans-sexual and queer theory has again contested early feminist readings of *The Well of Loneliness*, arguing, in turn, that the novel articulates a subject neither thinkable nor desirable. Two recent studies published within the same year, Judith Halberstam's (1998) *Female Masculinity* and Jay Prosser's (1998) *Second Skins: The Body Narratives of Transsexuality*, claim that the modern origins of their respective subjects do not overlap and are to be found in Hall's banned novel. I argue that the genealogies of both subjects can indeed make a twentieth-century home in *The Well of Loneliness*, whose subject is neither exclusively but *both*.

The very acrimonious disputes between trans-sexual and queer theorists that have often exploded into full-fledged border wars erupted most profoundly over the ownership of Brandon Teena. In Toronto ownership battles flared in May 1998 following a showing of *The Brandon Teena Story* (Susan Muska and Greta Olafsdottir, USA, 1998) at Inside/Out, the Lesbian and Gay Film and Video Festival of Toronto, the third event I want to use to theorize the No Man's Land of masculinity. Brandon Teena was a white, working-class Nebraska youth who was murdered along with two friends (a white female friend named Lisa Lambert and a young black man, Phillip DeVine) in 1993.[3] Audience members at the Inside/Out screening continued to speak about Brandon as "female" and "lesbian" when asking questions of the filmmakers who were in attendance, even though Brandon identified as heterosexual and male and disidentified with lesbianism and femaleness. The murders of Teena, Lambert, and DeVine attracted enormous media attention. The gay press coverage of the event evolved into a discussion of violence against lesbians and women as well as a debate over lesbian and gay civil rights: it specifically omitted discussion of violence against trans-sexuals. Donna Minkowitz's (1994) *Village Voice* narrative of Brandon's death, for instance, acknowledges the fact that Brandon himself identified neither as lesbian nor female, yet she continues to use a female pronoun to fetishize Brandon's masculinity as lesbian and to characterize him as a confused but sexy cross-dressing butch: "From photos of the wonder-boychic [sic] playing pool, kissing babes, and lifting a straight male neighbor high up in the air to impress party goers ... Brandon looks to be the handsomest butch item in history – not just good looking, but arrogant, audacious, cocky – everything they, and I, look for in lovers" (27). In subsequent interviews, those "babes," the white working-class women who were Brandon's lovers, make it very clear that they identify as heterosexual, that Brandon frequently talked with lovers and friends about being trans-sexual, and that he repeatedly talked about understanding himself as a man rather than as a butch lesbian. As I show in Chapter 5 – which considers these issues again as they are raised by Kimberly Peirce's very successful 1999 film, *Boys Don't Cry* – these quarrels continue.

What I find so profoundly disturbing about the border war that has erupted over Brandon Teena is its insistent and compulsory singularity, indeterminacy, and need for possession. Not only is Brandon misrepresented as something he seemed not to be, but his lovers – young, working-class white women who have clearly and articulately named themselves – are also misrepresented and characterized as self-hating closeted lesbians or "duped" heterosexual girls. By constructing the border war between two camps (butches and FTMs) as being solely over gender (specifically, masculinity in No Man's Land), such arguments must either ignore or repudiate other sites of contest – in this case, contests of meaning between lesbian-identified femmes and the, for all intents and purposes, heterosexual, working-class women who were Brandon's lovers and who have been delegated to the sidelines throughout the press coverage. One of the most frequent questions about Brandon concerns why he chose to stay in Nebraska instead of going west to the gay Mecca of San Francisco – a question that refuses to recognize that similarities in class might have been more important to Brandon than similarities in sexuality.[4] Brandon seems to have found himself in a non-queer but working-class rural community where he could more readily pass as male because he did not identify either himself or his desires as "female" or "queer." The border wars over

Brandon, by focusing on his supposedly self-evident queer orientation, completely disavow equally important facets of Brandon's identity, which remain contentious within gender and sexual debates.

Finally, the fourth skirmish that I want to discuss took place when the CBC aired the Bester Cramm documentary *You Don't Know Dick: Courageous Hearts of Transsexual Men* in late June 1998. On 2 July, *Xtra! Toronto's Gay and Lesbian Biweekly* featured a rather contentious review of the documentary by gay critic Brent Ledger (1998). It is entitled "Getting to Know Dick: Transsexuals as Guardian of Gender Status Quo," and it ups the ante on the stakes of the border wars in No Man's Land by shifting the focus of those wars from butch lesbians and FTM trans-sexual men to gay men and trans-sexual men over the right to define "maleness." "This wide-eyed doc," Ledger writes, "left me feeling as if I'd stumbled into a time warp. Maleness hasn't felt this claustrophobic since the fifties" (37). Ledger's primary quarrel with the documentary seems to rest with trans-sexual men seemingly conforming to heterosexual and, therefore, in Ledger's estimation, heteronormative notions of masculinity. "The real question," he writes, "is what are these guys chasing? For many gay men, maleness is a chimera, an illusion invented by a culture bent on endowing one segment of the population with a taste for aggression, control and dominance" (37). Ledger unproblematically equates gay masculinity with a critique of heteronormativity and compulsory heterosexuality when he simultaneously realigns all forms of heterosexual masculinity with aggression, control, and dominance, repudiating – indeed, disavowing – the ways in which gay men are often accorded forms of social power vis-à-vis class and race.

In his ironic accusation – "Instead of questioning standard gender roles and images these men embrace them – and the more conservative the better" – Ledger disavows Leo Bersani's (1995, 117) claim that, for white, gay, middle-class men, "there may have been no time at which the object of [their] desire did not include a socially determined and socially pervasive definition of what it means to be a man." Bersani makes it clear that, for many gay men, the struggle against those definitions, like the struggle against white supremacy for many white subjects, includes the ways that those struggles are ambivalently mapped onto their bodies: "An authentic, gay, male, political identity therefore implies a struggle not only against definitions of maleness and of homosexuality as they are reiterated and imposed in a heterosexist social discourse, but also against those very same definitions so seductively and so faithfully reflected by those male bodies that we carry within us as permanently renewable sources of excitement" (117).

Part of what Ledger misses in his reading of *You Don't Know Dick* are the ways the documentary and its subjects refuse to allow male bodies, authority, and power to stand as synonyms for each other. He notices yet misreads the fragility and instability that is constitutive of masculinity: "All of the men in the documentary share this sense of fragility. They're aware of the ways in which masculinity can be socially constructed. They talk about learning to be men, adopting a new personality. They're aware that their sex practices are not quite those of genetic men. They know they don't quite fit" (Ledger 1998, 37). What Ledger cannot know and, clearly, what he disavows is that all masculinities are fragile, markedly unstable, and continuously in process. In other words, if masculinity is no longer an essence that male bodies are naturally born with, then, as *Masculinities without Men?* suggests, becoming any gender is a process that is ongoing, contingent, non-foundational, and self-conscious: masculinity is the process by which men of any gender learn to identify and fit themselves into discourses of gender.[5] As Eve Kosofsky Sedgwick (1995, 12) argues, "sometimes, masculinity has nothing to do with men"; the trans-sexual men in *You Don't Know Dick* drive a wedge between masculinity as a cultural identification and masculinity as the sole prerogative of male bodies. Ledger pathologizes trans-sexual masculinity as the pale imitation of the original heterosexual and heteronormative masculinity that he himself, as a gay man, refuses. He constructs the female lovers of trans-sexual men as homophobic women who pander to phallic penetration while remaining entirely passive sexually. According to Ledger, "Max [one FTM in the film] has a relationship with a woman who says: 'Max is just absolutely the most male man I've ever been with. Max uses hands, dildos and strap-ons for penetration.' Which makes you wonder what the lover would do with a butch dyke like Lea DeLaria." Moreover, Ledger collapses all forms of heterosexual masculinity, including trans-sexual masculinity, with "aggression, control and dominance" – qualities that apparently all gay men essentially reject (37).

More important, Ledger also misses the very contingent and ironic status of the masculinity suggested by the film's title, *You Don't Know Dick*. The title, which resonates with "you cannot know" (the supposedly self-evident truth about bodies and subjects) as much as with "you do not know" (what you think you know about masculinity), foregrounds the crisis of knowledge and certainty that I argue is a constitutive feature of masculinity but that percolates most productively in, around, and through the bodies of trans-sexual men and butch women. As Holly Devor (1997) and others have noted, the transition from female to male is a process far more fraught with difficulties than is its male to female counterpart. Current medical technologies have not been as successful at constructing a full-functioning penis as they have been at constructing a vagina from a penis; the result for many FTM trans-sexuals is intersexed bodies – bodies that are marked as masculine through facial hair, primarily flat chests, dense muscle tone, masculine clothing, and so forth but that do not seem to bear that supposedly ultimate signifier of maleness: a stereotypical, conventional-looking penis. As one self-fashioned transman writes, "I call myself 'Intersex by Design' in order to call attention to the fact that it is a choice I am proud to make ... I find it a far more effective strategy [though] to be accepted as a regular guy first and then to reveal myself as something a wee bit different" (Volcano n.d., n.p.).

Del LaGrace Volcano acknowledges that, for many intersexuals, self-determination and control over one's own body has been violently stripped away by surgeons and family members. Morgan Holmes (1995), Suzanne Kessler (1998), and others have documented and theorized the surgical and psychological violences done to intersexed babies by paediatric surgeons, endocrinologists, and parents who need to stabilize meanings between gender, genitals, and sexualities. The intersexed bodies that medical technologies forcibly produce are radically different from manufactured FTM bodies. Nevertheless, they remain intersexed. In Chapter 3 I pay particular attention to intersexed bodies created by removing the most obvious and immediate visual signifiers of femininity: breasts. Reading the breast-removal scenes in the two novels under consideration in that chapter, I argue that, within what I call a mamillian economy, the absence of breasts changes these subjects' experience of a lack. By removing the signifiers of objectification and without adding the requisite penis, the subjects of female masculinity resignify lack (the lack of breasts) as both a refusal of but also a disidentification with masculinity's objectifying gaze.

The questions raised by both Ledger and the transmen in *You Don't Know Dick* are the questions of contemporary scholarship in gender and sexuality studies: What is masculinity? What is gender? And how is gender related to bodies? Indeed, what is that "something a wee bit different" referenced by the transman above? And how is it possible to know or articulate that "something a wee bit different"? Answers to these questions are to be found in cultural artefacts: texts, performances, and/or images that explore gender-variant subjects. Those artefacts – drag king shows, butch theatrical roles, documentaries, newspaper articles, FTM autobiographies, and novels articulating female masculinity – set the stage for the narratives I query. In short, those answers are found in the "trenching" in No Man's Land, where "to trench upon" means "to encroach upon a person's rights, privacy, etc.; or to verge upon [the] borders" (*Oxford English Dictionary*) between queers and transfolks; between FTM but gay transsexual men and gay men; between heterosexual women and heterogendered women; between non-operative FTM transmen and butch/lesbians and the bisexual and (sometimes lesbian) femmes who seek out both.

But those answers can also be found in the work of Mikhail Bakhtin. One of the central premises of Bakhtin's work is the parallel between the construction of texts and the construction of the self. Both centripetal and centrifugal forces intersect in and as utterances that are not the product of a closed system but of social acts or "active participant[s]" that respond to and anticipate other utterances (Bakhtin 1981, 233). Because Bakhtin's concern rests far more with language as living speech in its concrete totality (this is what Bakhtin means by "discourse"), he suggests that the meaning of any linguistic sign is diachronic and relational, involving different speakers and their use of words within sentences. He goes so far as to argue that language is inseparable from its specific socio-historical context: "Language acquires life and historically evolves ... in concrete verbal communication, and not in the abstract linguistic system of language forms" (Bakhtin and Medvedev 1978, 129). The results of these context-determined utterances are meaning-making processes dependent upon contexts. Language as discourse is productive, and relations of language evoke present, past, and possible future contexts as well. Thus, it follows that the constitutive nature of a word itself embodies a multiplicity of meanings and traces of its past usages. "Utterances are not indifferent to one another, and are not self-sufficient; they are aware of and mutually reflect one another. Each utterance is filled with echoes and reverberations of other utterances to which it is related by the communality of the sphere of communication ... Each utterance refutes, affirms, supplements, and relies on others ... and somehow takes them into account" (Bakhtin 1986, 91).

If language is the space of confrontation between differently oriented accents, then, by speaking and hence rearticulating and "languaging," subjects transform both the social context in which speech occurs and themselves. These transformations are what constitute language as dialogic. Stuart Hall rereads Bakhtin to posit that subjects are formed and, by implication, reformed "new" vis-à-vis discourses and utterances. Conversely, since subjects are "languaged" by discourse, so they must use and reconfigure those same discourses to, as Hall (1996a, 143) puts it, "construct some narrative, however impoverished and impure, to connect the past and the present: where they came from with where they are" and, indeed, where they are bound. In turning these texts, discourses, and dialogic languaging processes upside-down, subjects remake themselves, becoming and exceeding what they are, finding a meaning that *fits,* however temporarily, and only, as Bakhtin reminds us, until its next moment of refraction. "When a member of a speaking collective comes upon a word his own thought finds the word already inhabited ... there is no access to one's own personal 'ultimate' word ... every thought, feeling, experience must be refracted through the medium of someone else's discourse, someone else's style, someone else's manner ... almost no word is without its intense sideward glance at someone else's" (Bakhtin 1984, 202-3).

The larger question at stake in performances of female masculinity, especially when they emerge in lesbian contexts and then repudiate those contexts, is similar to one asked by Stuart Hall. Hall rereads Stallybrass and White (1986), who draw on Bakhtin to theorize metaphors of transformation, including those of the self. Stallybrass and White ask a question that I cannot fully answer here, nevertheless, it is one that informs my own reading and writing practices: "Why is it that the thing we deem socially peripheral has be[come] symbolically central"? (Hall 1996a, 303) Anyone who has watched lesbian-feminist communities and subjects transform themselves over the last twenty years would recognize the ways that performances of gender (especially masculinity) once "Othered" and banished have now returned to become symbolically central. These failures trouble constructions of the subject and allow me to flesh out Bakhtin's assertion that the subject is constituted by the "impossibility of a direct relation with oneself" (quoted in Stam 1989, 4).

Like many of the poststructuralists who followed him, Bakhtin (1986, 7) argues that there will always be an element of "outsideness" to any self; that is, the consummation of the whole, either a self or a text (which, with the poststructuralists, Bakhtin understands as any coherent complex of signs), can never be complete. In other words, as I become and realize myself as a "self," I become aware of my relations with others in the very moment that I transform myself through the operations of language. Without those "others" the self could not exist. For Bakhtin, the self-other relation is also dialogic in that the self does not and cannot exist as a fixed, finished, or finalized entity but, rather, is in a state of constant activity. While the building of a self constitutes a process that is dialogic, the self nevertheless remains partly outside the self. Thus, dialogism is grounded in alterity, where subjectivity constantly seeks to evoke or engage the words of others that might "externalize" and "finalize" its sense of self. "The hero's attitude toward himself is inseparably bound up with his attitude toward another, and with the attitude of another toward him. His consciousness of self is constantly perceived against the background of the other's consciousness of him – 'I for myself' against the background of 'I for another.' Thus the hero's words about himself are structured under the continuous influence of someone else's words about him" (Bakhtin 1984, 207). This self, then, exists on the boundaries between its own and the other's consciousness, between its words and the words of others. It is this other that enables the self to reflect on its others and to respond, so that the other's words become part of oneself. As Bakhtin puts it, I need the other to "author" myself.

If the word, as Bakhtin suggests, is both already inhabited and a social event – the expression and product of listeners and speakers – then the resignification of words and the performances of those resignifying practices are precisely what is at stake in both the code-crossing and riots of meanings that are fought on and over the words "man," "woman," "lesbian," "butch," "female-to-male trans-sexual," and so on. At its most conservative and violent, the sex/gender system cannot make provisions for the crises of meaning inherent in the nature of language, or what I name as a dialogic, or double-, indeed, multi-voiced collision of utterances and discourses articulating female masculinity in the twentieth century.

"Female Masculinity"

That collision of utterances and discourse is nowhere more evident than in the work of Judith Halberstam. There can be no denying the importance and significance of Halberstam's (1998a) *Female Masculinity*. Besides being the source of my own book's title, it is the first book-length study of subjects heretofore neglected in academic inquiry. Halberstam has, in essence, set the parameters of this field of inquiry. Until the publication of *Female Masculinity* there had been no comprehensive study of this subject, so one of its key goals is to theorize, document, and catalogue the diversity of masculine expression in primarily lesbian women. To this end, the book has been quite successful. While Halberstam nods towards trans-gendered and trans-sexual men, her theoretical project is most successful when she focuses on the range of expressions that encompass masculinity in women, each with its own history, characteristics, and representations.

Female Masculinity makes several important interventions in both the content and the methodologies of sexuality studies. First, after coining the phrase "female masculinity," which works through juxtaposition and paradoxical relation (i.e., through categorical indeterminacy), Halberstam constructs and then deconstructs the subjects who are now visible by and through the contradiction it names. Halberstam herself notes the misrecognition that has overdetermined or collapsed the very significant differences between subjects hailed by the phrase "female masculinity" – butch masculinity, trans-sexual masculinity, trans-gendered subjects, drag kings, and so on. She argues, as remedy, that while these subjectivities might look similar, each has different representational and discursive histories. Where some of the work theorizing these subjects challenges a binary, or two-genders, system by positing a third gender, Halberstam's work, like Anne Fausto-Sterling's (1995) and my own, instead gives us multiple engenderings; that is, her work is most potent when she suggests that, instead of conceptualizing female masculinity and lesbianism as coterminous and, thus, as a singular figure between masculinity and femininity, critics benefit, as do gender and sexuality studies, when female masculinity itself is understood as multiple, contradictory, and inherently plural. That said, and despite its predictability vis-à-vis queer fem(me)ininities – and Halberstam (1998a) has been taken to task by a number of queer femme scholars for her assertion that being tomboyish and/or butch is far more desirable than being feminine ("the excessive conventional femininity often associated with female heterosexuality can be bad for your health" and "it seems to me that at least early on in life, girls should avoid femininity ... femininity and its accessories should be chosen later on, like a sex toy or a hairstyle" [268-9]) – *Female Masculinity* makes an important contribution to depathologizing and complicating subjects who, at best, have been relegated to political non-importance.

At the same time, Halberstam has been very much influenced by the work of Sedgwick (1990) and Butler (1993) and their reluctance to stabilize the relation between signifier, signified, and supposed referent. Both Sedgwick and Butler, whose work has been so important to establishing the field of queer theory, share a deep suspicion of stabilizing the contemporary and historical meanings behind signs such as "lesbian," "queer," "butch," "trans-sexual," and so on. Besides the fact that linguistic fixity is, by definition, impossible, both Sedgwick and Butler are critical of essentialist identity politics that attempt to secure political certainty by making foundational claims about what counts, or, more important, does not count, as an identity. Such refusals, informed by semiotics and deconstruction as much as by poststructuralist theory, suggest, as does Halberstam, that triangulations between politics, language, and the "real" can never be innocent. Hence the importance of what Halberstam calls a "perversely presentist" model of historical and theoretical argumentation. According to Halberstam, her method of perverse presentism is an attempt to correct oversights in previous methodologies, which look for contemporary configurations of desire, sexuality, and gender in past constructions of lesbianism and define them as being synonymous with masculinity. Her method, in other words, avoids the trap of simply projecting contemporary understandings back in time as a way of attempting to secure current knowledge regimes. The problem with these configurations, she writes, is that "what we do not know for sure today about the relationship between masculinity and lesbianism, we cannot know for sure about historical relations between same-sex desire and female masculinities" (Halberstam 1998a, 54). Perverse presentism allows for both a denaturalization of the present and a history of the present rather than, to quote Michel Foucault, "a history of the past in terms of the present" (quoted in Halberstam 1998a, 53).

Another important goal of Halberstam's work involves distinguishing female masculinity from male masculinity, or, as she says in an oft-quoted expression, "conceptualizing masculinity without men" (Halberstam 1998a, 2). In the end, she wants to make masculinity safe for women and girls, even heterosexual women, so that, with more gender freedom, perhaps even men will be able to recreate masculinity using her model of female masculinity. A number of critics have read the phrase "masculinities without men" to mean "without relation to men." For instance, in his review for the *Journal of Men's Studies*, Daryl B. Hill (2002, 237) comments that "the assertion that [female] masculinity is 'masculinity without men' is problematic." What Hill seems to be identifying here is how Halberstam's work, like my own, is predicated upon a rupture, or distinction, between "masculinity" and "men." If the term "men" is successful as both an ideology and a signifier, then the referent it imagines itself marking is the male body, complete with penis as supposedly self-evident referent. If, however, the term "masculinity" accomplishes its work, then "men" no longer references a self-evident penis. What it references instead is the sex/gender system. "Men" collapses the distinction between signifier and referent whereas "masculinity" not only reasserts it but also suggests that the possession of a conventionally defined penis has nothing to do with securing manhood. Masculinity is a free-floating signifier, detached from the referent, which, as Stuart Hall (1997), Jean Baudrillard (1995), Roland Barthes (1993), and others have suggested, is itself a prior set of signifiers naturalized, and thus passing, as referents. So when Halberstam or I argue, as does Sedgwick, that sometimes masculinity has nothing to do with men, we are not necessarily arguing, literally, "that female masculinity isn't related to male masculinity"; rather, we are arguing that, since masculinity now has nothing to do with the male body, female masculinity is just another materialization, or form, of manhood – one among many, none of which is secured (or privileged) by a referent.

That said, the irony of Halberstam's accomplishment is that it is achieved through a series of problematic disavowals that have yet to be deconstructed in the reviews of her book. The major difference between Halberstam's work and mine is that *Masculinities without Men?* cannot and will not sustain the two disavowals at the heart of Halberstam's argument. First, and perhaps less immediately significant (albeit still glaringly problematic), is the question of the taxonimizing impulse that organizes Halberstam's inquiry. That this categorical imperative is confusing has already been noted in a number of reviews, including one by Rachel Adams (2000) for *GLQ: A Journal of Lesbian and Gay Studies*. Adams gives *Female Masculinity* a fair read, arguing that, while it suffers from certain shortcomings – the most important of which I discuss below – its accomplishments and contributions are both original and important. But those shortcomings, she suggests, actively conspire against the deconstructive claim implied by the contradiction in the title. Adams notes that *Female Masculinity* suffers from an "excessively schematic taxonomy ... characteristic of gay and lesbian identity politics" (473). She reiterates and celebrates Halberstam's argument that the phrase "female masculinity" works because it calls into being a subject previously eclipsed by both heteronormative and lesbian categorical imperatives. But she also questions why "Halberstam's solution to the problem of categorical thinking is to come up with still more categories." This, she argues, is the book's biggest limitation: "The tension that troubles [Halberstam's] work, between a capaciously flexible model of sexuality and one that is fractured endlessly in an attempt to account for every possible variant of experience, is characteristic of gay and lesbian identity politics ... Halberstam wants to have it both ways, to criticize existent categories for not doing justice to the diversity of sexual experience and identification but then to produce ever more exacting taxonomies as a corrective" (473).

Adams does not fully answer her own question – that is, why does Halberstam choose this particular tactic? – but she does give the book a close and generous reading and reviews it well. My answer to Adams's question marks the fundamental difference between *Female Masculinity* and *Masculinities without Men?* – namely, that the former is primarily concerned with lesbian masculinity while the latter seeks a post-identity politic and, at times, post-queer, anti-heteronormative but trans-ed materialization of masculinity. Adams remarks that, despite Halberstam's categorical imperative, what remains most queer about female masculinity is that it produces an "odd alignment of sex and gender," which is most powerful when it refuses categorization altogether (473). What I argue is that the subjects under discussion not only refuse categorization as a teleology but that they also rearticulate, or reassemble, the intelligibility of categorization itself. Post-queer (i.e., trans-gendered and/or trans-sexual but not gay and/or lesbian) subjects like Martin from *Sacred Country* and Jess from *Stone Butch Blues* are, by definition, newly configured bodies that at once realign and dealign the terms of gendered embodiment – alignments to which *Female Masculinity* attributes definitional self-evidence.

Second, Halberstam's argument begins to betray its lesbian identity politics through its second major disavowal during the discussion of Terry Castle's (1996) *Noel Coward and Radclyffe Hall: Kindred Spirits*. In this curious but significant text, Castle posits and documents a kind of kindred spiritedness between John Radclyffe Hall and Noel Coward by reading their work, aesthetics, and personal styles dialogically. Castle suggests that Coward and Hall shared a masculine sensibility that demonstrates "vibrant cross-gender relationships" amongst differently gendered and queer artists, friends, and colleagues (12). Halberstam (1998a, 88-9) dismisses such dialogic conversations between men of different genders, suggesting that "this is an admirable project in some respects, with regard to the question of Hall's masculinity and indeed Coward's femininity, Castle links female masculinity to the imitation of queer maleness and male femininity to the imitation of queer femaleness and thereby renders cross-gender expressions as wholly derivative." Her thesis seems to be that female masculinity (why does she continue to use the singular form when her own articulation is plural?) is complex and, as such, is a "copy" neither of male homosexuality nor of male heterosexuality; instead, it "carves out its own gender expression" (90). While this may be true, what is it carved out of? With what tools? By which (by Halberstam's account) pre-interpellated subjects? Why insist that only female masculinity is a unique articulation of masculinity?

This is an all too easy dismissal of an increasingly queer cross-polinization of subjectivities not just between butches, FTM trans-sexuals, trans-gendered men, and heterosexual men, but also between and amongst gay men and butches, tranny-fags and gay men, FTM trans-sexual men and heterosexual "bio" men, and many other possible arrangements of which we cannot yet conceive. Moreover, what seems to be at stake here for Halberstam is the pernicious belief, despite sentiment to the contrary, that male masculinity is the original and female masculinity the derivative. While Halberstam argues the opposite, as is indicated above, what she seems to disavow is precisely what masculinity studies has suggested all along – that male masculinity, for lack of a better term, is itself derivative. If there is no "original," as Butler has repeatedly reminded us, then why continue to claim that female masculinity is not derivative, there being no argument to the contrary? Female masculinity, I argue, does indeed carve out its own gender expressions, but so does male masculinity, gay masculinity, working-class masculinity, masculinities of many colours, and all combinations of the above. Each, to borrow the language of both Hall and Butler, is always already a rearticulation of engendering discourses. No one articulation is original: all are derivative. And, thus, each is capable of rearticulation and/or reconstruction.

Moreover, given the first premise of social construction theory – that each gender will be articulated through discourses of class, race, sexuality, and so on – each subject of female masculinity that I theorize is bound by the materialization of manhood as it appears in and is, as it were, spoken through different classes, races, sexualities, and bodies. These relationships amongst men of different genders within similar classes, races, sexual orientations, and so on are the stuff of female masculinity. Halberstam suggests and declares a performative indifference towards male masculinity, which she hopes will pass as an affirmation of female masculinity. "Such affirmations," Halberstam (1998a, 9) writes of female masculinity, "begin not by subverting masculine power or taking up a position against masculine power but by turning a blind eye to conventional masculinities and refusing to engage ... [P]ower may inhere within different forms of refusal: 'Well, I don't care.'" On the contrary, I make no such disavowals. In fact, I am interested in taking up power precisely in and as masculine power. Each of my subjects finds power not by feigning indifference but, rather, by cultivating proximity, identification, and similarity with other subjects of masculinity.

Can we really suggest that Stephen Gordon refuses kinship with his father and with his childhood friend Martin Hallam? Does Jess Goldberg not look into the faces of fellow-labourer Ben and of union organizer Duffy and see him-self? *Sacred Country*'s Mary Martin Ward refuses her father, yes, but her grandfather, Cord, gives him his name – a name that brings him into existence. The novel ends, in fact, with Martin finding ironic kinship, solace, self with Judge Riveaux, Jeremiah, and Walter. And isn't the horrific and painful irony of the film *Boys Don't Cry* the fact that it was the boys who mentored Brandon who were eventually responsible for killing him? Can we entertain the possibility that sometimes, as my opening epigraph suggests, some "lesbians" actually *do* want to become men? That each of the characters in these and the many texts I discuss all cultivate profound and important relationships with women cannot be disputed. But the argument that female masculinity does not notice, or is not influenced by, or does not reciprocate or return the gaze to male masculinity cannot be supported. Each is unquestioningly informed, influenced, mentored, and otherwise learns to become a man from other men in their class. Stephen, Jess, Martin, and Brandon, as trans-gendered and possibly trans-sexual men, not only have to directly "engage" the men around them but must also, to turn a clichéd phrase, embrace the boy within themselves in order to move closer to becoming that boy. Halberstam's "I don't care" might work as a rhetorical disavowal; but, like all disavowals – moments where subjects cannot know what it is they both already know and are always already constituted by – it certainly raises the question of psychic proximity to and identification with masculinity.

In *Masculinities without Men?* I do not just map these proximities; I advocate for the social, psychic, and political necessity of these relationships. Post-queer relationships amongst men are often at different angles to each other politically, but even though we are not likely to see the masculine version of the television show *Will and Grace* (could we even imagine, let's say, *Bubba and Butch* or *Spike and Mike*), each text I discuss cultivates the space between men and butches – male masculinity and female masculinity – as vitally important spaces. Halberstam is right to suggest that an examination of female masculinity has much to tell us about masculinity in general. But she is wrong to suggest that, somehow, masculinities can be reduced to the categorical imperatives of body types. As Sedgwick (1990) notes, each instance of a gender has to be understood through the specificities of other axes of identity (e.g., race, class, sexuality, etc.). As such, it is entirely conceivable that heterogendered working-class FTM trans-sexual men might have far more in common with heterosexual working-class "biological" men than with FTM trans-sexual men of a different class. And trans-sexual men of colour might have more in common with men of colour than with white trans-sexual men. To continue to privilege "female embodied" masculinity over other instances of masculinity is to capitulate to essentialist constructions of gender as limited by bodies rather than as limited by discourse. Finally, *if* Butler (1997a) is correct in her assertion that gender performatives mark the space of unmournable loss rather than positivist identities, then female masculinity and Halberstam's "I don't care" disavowal mark far more complex relations than its subjects could ever know. Masculinity, regardless of what type of body it is articulated through, by definition marks a space of proximity with men; it is *this* space that I theorize in *Masculinities without Men?*

Masculinities without Men?

1
Alibis of Essence and Enemies Within: At the Well of Obscenity

Alibis of Essence and Enemies Within

In 1948 George W. Henry, MD, member of the executive of the (American) Committee for the Study of Sex Variants, Inc., published a huge volume of the committee's research entitled simply *Sex Variants: A Study of Homosexual Patterns* (hereafter *Sex Variants*). The Committee for the Study of Sex Variants, Inc., was composed of both an executive committee and a research committee, and members, authorized by the traces "MD" and "PhD" that followed their signatures, hailed from prestigious universities and medical research committees, including Yale, Columbia, Harvard, Johns Hopkins, Stanford, and the University of Pennsylvania as well as the psychiatric division of New York's Bellevue Hospital.

The research undertaken by the committee is vast and includes the study of numerous male and female homo- and bisexual males and females. Structured around basic types of deviancy – "Homosexual Cases," "Bisexual Cases," and "Narcissistic Cases" – the sex variant study followed the rigorous methodologies established by turn-of-the-century sexology and included detailed interviews as well as extensive structural, physiological, psychological, gynaecological, and skeletal examinations. The case studies in *Sex Variants* follow a consistent format and are organized around the following: general impressions, family background, personal history, physical examination, gynaecological examination, X-ray examination, (expert) comment, and, finally, (familial) résumé. Each section is often appended with an additional "commentary" or "impression," consisting of notes by those conducting the research on each particular case. Moreover, each case is accompanied by detailed genealogical maps that outline, in numerous symbols and codes, the particular psychological history of the case's family. For instance, the genealogical map for "Rebecca R ... an attractive, tall, slender blonde woman of twenty-five," shows a long history of artistic, bisexual, neurotic, psychotic, mentally retarded, suicidal, promiscuous, separated, and divorced individuals in her family, with Rebecca placed precisely at the intersection of such types (962).

What is particularly noteworthy about the case studies collected in *Sex Variants* are the detailed pen drawings reproduced in "Appendix 6: The Gynaecology of Homosexuality" (1069-1130). Appendices 1 through 5 document the various "Masculinity-Femininity Tests," inventory charts of "Physical Characteristics Suggesting Masculinity or Femininity," "Anthropological Data" for all case studies, and the "Internal Pelvic Measurements of Sex Variants." Again, this provides more qualitative and quantitative statistical and classificatory inventories of the data collected from the subjects, including reproductions of numerous tables, graphs, X-rays, and photographs. However, Appendix 6 is the pièce de résistance of the entire study. The drawings were made using measurements and tracings of both tumescent and detumescent vulva and breasts: "In addition to taking measurements of the parts, Dr. Moench made tracings by laying a glass plate on the vulva, and outlining the external genitals upon it in soft crayon – then tracing this outline on the record sheet ... [T]he Moench record, it will be noted, is very specific in the description of each condition" (1099). The more than thirty pages of remarkably detailed pen drawings document the anatomies of mostly female genitalia and accompany the descriptive, analytical, and statistical evidence. Taken as a whole, *Sex Variants* produces the female variant as Foucauldian species by generating a fictional narrative about one's *inside* truth via quantifiable *outside* anatomy – an imbrication of morphology with ontology – producing a text both written and read by the appropriately authorized expert.[1]

Once more, what is even more curious about "The Gynaecology of Homosexuality" in particular, and the entire sex variants study in general, are the ways in which it inadvertently functions as a "how-to" manual for abjected sex practices. One section of "The Gynaecology of Homosexuality," with the strange subheading "Suggestions for Detailed Case History of Sex Behavior," offers detailed descriptions of sexual activity, observed by the doctors, between several participants in the study, producing the so-called natural (albeit deviant) practices it claims to be unearthing: "Location of touch alongside clitoris, beneath and lifting stroke; both sides at once; above clitoris, on lesser lips ... Vaginal entry with finger a little at first, then freely and full length, gradual process; two fingers or three; stroke gentle, strong, slow, rapid, increasing thrust; with clitoris pressures at same time" (1098). This section continues its narrative for several pages, lesbianism giving a now discursive and "detailed account of itself" before the watchful witness, and finally refers to a pen drawing.[2] "Figure 31" depicts "woman above" and "woman below" sharing a double dildo in quite remarkable detail (1130).

Published twenty years after *The Well of Loneliness*, the case studies in *Sex Variants* also provide a very rich description of the productive effect of early twentieth-century fiction that was exploring female same-sex desire. Here is part of one account, again Rebecca R.'s, which is now seen as a class-based narrative of the almost mythical currency accorded novels like *The Well of Loneliness* in the United States some time after their publication.

> As I grow older I am beginning to realize that I am typical of a most obvious group of young American women who have homosexual tendencies. With minor variations my history duplicates that of girls seen in rendezvous in half a dozen shabby cafés in the region of Washington Square, on the terrace of the Dome in Paris or on the Island of Capri. Most of them have had a pampered childhood; several years in girls' camps or schools and with a series of crushes on girls, usually older; incomplete, or unpleasant relations with a man in their late teens or early twenties; and recollections of the greater tenderness of the intimacies with girls. By this time they have read "The Well of Loneliness" or "Extraordinary Women"[3] and they have been introduced to a circle of girls who profess to be Lesbian and who swagger a good deal in mannish clothes. (Henry 1948, 969)

There are numerous references throughout *Sex Variants* to these two novels, and to others, including Rosamond Lehmann's *Dusty Answer* and Clemence Dane's *Regiment of Women*, suggesting an overdetermined relationship between reading practices and identity formation.[4] As Jennifer Terry (1991, 60) has noted, extant historical texts that document homosexual identity formation and questions of the "self" are rare, and, ironically, texts such as *Sex Variants* often provide some of the richest and most detailed accounts of homosexuality in the late nineteenth and early twentieth centuries. Terry names the value of such texts and inadvertently outlines my methodology: "While it may be depressing to think that these [texts] account for the largest number of sources on homosexuality from the late nineteenth century until at least the beginning of the homophile movement, these sources are ripe for destabilizing strategies of reading for difference. They constitute the hegemonic discursive field for watching the conflictual interplay between scientists, doctors, police, and clergy on the one hand, and deviants on the other" (59).

Terry's project is limited to readings of sexological texts; in this chapter, I explore those same discourses in conjunction with one fictional text produced around the same historical moment, reading for power/knowledge regimes and strategies of resistance in both. More precisely, I analyze the trajectory of one prose narrative, *The Well of Loneliness* (hereafter *The Well*), through its collisions with the discursive fields of sexology, the British Obscene Publications Act, the subsequent obscenity trial, and critical dialogues and newspaper coverage. The second part of this chapter, "The

Codifications of Inversion," interrogates the late nineteenth- and early twentieth-century fields of sexology, examining the discourses in some detail. The third part, "Ironic Proliferations and Shame/less Practices of Freedom," analyzes the British obscenity trial and the *London Times* coverage, demonstrating that the figure of the invert as he[5] was first produced in sexological discourse, then reconfigured by *The Well*, represents a productive contradiction and constitutes both an overdetermined identity-space (or subject position) as well as a strategy of resistance (Terry 59-60). And finally in "The Outsider Within," I explore this historical moment as one obsessively concerned with questions of nationality.

In setting *The Well* obscenity trial in the context of a previous libel case, the 1918 Pemberton Billing trial, I argue that both the context of production and the reception of *The Well* was overdetermined by post-First World War anxieties about nationalities and racialized identities. In other words, the trial that banned *The Well* as obscene functioned as a micro-site where discourses of sexuality were articulated within a politics of race. Laura Stoler (1995, 11) names what was at stake in these kinds of discursive events: "[This was a] micro-site where designations of racial membership were subject to gendered appraisals and where 'character' [and] 'good breeding' were implicitly raced. These discourses do more than prescribe suitable behavior; they locate how fundamentally bourgeois identity has been tied to notions of being 'European' and being 'white' and how sexual prescription served to secure and delineate the authentic, first-class citizens of the nation-state". Hall's novel is banned not so much because it articulates supposedly unsuitable desires (although it does) as because it legitimates Stephen's sexual and gender identity by deploying the alibi of essence provided by German sexologists – the same thinkers who, according to Billing in 1918, constituted one of the biggest and most potent threats to England during the final year of the First World War.

To argue that the technologies producing female masculinity coalesced around Hall's novel, it is necessary to situate *The Well* within the context of the late nineteenth- and early twentieth-century notions of inversion as theorized in the writings of sexologists such as Richard von Krafft-Ebing (1965), Karl Heinrich Ulrichs (1977), and Havelock Ellis (1926, 1929). Hall's novel poaches its raison d'être from sexology, positing that the invert is an innate and supposedly natural subject, the product of the inversion of normal sexuality and, thus, a subject that ought to be tolerated because it cannot be helped (Ruehl 1982). Hall traces the life of a young invert, Stephen Gordon, from his birth into British moneyed country gentry, through adulthood and an inverted sexuality, and follows him through a small circle of sophisticated lesbians to the bar life of British and American expatriate lesbian culture in Paris (Newton 1989). Ostensibly alone at the end of the novel, Stephen discovers that his true vocation is to challenge the social ostracism that "distorts the lives of lesbians like herself, whom God created and who are, Hall declares, normal in their inversion of heterosexuality" (MacPike 1994, 219). Upon publication, Hall's novel was immediately denounced as "insidious moral poison" and was, within six weeks, prosecuted for obscenity and eventually banned (Brittain 1968, 86). As Ruehl (1982, 15) notes, "the trial and surrounding publicity about the book put lesbianism on the map. A battle over competing definitions of lesbianism was engaged and, for the first time, the idea of 'the lesbian' as a specific identity and image was given wide public currency."

Hall's novel remains one of the most popular and, indeed, in 1999 is still listed as one of the most notorious lesbian novels (Boutilier 1995; MacPike 1994; Ruehl 1982). As Loralee MacPike (1994, 219) notes, Stephen's masculinized self, which embodies the sexologist's theories of inversion, has been and continues to be the focus of most critical response to the novel. For instance, even though they were writing within fifteen years of each other, lesbian-feminist critics Jane Rule (1975) and Dolores Klaich (1974) lament that the novel is depressing and anti-feminist because it oversexualizes the idyllic homosocial world of female friendship, love, and work. Lillian Faderman (1981) concurs with Klaich and Rule. She argues that the predominantly working-class lesbians who identified with the model of female same-sex desire represented in the novel – that is, desire that is heterogendered, that operates within the realm of gender (but not necessarily body or sex) difference (what is more commonly known today as butch-femme) – were misled by the sexologists and thus were complicit in destroying the innocence and safety of female friendships.

More recent readings of *The Well*, influenced by the separation of sexuality from gender, invest it with a new importance. An entire afternoon session of five papers was devoted to Hall's novel at the three-day Sixth Annual North American Lesbian, Gay and Bisexual Studies Conference in November 1994. In addition, Sonia Ruehl (1982), Esther Newton (1989), and Lisa Duggan (1992) argue against the feminist readings of critics like Klaich and Rule and suggest instead that the novel initiated a productive rupture with existing definitions of lesbianism as the "female world of love and ritual" (Smith-Rosenberg 1975). Ruehl reviews both the medical-psychological discourses that organized the new field of knowledge about deviant sexual practices (i.e., nineteenth- and early twentieth-century sexology) and the practices of power (i.e., the Obscene Publications Act, 1857) that banned Hall's novel, to argue that *The Well* could be read as the start of a Foucauldian reverse discourse, the process by which a category produced by discourse is initially adopted and then eventually transformed by those originally defined by it. Thus, Ruehl (1982, 27) suggests that the definition of lesbianism inherent in Hall's novel laid the groundwork for an important moment of political mobilization.

While Ruehl's well-crafted analytics of the production of lesbian sexuality reads *The Well* in terms of the knowledge/power regimes referring to sexuality, I suggest that it does not go far enough. Ruehl presumes a far too stable and, ironically, ahistorical definition of gender and sexual identity. She also posits the erotics at work in Hall's novel as exclusively "lesbian." Such an argument misreads Stephen as only, or simply, "female"; instead, I place Stephen at the critical aporia between "trans-sexual," "butch," and "man." If we understand Stephen as an example of female masculinity, then he must inhabit the space between "female" and "masculine," neither fully one nor the other but citing both. The specific practice referenced by Hall is a gendered erotic system that pre-dates lesbian-feminism, and Stephen realizes the first term of "butch-femme" sexual practices as well as a "trans-gendered" subject who imagines and defends its own ontological being with an alibi of essence.

The Codifications of Inversion

The collisions between *The Well* and the nineteenth-century sexologists mentioned by name in Hall's text – Richard von Krafft-Ebing, Karl Heinrich Ulrichs, and Havelock Ellis – constitute not only a productive moment for sexual subjectivities but also an intertextual arena wherein texts become virtual microcosms of the overall field of competing discourses (Collins 1989). Stephen Gordon, the protagonist of Hall's novel, was rewritten by these texts as much as they were rewritten by Hall, who foregrounded the ways in which sexual subjects are made to speak and be spoken through the imperatives of subjectivity played out in those collisions. This part of Chapter 1 concurs with Collins, who writes, "these collisions share a common purpose – to demonstrate that our cultures are so thoroughly discourse-based that we cannot even hope to encounter 'real life' unless we investigate the ways discourses fundamentally shape our experience" (60).

Turn-of-the-century sexology was preoccupied with empirically identifying, describing, and understanding sexual perversion and inversion. The scientific study of sexual inversion is usually dated from the 1869 publication by Carl von Westphal of a case study of a woman suffering from "a contrary sexual instinct" (Duggan 1992, 265). Westphal, a professor of psychiatry in Berlin, believed the patient's condition was congenital, the result of hereditary degeneration. He had been influenced by the initiatives of other psychiatrists, mainly in France, who had been developing and applying the notion of hereditary degeneration as an explanatory model for a wide range of conditions and borderline diseases, including hysteria, neurasthenia, and sexual perversion. The model of hereditary degeneration as it was applied to mental and nervous diseases also became a major activity of the new medical specialty of neurology. As Duggan notes, many well-known European neurologists were also involved in defining and explaining the new sexual perversions, particularly "contrary sexual instinct," or sexual inversion (265-7).

The burgeoning field of sexology viewed sexual perversion as a combination of vice and disease, but it did so, as Doan and Bland (1998, 2) suggest, in order to displace the old view of sexual practices as sinful and, hence, under the jurisdiction of the Church. Psychiatrist A.B. Morel and criminologist Cesare Lombroso had been quick to link sexual perversion, as disease, with vices such as alcoholism, pauperism, and prostitution, combining theories of criminality with theories of degeneration. Bad habits and immorality, Morel wrote in 1857, could be passed to offspring in the form of a constitutional weakness, or neuropathic weakness, thus functioning as a predisposition to disease (Duggan 1992, 265-6). Gender, it was argued, was rooted in biology, evolution, and heredity, and, thus, gender deviations must be similarly rooted. Lynda Hart (1994, 4) has also traced this coupling of sexual perversion with vice, arguing that, from her initial entry into sexological discourse, the female invert, as an ahistorical construct, was always already both pathologized and criminalized.

Sexological discourse was not only interested in documenting so-called deviant sexualities (i.e., separating "normal" from "deviant"); it was also preoccupied with the idea of "normality" in and of itself. Jonathan Ned Katz (1995) notes that the term "hetero-sexual" first appeared in the United States in an 1892 article by Dr. James G. Kiernan. In this context "heterosexual" did not signify non-deviant (or normal) sexual identity but, rather, suggested yet another "abnormal manifestation of the sexual appetite" in a catalogue of "sexual perversions" (20). Thus, heterosexuality was a kind of "psychical hermaphroditism" wherein the subject experienced both a male erotic attraction to females and a female erotic attraction to males. In other words, emotions were presumed to have a biological sex, and those who were identified as heterosexual had "inclinations to both sexes," the "hetero" referring not to a desire for the opposite sex but to a desire for two different sexes (20). Katz's genealogy of heterosexuality reveals a kind of contest of meaning taking place within the category heterosexual. Kiernan, Richard von Krafft-Ebing, and Havelock Ellis all note that sexual instinct was generally identified as a procreative desire of men and women. What emerges as heterosexuality in their respective works was an ambivalent, and not always reproductive, sexuality, clearly constructed as "abnormal" for its reproductive deviance. According to Katz, "[Kiernan's] heterosexual described a mixed person and compound urge – at once sex-differentiated, eros-oriented, and [ambivalently] reproductive ... heterosexuals' ambivalent procreative desire made them absolutely abnormal" (20).

Kiernan was influenced by Richard von Krafft-Ebing's (1965) famous *Psychopathia Sexualis, with Especial Reference to Contrary Sexual Instinct: A Medico-Legal Study* (first published in 1836 and hereafter referred to as *Psychopathia*

Sexualis). With Krafft-Ebing's work, it becomes clear that not all sexologists were interested in ensuring that sexual perversion and criminality necessarily were imbricated. As Doan and Bland (1998, 4) note, one of the most erroneous assumptions made about the field of sexology is that it can and should be read as monolithic; thus, many of the thinkers in the field are lumped together as if they were somehow all in agreement. In fact, many of the sexologists represented and produced diverse and contradictory theoretical positions. A disciple of Wesphal, Krafft-Ebing developed a classificatory scheme around several distinct and important axes. "Pathological sexual instinct" and "contrary sexual instinct" both refer to non-procreative desire and are set in simple opposition to "sexual instinct," or reproductive desire (9). Non-procreative desires are further divided into "congenital sexual perversion" (i.e., congenital hereditary behaviour for which the subject could not be held responsible) as distinguished from "acquired sexual perversity" (i.e., willed immoral behaviour for which the subject could be held accountable). These are important distinctions, and, paradoxically, they allow Krafft-Ebing to propose and to substantiate the notion of a healthy sexual instinct as opposed to a pathological instinct.

Havelock Ellis (1926) also interrogated heterosexuality long before he interrogated inversion. His *Man and Woman* (first published in 1893) concurred with Krafft-Ebing with regard to the assertion that, in nature, there is a "cosmic conservatism," or natural harmony, in the two genders; hence, there are gender roles and spheres: "woman breeds and tends; man provides; it remains so even when the spheres tend to overlap" (440). While Ellis did focus on reproduction as the source of that "natural harmony," Krafft-Ebing elevated desire between men and women to great heights. It is fitting that Krafft-Ebing begins his 436-page tome with the following admonishment regarding both chastity and purely procreative desires.

> The propagation of the human race is not left to mere accident or the caprices of the individual, but is guaranteed by the hidden laws of nature which are enforced by a mighty, irresistible impulse. Sensual enjoyment and physical fitness are not the only conditions for the enforcement of these laws, but higher motives and aims ... man puts himself at once on a level with the beast if he seeks to gratify lust alone, but he elevates his superior position when by curbing the animal desire, he combines with the sexual functions ideas of morality, of the sublime, and the beautiful. Placed upon this lofty pedestal, he stands far above nature ... if man were deprived of sexual fulfillment and the nobler enjoyments arising there from, all poetry and probably all moral tendency would be eliminated from his life. (1)

Krafft-Ebing continues to toggle between the healthy and the pathological, often on the same page, establishing the contradictory and discursive terms by which *The Well* is not only produced but, later, both praised and condemned.

> Sexual feeling is really the root of all ethics, and no doubt of aestheticism and religion. The sublimist virtues, even the sacrifice of self, may spring from sexual life, which, however, on account of its sensual power, may easily degenerate into the lowest passion and basest vice. Love unbridled is a volcano that burns down and lays waste all around it: it is an abyss that devours all – honour, substance and health ... Life is a never-ceasing duel between the animal instinct and morality. Only will-power and a strong character can emancipate man from the meanness of his corrupt nature, and teach him how to enjoy the pure pleasures of love and pluck the noble fruits of earthly existence. (1-3)

In other words, the questions of "sublimist virtues," "sacrifice of self," and the "never ceasing duel between the animal instinct and morality" become the foundation upon which the condemnation and eventual banning of Hall's novel were successfully constructed.

In addition to seeing how his theories drew important distinctions between the categories "healthy" and "pathological" as well as "perversity" and "perversion," it is worth examining Krafft-Ebing's theories of female inversion. Krafft-Ebing draws his own conclusions from his case studies, and he also documents cases of inversion from other sexologists. He is, however, quick to read extant case studies according to his own distinction between perversity and perversion: "I cannot lay sufficient stress upon the fact that sexual acts between persons of the same-sex do not necessarily constitute antipathic sexual instinct" (262); rather, the latter only exists when "the physical and psychical secondary sexual characteristics of the same-sex exert an attracting influence over the individual and provoke in him or her the impulse to sexual acts." In other words, inversion is antipathic only when two conditions exist. First, Krafft-Ebing makes a distinction between (1) the "sexual meeting of women," or what he calls "Lesbian Love," that takes place in female homosocial sites such as "the harem, in female prisons, brothels and young ladies' seminaries," and (2) inversion, or what he calls "viraginity" (262-3). "Lesbian Love" is not antipathic but merely circumstantial. These abnormal, but not congenital, inclinations can be corrected as the subject is "forc[ed] ... into the ways of normal sexual intercourse" (263). It is "viraginity" that concerns him the most, and it is this that qualifies as perversion. Clearly, it is provocation via the usurpation of masculinity, or those "physical and psychical secondary sexual characteristics" in viraginious women that "exert an attracting influence over the individual and provoke in him or her the impulse to sexual acts," that troubles Krafft-Ebing.

Krafft-Ebing details, in much the same way that Ellis will later, the female masculinity that signals inversion, although he cautions that not all "homosexual women ... betray their anomaly by external appearances nor by mental (masculine) sexual characteristics" (263). In fact, when read against their own clinical and regulatory discursive contexts, these texts can also function as how-to manuals, textually producing in rich detail the specificities of an erotic signifying system: "Uranism may nearly always be suspected in females wearing their hair short, or who dress in the fashion of men, or pursue the sports and pastimes of their male acquaintances; also in opera singers and actresses, who appear in male attire on the stage ... The female homosexual may be found in the haunts of boys ... perfumes and sweetmeats are disdained ... [and] the masculine soul ... finds pleasure in the pursuit of manly sports" (263-4). Krafft-Ebing paradoxically describes not only the *how-to-signify* of female homosexuality but also the *where-to-find-it:* "Moll has given many interesting items about the mode of life led by these men-women, and about the way in which they satisfy their sexual needs ... [and] suspicion may always be turned towards homosexuality when one reads in the advertisement columns of the daily papers: 'Wanted, by a lady, a lady friend and companion'" (264-5).

Texts like *Psychopathia Sexualis,* Ellis's *Sexual Inversion* and, later, *Sex Variants,* circulated primarily, but not exclusively, within clinical, discursive, and legal contexts. But Stephen Gordon, via Radclyffe Hall, was also subject to this "game of truth" and, in Foucault's (1985, 5-27) words, he not only recognized himself precisely as a "desiring man" but also came to decipher and acknowledge the "truth of his being, be it natural or fallen," transforming that self into an ethical subject. The figures that emerge from Krafft-Ebing's text are very precisely both gendered and sexed subjects. Female same-sex desire is no longer that of simply forbidden friendships, "Lesbian Love," or what Krafft-Ebing (1965, 406) ironically calls "homosexuality by cultivation"; rather, what emerges are the tropes of the active invert: "Where viraginity is fully developed, the woman so acting assumes definitely the masculine role ... [and that] desire to adopt the active role towards the beloved person of the same-sex seems to invite the use of the priapus." The "passive" woman to whom the active invert is attracted, "the woman of this type possesses ... the feminine qualities" (264).

The epistemological contradictions that structure texts by Krafft-Ebing, Ellis and, eventually, Ulrichs, or tensions between "homosexuality by cultivation" and "viraginity," are those that Eve Kosofsky Sedgwick (1990, 83-90) identifies as tropes of "gender-separatism" and "gender inversion." Within more recent understandings of female same-sex desire, which privilege tropes of gender-separatism (e.g., twentieth-century second-wave lesbian-feminism), lesbianism came to be understood as a "diacritical mark of social organization," where people within one gender (female) were seen to have "economic, institutional, emotional, physical needs and knowledge ... [that had] so much in common ... they [were expected to] bond together also on the axis of sexual desire" (87). Under such a gender-separatist paradigm butch-femme practices that clearly relied on queered notions of gender were only intelligible as less than pure imitative heterosexual practices that threatened a lesbian-feminist agenda. Lesbian-feminist scholars revisited the texts of Hall and the sexologists and argued that the subject positions opened up in these works destroyed previous gender-separatist sites. Thus, the critiques levelled against butch-femme practices argue that they do little more than reify and consolidate gender identities. On the other hand, tropes of gender-inversion or liminality between gender – those conceptual registers surrounding "the sissy boys and their mannish sisters" so popular under the banner of "queer theory" – radically destabilize the naturalness of gender identities but preserve an essential heterosexuality within a butch-femme erotic signifying system: "Desire, in this view, by definition subsists in the current that runs between one male self and one female self, in whatever sex of bodies these selves may be manifested" (87).

Clearly, these are epistemological contradictions that structure nineteenth-century sexology, contemporary queer theory, and much of the recent scholarship on butch-femme. What is at stake in my return to both sexology and *The Well*, and despite queer theory's necessary theoretical and strategic separation between the axes of "sex" and "gender," is a momentary insistence on a contingent and strategic reconsolidation of sex and gender. What troubles and eventually emerges from sexology is not necessarily just the privileging of a sexual practice (i.e., heterosexuality) via the pathologization of its "Other" (i.e., homosexuality), although that does occur; rather, what is also reified and naturalized in these writings are gender subjectivities. Krafft-Ebing, Ellis, and others are preoccupied by the presumption of masculinity in inverted subjects. Judge Chartres Biron, who presides over the obscenity trial that eventually bans *The Well*, betrays a similar preoccupation with Stephen as mannish. If sexology succeeds at codifying gender identities, as I suggest it does, then resistance to such a power/knowledge regime can only turn those gender identities against themselves. Indeed, as Doan and Bland (1998) note, critical assessment of the sexological project often focuses on the question of whether sexology constituted a bold innovation and emancipatory investigation into human sexuality or whether it was merely another social repression. This question is supplemented by the additional question of sexology's audience.

Some have argued that, because it was such a specialized field, only clinicians and theorists could gain access to this body of work (Chauncey

1989). Doan and Bland are amongst those who would challenge those assertions, answering that many of the ideas emerging in sexological writing circulated in and around fiction (certainly in *The Well*) but also in obscenity trials, where sexology was deployed as a scientific discourse to either prove or disprove perversity (Doan 1998, 211). Thus, I concur with Doan when she writes that "sexology could thus be simultaneously empowering and disempowering, for it offered not a homogeneous ideology but the potential to be all things to all people" (3). She goes on to say: "Although sexology may not have engendered universal sexual 'emancipation,' we would suggest that it is equally wrong to conclude, as have some historians, that sexology has been simply harmful in its effects. It is clearly the case that sexology has contributed to the control of certain sexual behaviors and sexual subjectivities, but it has also proved positive for many in its offer of identities and a language of expression" (4).

If, as Foucault (1977a, 150-3) suggests, even the so-called "truth" of the biological, or the body, is unstable and cannot "serve as the basis for self-recognition," then what I trace here are the ways in which a system of abstracted violences, or what Foucault calls "the endlessly repeated play of dominations," are staged over the "female" body as it is represented in Hall's text. Truth regimes – systems of interpretations and rules that force gender to signify according to so-called biological truths – are, in fact, the very thing that Hall contests. My genealogy of the contradictions signalled by female masculinity challenges the supposed self-evidence of the act of interpretation itself and concurs with Foucault's following comment:

> If interpretation were the slow exposure of the meaning hidden in an origin, then only metaphysics could interpret the development of humanity. But if interpretation is the violent or surreptitious appropriation of a system of rules, which in itself has no essential meaning, in order to impose a direction, to bend it to a new will, to force its participation in a different game, and to subject it to secondary rules, then the development of humanity is a series of interpretations. The role of genealogy is to record its history. (151-2)

With its denaturalized and differently gendered bodies, *The Well* reinterprets such resistances with the alibi of essence provided by sexological discourse. Inversion, or female masculinity, constitutes a productive contradiction between supposedly natural (or biological) truths (or rules) and culturally gendered subject positions in this text – a contradiction that not only hijacks the technologies of its own imagined origins but that also jams that machinery, almost making it "function so as to overcome the rulers through their own rules" (151).

But texts such as the sexologists' also reveal the discontinuities, contradictions, and tensions structured within that complex mechanism as a system at war with itself. In "Congenital Inversion in Woman," from *Psychopathia Sexualis*, Krafft-Ebing (1965, 262) laments: "Science in its present stage has but few data to fall back on, so far as the occurrence of homosexual instinct in woman is concerned as compared with man." This does not suggest, he asserts, that inversion in women is rare since the "degenerative influences will prevail alike in the female as well as in the male" (262). What it does suggest, however, and what is crucial for my purposes here, is that: "This anomaly, in so far as it leads to sexual intercourse, among women, does not fall ... under the criminal code, and therefore remains hidden from public knowledge" (262). *Psychopathia Sexualis*, in conjunction with other sexological texts and the obscenity trials that publicized *The Well*, unknowingly displays and, in fact, legitimates the very thing it sought to regulate through epistemological domination, that is, the gendered and unwittingly queered subject positions articulated in and across a number of texts, including Hall's. Again, Foucault (1977a, 150) reminds us that the endlessly repeated play of dominations leads to differentiation of ideas: "class domination generates the idea of liberty" and so on. Thus, relationships of domination are fixed in rituals, "in meticulous procedures that impose rights and obligations," establishing marks of its power on bodies: "The law is a calculated and relentless pleasure ... which permits the perpetual instigation of new dominations and the staging of meticulously repeated scenes of violence" (151). An analysis of these procedures of law as the interstitial non-place of confrontation both contests and seizes inscriptions while, at the same time, installing a new system of rules regarding nationhood.

Not only did Krafft-Ebing (1965, 1) and, later, Havelock Ellis cast their empirical and scientific gazes towards the imbrication of gender and sexuality identities in general, but they also scrutinized the "savage races" in their textual production of the heterosexual, "healthy," and Christian subject. By the end of the first page of his text, Krafft-Ebing writes: "The gratification of the sexual instinct seems to be the primary motive in man as well as beast. Sexual intercourse is done openly, and men and women are not ashamed of their nakedness" (1). At the end of this passage, he proceeds to cite numerous "savage races ... who are still in this stage" and teleologically reads these "lower" races through those "Greek" and "Teutonic" races whose so-called superior and civilized institutions propelled them into a highly evolved sexual ethos.

> This development is hastened wherever nomadic habits yield to ... colonization ... Christianity raised the union of the sexes to a sublime position

> by making woman socially the equal of man and by elevating the bond of love to a moral and religious institution ... Even though nature should claim merely the law of propagation, a community ... cannot subsist without the guarantee that the offspring thrive ... [and] in comparing the various stages of civilization it becomes evident that, despite periodical relapses, public morality has made steady progress, and that Christianity is the chief factor in this advance. (2-3)

Havelock Ellis's (1929) "Sexual Inversion in Women" not only fixes the female subaltern in his gaze but also sexually marginalizes her. For Ellis, female homosexuality emerges out of both colonized and "lower" races. Out of approximately twenty-six case studies and citations of female inversion in his work, more than half are from colonized nations, including Brazil, North America, Bali, India, Zanzibar, Arabic and French Creole countries, Madagascar, and China. The remainder are accounts of inversion taken from prostitutes, female prisoners, female college students, and women from other sex-segregated sites. A few cases are referenced in German sexology, French literature, and sensational American newspapers (Duggan 1992). The female invert was not merely a sexual subject but always already a race- and class-specific entity. Thus, the threat of female deviance was safely displaced onto women who were always already considered to be socially marginal. "It would seem to be precisely when the threat of lesbianism became an area of concern for white middle-class European men that lesbianism was construed as a secret that must be withheld from its potential practitioners. That is to say, when the objects of concern become white, middle- and upper-class women, lesbianism became foreclosed" (Hart 1994, 4).

Unlike Krafft-Ebing and Ellis, Karl Heinrich Ulrichs was a German lawyer and writer, although, like Krafft-Ebing, he, too, argued that female homosexuality could be discerned in those women possessing "mental (masculine) sexual characteristics" (Krafft-Ebing 1965, 263). Beginning in 1864 Ulrichs developed his own congenital theory of sexual inversion and published his theories in twelve books, with the collective title *Researches on the Riddle of Love between Men*, which was written and printed at his own expense (Katz 1995, 51). Like Krafft-Ebing, Ulrichs asserted that erotic feelings are gender-specific, arguing throughout his many texts that the "urning" was the product of an unusual development in the human embryo, where the brain of the infant was actually cross-gendered. In other words, the urning was characterized by the growth of a female brain in a male body, and vice versa. Duggan (1992, 268-9) explains the strategic impact of Ulrichs's influential theory: "Ulrichs, himself an 'urning,' could thus proclaim the congenital basis of his condition in a way that freed him from association with vice or disease. The anomaly was benign, and the urning's love for his own sex was perfectly 'natural' under the circumstances." While it is no accident that Ulrichs is the first of several sexologists mentioned by name in *The Well*, his work was not as well known as was that of Krafft-Ebing and Ellis, and he was not published in English until well after the obscenity trials (Weeks and Rowbotham 1977, 150). Clearly, though, his influence on Hall's text cannot be underestimated. The few extant English texts by Ulrichs were published as "briefs" in the Urania Manuscripts series.[6]

Ulrichs's *Raging Sword: The Riddle of Nature, and of Uranian Love* (hereafter *Raging Sword*) is a remarkable text that combines his 1868 address and recommendations to the Legislative Assembly of Germany, including the Tewes-Ulrichs Proposal; several appendices that document the scientific, anthropological, and statistical claims made in the address; as well as Lombardi's 1977 notes and annotations. Ulrichs's address was occasioned by an opportunity to amend the German criminal code to include protection for homosexuals. Lombardi writes of the outcome of Ulrichs's efforts: "Ulrichs ... indicated what was wrong with the governing system in nineteenth-century Germany. An elaborate magistrate, he attempted to describe in detail to his fellow legislators how they might approach the subject of homosexuality and seek a suitable answer to the legal problems which concern it. But the legislators silenced his speech" (Lombardi, in Ulrichs 1977, 1). *Raging Sword* begins with a preface in which Ulrichs cites both medical and legal terminology, statistics, and the "scientific texts by Numa Numantius" to support the legal positions that are to follow. "After the fashion of our predecessors, this text names men Uranians who feel that their innate sexual love drives them without exception towards persons of the male sex. They are not men in the exact sense of the word because they possess the love drives of women ... Among 2,000 people there are approximately 500 adult males among which there is on the average 1 Uranian" (n.p.). The irony of Ulrichs's evocation of *science* here is that "Numa Numantius" was Ulrichs's own pen name under which he published some of his "scientific" findings (Lombardi, in Ulrichs 1977, iv).

Once more, what is particularly fascinating about Ulrichs's highly rhetorical address are the ways in which Ulrichs, as both speaker and urning, heeds the imperatives of subjectivity and forces the "nineteenth-century homosexual [as] personage, a past, a case history, and a childhood," indeed as "a life form," to both speak and be spoken (Foucault 1978, 43). Clearly, a trope of speech or audibility predating that of late twentieth-century AIDS activism (i.e., SILENCE = DEATH) overdetermines Ulrichs's text. Similarly, it is possible to trace a genealogy of the political strategies of contemporary identitarian liberatory movements in the strategies he deploys to gain visibility for his fellow urnings. "I found courage to come face to face in battle against an age old, wrathful hydra which for time immemorial had injected poison and spectres into me and into men of my nature. Many were driven to suicide because all their happiness in life was poisoned. Indeed I am proud that I found courage to deal the initial blow to the hydra of public contempt. What gave me strength ... was the awareness that at that very moment the distant gaze of comrades of my nature was fixed on me" (Ulrichs 1977, 1).

What follows in both the main text and appendices is a catalogue of the tragic harms and injustices endured by those urnings who, because they are constructed as immoral or, in some places, illegal, suffer unnecessarily: "Before my eyes appeared the images of the persecuted and of those already damned who are yet unborn, and I behold the unhappy mothers beside their cradles rocking cursed, innocent children! Then I saw our judges and their blind-folded eyes" (2). Ulrichs's text is splattered with metaphors and tropes of war and battle as individual urnings come together to form one body at war: "The present battle situation has totally changed. Prior to this we were a dismembered body of defenceless weaklings, persecuted and mangled, seeking our salvation miserably in exile and in hiding places ... We simply refuse to allow ourselves to be persecuted!! ... Out with you, you miserable persecutors, and do battle in an honorable way! We shall reveal that our sword is wrought of genuine might and right" (16).

Writing just after Ulrichs and Krafft-Ebing, Havelock Ellis's seven-volume *Studies in the Psychology of Sex*, with volume 2 solely devoted to sexual inversion, was highly influential. Duggan (1992), along with many others, has already explored the content of Ellis's work in relation to early twentieth-century sexual discourses.[7] What interests me here are Ellis's own encounters with the juridical process – encounters that demonstrate how such a relatively small and highly specialized literature came to accrue the cultural authority and capital it eventually did, both inside and outside Judge Biron's courtroom.

Havelock Ellis wrote the preface to *The Well*, and it was hoped that this would keep the book from being read as a mere "salacious diversion by undesirable elements of the public" (Baker 1985, 203). Ellis's own work on sexual inversion had been seized by Scotland Yard in 1898 and, although Ellis was not charged, his book did have obscenity charges successfully brought against it in a sensational and very damaging trial known as *Regina* v. *Bedborough*.

George Bedborough was part of a group in London called the Legitimation League, a society dedicated to sex reform. The league looked favourably on Ellis's work and stocked copies of his *Sexual Inversion*. However, the league had previously attracted the attention of the police, who were convinced that it was the haunt of another London group known as the Anarchists. Capitalizing upon this opportunity to close down both the league and the Anarchists, an undercover Scotland Yard officer approached Bedborough and purchased a copy of Ellis's *Sexual Inversion*. Bedborough was arrested on 31 May 1898. Ellis was also supposed to be arrested (although he was not), and in 1898 Bedborough was charged with possessing and selling "a certain lewd wicked bawdy scandalous and obscene libel in the form of a book entitled *Studies in the Psychology of Sex: Sexual Inversion*" (Ellis 1967, 309).

A Free Press Defence Committee was established to defend both Bedborough and Ellis's text, but the case ended in anti-climax (Weeks 1981, 181). Bedborough was persuaded to plead guilty and was released. The effect of his release was that Ellis's book was left undefended and labelled scandalous and obscene (154). The judge had this to say upon Bedborough's release: "You might at the outset say that this was a scientific book. But it is impossible for anybody with a head on his shoulders to open the book without seeing that it is a pretence and a sham" (Ellis 1967, 369). After the trial, an editorial in the *London Daily Chronicle* also condemned Ellis's book, anticipating the contradictory press coverage of *The Well* trial: "The courts of the law and the criticisms of the Press are the responsible organs of public opinion in such matters ... we cannot take the view that the book has any scientific value whatever[; to the contrary] in the discharge of our duty to the public we feel bound to say that the book in question ought never to have been written or printed ... [it is] a highly morbid production, worthless as science even if the science it professes to advance were worth studying" (310).

Ironically enough, *Sexual Inversion* had been elevated to the status of *scientific* treatise by the time of *The Well* obscenity trial just thirty years later. In an American trial, *People* v. *Friede et al.*, 21 February 1929, the judge had a substantially different *Sexual Inversion* in front of him: "Although the book in evidence [*The Well of Loneliness*] is prefaced by a laudatory commentary by Havelock Ellis, yet it is he who, in his scientific treatise on the subject, states: 'We are bound to protect the helpless members of society against the invert.' Havelock Ellis, *Studies in the Psychology of Sex*, vol. 2, 356. The Court is charged with that precise duty here" (*People* v. *Friede et al.*, 78).

Clearly, by 1929 sexology has not only accumulated a great deal of capital and prestige but has also authorized a judiciary to act in its own and in society's best interest. Sexology's appeal to supposed objective truth in the name of both "science" and "knowledge" was supported by rhetoric from scientific humanitarianism in general and by the way science was increasingly evoked as a signifier and discourse of truth.[8] In its search for biologically based truths based on the rational activities of observing, describing, and classifying sexual species – as well as in drawing its images, metaphors, assumptions, and supposedly self-evident facts from the culture that produced it – sexology sought to make important distinctions between vice and disease and to provide, in a sense, a more humane treatment for those unfortunate sufferers (Duggan 1992, 259). What it (re)produced, however, were the very cultural narratives about gender and sexuality that it had purported to "scientifically" discover. In doing so, it inadvertently proliferated the possibilities not only for resisting those narratives but also for deploying the truths, metaphors, rhetoric, images, and facts that turned those narratives against themselves – a paradoxical strategy of resistance that Hall mobilized in *The Well of Loneliness.*

Ironic Proliferations and Shame/less Practices of Freedom

In her book, *Radclyffe Hall: A Case of Obscenity?*, which was written some forty years after she favourably reviewed *The Well* in *Time and Tide*, Vera Brittain (1968, 9-10) wrote the following summary of the British trial banning Hall's novel.

> In November, 1928, one of the most sensational prosecutions in the history of publishing centred upon Bow Street Police Court. The action was initiated by the Home Secretary, Sir William Joynson-Hicks (popularly known as "Jix"), after an attack by James Douglas, the Editor of the Sunday Express, on August 19th, 1928, upon a novel entitled *The Well of Loneliness*, written by Radclyffe Hall and published by Jonathan Cape Limited. Sir Chartres Biron, the Bow Street magistrate, heard the case and pronounced the book obscene. Mr Norman Birkett ... called Mr Desmond MacCarthy, Editor of Life and Letters, [to the witness stand] and asked him only one question: "In your opinion is this book obscene?" This was promptly disallowed. He asked him no other questions and Mr MacCarthy left the witness box without giving any evidence. Mr Birkett then announced that he had thirty-nine other witnesses whom he formally tendered, telling the magistrate that he intended asking them the very same question. Sir Chartres Biron would not admit their evidence and the witnesses were not called ... The magistrate ordered the book to be destroyed.

My analysis of the obscenity trial is threefold: first, my reading of the transcripts argues that this exercise of juridical power generates, indeed proliferates, the desires and pleasures it renounces and seeks to regulate. Thus, the invert as subject is constructed in a moment that simultaneously paves the way for its resistance.[9] "Radclyffe Hall," now functioning discursively as both "Invert" and "Author," embodies that resistance the moment Judge Biron attempts to shame Hall and bans *The Well* – it is a moment of excess and, hence, disruptive resistance that the *London Times,* unwittingly and rather paradoxically, mobilizes by reporting it. In the trial transcripts themselves, the moments of subjugation and resistance occur, ironically, in statements by counsel for the prosecution as well as by Judge Biron and not in statements by the defence counsel.

Second, the trial stages an elaborate theatre where contests of literary meaning meet matters of national security as both defence and prosecution present their very different readings of the same text, the latter authorized by Judge Biron's own reading, which, paradoxically, is very similar to my own. What emerges in Judge Biron's reading of *The Well* are the simultaneous disavowals and sanctions of the supposed truths of sexological discourse. On the one hand, Judge Biron refuses the alibi of essence as it was deployed in Hall's text vis-à-vis sexology while, on the other, he suggests that "such horrible instincts" do exist and that "these women" may be "unable to resist them" (4). Judge Biron imagines books that he argues could deal with these instincts in a way that he would not find objectionable – books that "might have a strong moral influence." "I can imagine a book written dealing with this subject that would present the whole matter as a tragedy ... presenting these women as the prisoners of circumstances which, however much they fight against them, they are unable to resist – I can imagine a book" ("Judgement," 3-4). Judge Biron, in essence, writes his own novel and his overdetermined text clearly anticipates how he reads the novel he is asked to adjudicate. He reads *The Well* against the text he discursively imagines, seemingly, but not quite, ad infinitum. The reading he eventually produces of Hall's text is exactly the same (meta)text written by Stephen Gordon via Hall in *The Well*, a text that remains bound by the same discursive, narratological, and epistemological machinery delineating what was thinkable about inversion in the twentieth century. Judge Biron bans *The Well* because it is both a success and a failure: it is a success because it deploys an alibi of essence that judicial and sexological discourses cannot contain but ultimately authorize, and it is a failure because it is not the text he imagines it should be.

Third, my reading of these transcripts argues that an understanding of the collisions between sexological discourse, juridical proceedings, and *The Well* must filter them through the lens of gender, race/nationality, and sexuality, where gender is the privileged theoretical axis that is intelligible only through race and nationality. In other words, inversion, already medicalized, is now "nationalized" as well. Coming ten years after the Pemberton Billing trial, *The Well* obscenity trial remains caught in a panicked epistemological contradiction where Englishness is whiteness is heterosexual, with perversion and inversion being its necessary national Other.

Charges of obscenity were not actually brought against *The Well* or Radclyffe Hall but, rather, against the two publishers. Thus, counsel retained for the defendants, the London publisher Jonathan Cape Ltd. (represented by Norman Birkett and Herbert Metcalfe) and Leopold Hill of the Paris publisher Pegasus Press (represented by J.B. Melville), sought to defend their clients against obscene libel; they did not seek to defend *The Well* against charges of perversion. The strategic position of the defence counsel, one with which Radclyffe Hall herself vehemently disagreed, can be summed up as follows: "Whilst in [*The Well of Loneliness*] there is a very definite description of a phase of life that exists and which, it is not in question it exists, there are no descriptions of acts which would bring this book within the bounds of pornographic work" (9 November 1928, 1).

J.B. Melville, in particular, secures his opening statement in the reiterated and yet highly unstable positivism of sexology: "The book accepts inversion as a fact in life, as a fact of nature, more as a fact of God's own creation ... it is the law, as it were, or a fact of nature, it calls for no more apology in the sense of the novel than the law of gravity. It exists ... it is a fact – as truly a fact as ... the fact in the law of nature" (2). Curiously though, having asserted that inversion exists as a "fact of nature," Melville proceeds to disavow the very "fact" he himself so vehemently evokes. And in that disavowal Melville's somewhat detailed reading of *The Well* bears remarkable similarity to more recent and less favourable feminist criticism that dismisses *The Well* on the grounds that it presents a heteronormative picture of the tragedy of lesbianism before it was rescued by feminism. Melville summarizes his position as follows: "I am thinking of ... this association and relationship which grows up between Stephen and ... Mary ... what is the end of it? ... What happens upon that? ... You will remember that the heroine, Stephen, decides to give up ... Mary, and to see that she resumes or starts life in normal affection with the man Martin" (6). Melville emphasizes Stephen's supposed tragedy at the end of the novel, and argues incessantly that the "fact itself" is presented with religious reverence, social respectability, and, above all, sexual conservatism. "If it be a description of acts of sexual relationship, then that would be a very indecent thing ... and I should be sorry to be briefed to support [it]" (4).

Alternatively, *The Well* presented in Judge Biron's 16 November judgment differs dramatically from that of Melville's defence statements ("Judgement"). Ironically, it is Judge Biron's reading of the novel that highlights not only the "viraginious" eroticism of the text but also the thinly disguised physicality that structures the relationships between Stephen and his lovers. Judge Biron only partially refuses Melville's (and sexology's) discourse of naturalism and essentialism, replacing it instead with competing discourses of "vice," "disease," and "acts." Judge Biron begins with a self-referential and authorizing evocation of juridical power – "these unnatural offences between women which are the subject of this book involve acts which between men would be a criminal offence" – and he continues to describe in detail the moments, and effects, of viraginious sexual intimacy in the novel.

> There is not a single word from beginning to end of this book which suggests that anyone with these horrible tendencies is in the least blameworthy or that they should in any way resist them. Everybody, all characters who indulge in these horrible vices are presented to us as attractive people ... the actual physical acts of these women indulging in unnatural vices are described in the most alluring terms; their result is described as giving these women extraordinary rest, contentment and pleasure, and not merely that, but it is actually put forward that it improves their mental balance and capacity. (4)

Judge Biron rather incredulously documents the evidence from *The Well* that supports both his, and my own, reading of the text: "What does it go on to say? What is the result of these horrible practices? 'It made me feel terribly strong ... and gentle. It was good, good, good' – repeated three times, the last 'good' emphasized in that order that one may make no mistake about what is meant in this book" (5). Again, Judge Biron's reading of the text differs dramatically from the defence's reading. "Then there is another passage concluding this incident ... [Stephen] writes to her mother in these terms: 'You insulted what to me is natural and sacred.' 'What to me is sacred'? Natural and sacred! Then I am asked to say that this book is in no sense a defence of unnatural practices between women, or a glorification of them, or a praise of them ... 'Natural' and 'sacred'! 'Good' repeated three times" (6).

As Judge Biron continues, it is possible to trace precisely the trajectory of the reverse-discourse mobilized by Hall's text.

> Then what are the effects of this book which is said to have been written on a note of tragedy? What are the results of these horrible practices – not that there was tragedy in people's lives, but, on the contrary, what we are told: "They no longer felt desolate, hungry outcasts, unloved and unwanted, despised of the world ... Love had lifted them up as on wings of fire, had made them courageous, invincible, enduring." What are the results of these vices as described in this book, on Mary: "Yet there was something quite new in her face, a sort of wise expression that Stephen had put there." (8)

Furthermore, Judge Biron reads the text beyond the specificities of language and forces it to speak even when it remains silent.

> There is another passage ... "And although they could not have put it into words, could not have explained it to themselves or each other, they seemed at that moment to be looking beyond the turbulent flood of earthly passion; to be looking straight into the eyes of a love that was

> changed – a love made perfect, discarnate ..." In order that there may be no mistake what is meant by that passage there are four asterisks placed directly after it. (8)

In addition to reading for the erotic intimacy between lovers, Judge Biron highlights the ways in which gender is denaturalized and deflected back upon itself through an alibi of essentialism. The passages in the novel that incense Judge Biron are those in which Stephen identifies across genders – where he not only occupies sites of British aristocratic masculinity but also deploys those narratives to highlight the injustice done to all inverts. Quoting from the text where Stephen is confronted by his mother and eventually is forced away from his home at Morton Hall, Judge Biron reads:

> "This terrible slur upon her love" – what does that mean? Then again, addressing her mother, "She held up her hand, commanding silence, commanding that slow, quiet voice to cease speaking, and she says: 'As my father loved you I love'" – this practitioner of unnatural vice!! – "'As a man loves a woman that was how I loved – protectively like my father. I wanted to give all I had to give'". I am asked to say that this book is not a defence of these practices? (5)

Before Judge Biron concludes, he comments, rather ineffectively, on Stephen's supposed tragedy and plea for tolerance at the end of the text, at once disavowing Melville's reading and, ironically, demonstrating Hall's success.

> It concludes with a very singular hysterical passage in which God is introduced ... There are a good many other passages in which the name of the Deity is introduced in a way which is hardly appropriate ... I confess the way in which the Deity is introduced into this book seems to me singularly inappropriate and disgusting. There is a plea for existence at the end. That of course means a plea for existence in which the invert is to be recognized and tolerated, and not treated with condemnation, which they are at present, by all decent people. (10)

Judge Biron quickly follows this passage with his very brief decision: "This being the tenor of this book, I have no hesitation whatever in saying it is an obscene libel ... and I shall order it to be destroyed" (10).

The contradictions inherent in Judge Biron's decision emerge in his construction of the type of book dealing "with unnatural offences" that "would not in itself" be an "obscene libel" (3). Both in the trial and in the appeal, Melville unsuccessfully attempts to shape *The Well* to fit Judge Biron's description, which reads as follows:

> I can imagine a book written dealing with this subject that presents the whole matter as a tragedy, the tragedy being that there may be people so afflicted who try their best to fight against this horrible vice, find themselves impelled in that direction or unable to resist those tendencies, with the result of the moral and physical degradation which indulgence in those vices must necessarily involve ... I can imagine a book of that kind ... having anything but an immoral influence; it might have a strong moral influence ... it [would show] the tragedy of people fighting against horrible instincts and being unable to resist them. (3-4)

But as I indicated already, Judge Biron reads a different text when he reads *The Well*. Melville tries again with a new magistrate in the appeal of 14 December 1928, quoting Judge Biron's words from the 16 November "Judgement," followed by his own.

> My submission to the Bench here is that if one examines this book carefully one will see that the heroine, Stephen, whilst she succumbs to temptation at one stage, is finally able to go back and, with all the commendation that the author can put into the passages of the work, and does finally go back into what on the obvious reading of the book is the lot which the inverted woman must face and endure, and that is loneliness. That is why I take the book is called "The Well of Loneliness." (16 November, 5)

Clearly, Melville is trying to shape *The Well* as the "tragedy of people fighting against horrible instincts and being unable to resist," using one discursively authorized text to overdetermine the reading of another. "There is developed, or commences to develop, the tragedy of this book; and I remind your Lordship now of the words that I read of the learned Magistrate below. Here is the commencement of the tragedy of the person so constituted that she can neither associate with men nor be welcomed by women" (9).

Melville's manoeuvrings both in the appeal and in the trial, as well as the responses of the magistrates who so rigorously disavow such a reading of *The Well*, demonstrate the ways in which the power/knowledge regimes supporting these various interpretive paradigms are, to a certain extent, not really under question here at all. Judge Biron at once refuses the alibi of essence but deploys a language of "instincts"; Melville deliberately evokes the positivism of science and sexology, but his clients are eventually found guilty. What is at stake are competing discourses of sexuality and the needs of legal institutions to strengthen their position by governing sexuality through "pastoral power" (Foucault 1981, 229-30). What crystallizes in the transcripts are the ways in which the judiciary mandates itself by constructing the "flock" it is supposedly authorized to watch over. Judge Biron interprets his task as follows: "the test of obscenity is this, whether the tendency of the matter charged as obscenity is to deprave and corrupt those whose minds are open to such immoral influences, and into whose hands a publication of this sort may fall" ("Judgement," 2). Moreover, Judge Biron reacts strongly to how *The Well* constructs those who, like himself, are reasonable men and who disapprove of such practices: "all characters who indulge in these horrible vices are presented to us as attractive people ... [while] those who object to these vices are sneered at in the book as prejudiced, foolish and cruel" (4).

Similarly, during the appeal the attorney general prosecuting Hall's novel spends a great deal of time constructing the "pure woman or even a young man" who would be corrupted by reading *The Well*. Ironically, such constructions inevitably legitimate the very reading they are trying to regulate.

> "Then Angela forced herself to think quickly and she said just five words: 'Could you marry me, Stephen?'" What does that mean? Imagine a young person reading that, coming to the end of the page. Imagine a pure woman or even a young man of adolescence reading it: "Could you marry me, Stephen?" What is the picture conjured up at once? He says: What do those words mean? His mind revolves round libidinous thoughts and it depraves him and corrupts him as he conjures up the picture which the writer of this book intends. (14 December, 9-10)

Like Judge Biron, the attorney general reads beyond the specificity of the text, sanctioning not only the reading he seeks to control but also producing the supposedly pure subjectivized flock juridical power needs to watch over in order to strengthen its own power: "My Lord, I must use plainness of speech. What is the implication from that sentence: What is the search which anybody who reads those words will make for the explanation? Why – 'I swear I won't torment you' – the suggestion by Stephen to Angela that there is to be no physical interference with her. That is the sort of enquiry which readers of this are set upon" (12). Finally, echoing the imperial gaze of sexology and the nation-building imperative of humanitarian science at the end of the nineteenth century, "the pure woman or even young man" is inevitably white, colonial, Christian, and heterosexualized as well as subject to a totalizing and individualizing pastoral power.

> Obscenity is to be judged by the standard of the laws of this realm ... You might get a native of another race, be it a white race or a yellow race or a black race, accustomed to practices which are not merely tolerated but which are part of a religious ritual, and who might theoretically produce

> a book in this country which would not be obscene in their land, be it in Africa or any other land; and yet I apprehend that the Court, if it thought it obscene, would condemn it ... In this country we have standards laid down by the law ... If ... not ... it is obvious that every nation would be exposed to influences which it would be powerless to destroy. (14 December, 20-1)

The competing interpretive and epistemological paradigms in the transcripts reveal the power/knowledge regime that delimits what is thinkable about sexuality. I return to a discussion of how this particular quote reveals the nation as heterosexual trope in the final part of this chapter. For now, it is important to foreground how, not surprisingly, essentialism is reflected in the competing representations of female same-sex desire by Melville and the attorney general, respectively, as well as in sexological discourse itself. On the one hand, and much like the early second-wave feminist criticism of the text, the attorney general argues that *The Well* ought to be banned because it corrupts the "natural" and "pure" friendships that exist "woman to woman": "My Lord, it is passages like those which dispose of the suggestion that this is a study of a pure love, woman to woman, which is consistent with the natural uses of the body. The world does not call unclean women who have intimate and beautiful friendships" (14 December, 13).

Melville, on the other hand, deploys the trope of the invert who exists as a fact in nature and thus ought not to be punished, ironically disavowing both *The Well* as fiction and the very sexuality of the invert he argues exists as fact.

> If it was a book which said that while this woman Stephen realised that what she took pleasure in ... that what she was revelling in ... was beastly [and that] she none the less preferred to do it, that would be, would it not, pornographic, be obscene, be something disgusting? But that is not the character of the book. Stephen is not that. Nobody suggests that this authoress had invented some monster for the purpose of writing a fiction that does not exist in the world; but she says that this woman, being a type that does exist, feels that there is nothing strange or unholy in what she feels ... as naturally as it occurs to her nature to do so, there is the request, the invitation by Stephen to Angela that she should come away and live with her ... Up to this time nothing has happened between them that could not happen, properly happen, decently happen, between ordinary women. (14 December, 13)

Here epistemological contradictions between a gender-separatist and a gender-inversion understanding of same-sex desire overdetermine how it is possible for either Melville or the attorney general to talk about the contents of Hall's novel. In the newspaper and critical coverage of both *The Well* and the obscenity trial a different contradiction emerges. Here we see how Hall's novel became and remained an indeterminate and dialogic site where an alibi of essence does battle with a repudiation of essentialism in favour of metaphors of disease.

Newspaper reviews played a crucial role in bringing about the obscenity charges against Cape and Hill. As Brittain stated, advanced review copies were sent out and James Douglas, editor of the *Sunday Express,* condemned *The Well* as "insidious moral poison" (19 August 1928). It was Douglas who insisted that Hall's novel be cleared by the home secretary, and, from that moment on, "The Well of Loneliness" came to carry a great deal of currency as a newspaper headline. Of course, not all reviewers were as outraged as was Douglas. In fact, Melville himself deploys many of the favourable reviews as evidence in his defence:

> There are certain Press notices which I think are indicative of the general view of the Press. First of all, from the "Morning Post": "Miss Radclyffe Hall's beauty of style and delicate, yet vivid, presentation of character and mood do not desert her." Then from the "Times Literary Supplement": "Sincere, courageous, high-minded and often beautifully expressed" ... The "Sunday Times" considers that she has courage and honesty. Then there is Mr Arnold Bennett [1928] writing in the "Evening Standard," and then the "Saturday Review" saying: "Her appeal is a powerful one, and it is supported by passages of great force and beauty" ... it does not appear likely that a book which is an obviously pornographic book would receive the powerful commendation of these critics. (14 December, 3-4)

What emerges in these reviews are the ways in which a discourse of essentialism and an alibi of essence function to facilitate a kind of ontological will, or right, not just to visibility but also to counter-discursive voice. For instance, Bennett's review of 9 August in the *Evening Standard* praises the novel and glumly predicts the response it was to receive: "*The Well of Loneliness* is the story of one of the victims of one of Nature's caprices. Havelock Ellis stands by it ... I cannot disagree with him." In a clever and insightful review, Bennett goes on to acknowledge the importance of Hall's novel: "Nature has no prejudices, but human nature is less broadminded, and human nature, with its deep instinct for the protection of society, can put up a powerful defence of its own limitations ... What [*The Well*] amounts to is a cry for unprejudiced social recognition ... The future may hide highly strange things, and therefore conservative prophecy is dangerous; nevertheless, I must say that I do not think the cry will be effectively heard."

In his April 1929 review in *The Canadian Forum*, S.H. Hooke also evokes the positivism of science and the alibi of essence to favourably review *The Well*. In doing so, he collapses morphology with ontology in the same way as does the *Sex Variants* study: "We know that nature, careful of the type and careless of the single life, from time to time throws off sports, individuals whose physiological make-up does not conform to the normal type, and whose emotions, through no fault of their own, refuse to run in the normal channels of ordinary social sex-relations ... Science passes no moral judgement on the invert, any more than it does on the individual born with a superfluous number of fingers or toes" (Hooke 1929, 243). Moreover, Hooke also names the productive irony of the British obscenity trial banning *The Well*: "But by the irony of life, society's blind reaction in the censorship to certain facts of life defeats itself. As a result of the ban upon *The Well of Loneliness*, thousands of people have read the book and become aware of the facts of inversion who would ordinarily never have seen the book, nor become cognizant of the facts which it deals with" (244).

Finally, Dr. Clifford Allen's 1950 essay, "The Personality of Radclyffe Hall," published in *The International Journal of Sexology*, reveals the numerous identities that were produced as effects of the 1928 collisions between *The Well*, sexology, and the Obscene Publications Act, 1857. Allen explores the relationships between Radclyffe Hall as "artist," "invert," and "author." His argument is absolutely crucial to understanding her exchange with Judge Biron in the courtroom, an exchange the *London Times* ran on page 5 of its 17 November 1928 edition. Allen (1950, 95) likens the artist's creative process to that of science: "Every artist creates in a peculiar form because of the structure of his mind ... and [is] unaware that conscious motivation is controlled by deeper forces ... their carving was more in the nature of shaping a stone which was already naturally half way on the path to be a piece of finished sculpture. The theory was that of a *chose trouvée* – a thing discovered, and the artist was only completing nature's work."

Arguing that both the artist and scientist reveal and discover what already exists in nature, Allen constructs Radclyffe Hall as doing both. The writer, he asserts, is driven by the forces of (human) nature ("his innermost mental structure"), whether he is aware of it or not: "Radclyffe Hall as a novelist is interesting because it would seem that most of her work is an exploitation of her personal problems rather than the technically superior use of objective factors" (96). Thus, Hall's output as a writer will be completely overdetermined by the verity of her sexual essence and by her creative process as an artist. Allen praises her work not because she was unjustly treated by juridical proceedings but because "her true position is that of an honest writer" (98).

I have discussed in detail how Hall is produced as an invert. What is perhaps even more noteworthy in Allen's essay are the ways in which he constructs the figure of the author. In "What Is an Author?" Foucault (1977c) argues that the author's function cannot be understood simply as an element of speech; rather, it functions as a discursive and classificatory sign, allowing a number of texts to be grouped together and establishing relationships of homogeneity, filiation, reciprocal explanation, authentication, or common utilization among them. Finally, the author, or what Foucault calls the "author-function," signifies as a discursive practice in and of itself: "In this sense, the function of an author is to characterize the existence, circulation, and operation of certain discourses within a society" (124). What occurs in Allen's essay is a kind of "piggy-back" effect, where the discourse of the "author" is collapsed onto that of the "invert" and "species." "Radclyffe Hall" as "author" unwittingly emerges out of Allen's analysis as a "complex and variable function" of numerous discursive practices (138).

Thus, the exchange between "Radclyffe Hall" and Judge Biron becomes particularly critical. His banning of *The Well* forecloses on the collisions between the various discursive technologies transforming female same-sex desire into the discursive category "Invert." As such, however, he also facilitates resistance to that closure, and "Radclyffe Hall" challenges Judge Biron in a florid performance of that resistance and in an originary moment of a reverse-discourse. Here is that exchange as it appears in the trial transcripts, just as Judge Biron is about to render his decision:

> Then we come to the incident of Mary. This takes place at the Front where, according to the writer of this book, a number of women of position and admirable character, who were engaged in driving ambulances in the course of the war, were addicted to this vice.
> MISS RADCLYFFE-HALL: I protest. I am that writer.
> THE MAGISTRATE: I must ask people not to interrupt the Court.
> MISS RADCLYFFE-HALL: I am the author of this book.
> THE MAGISTRATE: If you cannot behave yourself in Court I shall have to have you removed.
> MISS RADCLYFFE-HALL: Shame! It is a shame! ("Judgement," 6-7; *London Times* 17 November 1928, 5)

Clearly, the juridical proceedings intended to shame both sexed and gendered subjects as they were constructed in *The Well*. However, as Sedgwick (1993, 12-13) notes, shame is an "affect that delineates identity – but delineates it without defining it or giving it content ... [it] is available for the work of metamorphosis, reframing, refiguration, transfiguration, affective and symbolic loading and deformation." What is delineated, transfigured, and queered in Hall's shaming of the court proceedings is not necessarily only the question of identity but also the very terms of resistance.

The Outsider(s) Within[10]

> White people are not white: part of the price of the white ticket is to delude themselves into believing that they are.
>
> – James Baldwin, *The Price of the Ticket*

It is no accident that such discursive spaces were carved out in a British courtroom. Ten years before the Hall proceedings, Oscar Wilde posthumously fought his last stand in a trial that ironically established the epistemological limitations that overdetermined this relationship between sexology and nation building.[11] It could be argued – in fact, should be argued – that what occurred during the Pemberton Billing trial of 1918 was as much a reflection of the paradoxes and passions of its time as what occurred at the O.J. Simpson trial was of its time (i.e., the mid-1990s). Both Michael Kettle's (1977) *Salome's Last Veil* and Philip Hoare's (1977) *Oscar Wilde's Last Stand: Decadence, Conspiracy, and the Most Outrageous Trial of the Century* agree on a basic set of facts that occurred in and around the spring of 1918 in London: the British authorities finally permitted a private performance of Oscar Wilde's previously banned *Salomé* to be danced by the American Maud Allan. The part of Salome had been danced elsewhere, but a version of this exotic and provocative play had not been seen in London. Noel Pemberton Billing, Member of Parliament and author/publisher of the right-wing newspaper the *Imperialist* (which later changed its name to the *Vigilante*), denounced Allan, accusing her and all *Salomé* audience members of being part of the "Cult of the Clitoris," a catchall for anyone guilty of degeneracy, perversion, and loyalty to the extant cult of Oscar Wilde, which, Billing argued, continued to infect the British Empire.

Billing had a secondary agenda that becomes clear in the 26 January 1918 edition of the *Imperialist*. I quote the passage at length.

> There exists in the Cabinet Noir of a certain German Prince a book compiled by the Secret Service from reports of German agents who have infested this country for the past 20 years, agents so vile and spreading such debauchery and such lasciviousness as only German minds can conceive and only German bodies execute ... In the beginning of the book is a précis of general instructions regarding the propagation of evils which all decent men thought had perished in Sodom and Lesbia ... There are the names of 47,000 English men and women ... Privy Councillors, wives of Cabinet Ministers, even Cabinet Ministers themselves, diplomats, poets,

> bankers, editors, newspaper proprietors, and members of His Majesty's Household ... prevented from putting their full strength into the war by corruption and blackmail and fear of exposure ... [T]he stamina of British sailors [has been] undermined ... Even to loiter in the streets was not immune ... agents of the Kaiser were stationed at such places as Marble Arch and Hyde Park Corner ... Wives of men in supreme position were entangled. In Lesbian ecstasy the most sacred secrets of State were betrayed. The sexual peculiarities of members of the peerage were used as a leverage to open fruitful fields for espionage. (n.p.)

The 16 February 1918 edition of the former *Imperialist,* now the *Vigilante* (appropriately named, given that the *Oxford English Dictionary* defines "vigilante" as "watchfulness, caution, circumspection" and a "vigilance committee" as a "self-appointed body for maintenance of order, etc., in an imperfectly organized community"), makes explicit the link between the list of 47,000 names, *Salomé,* and British nationalism.

> THE CULT OF THE CLITORIS
> To be a member of Maud Allan's private performances in Oscar Wilde's *Salomé* one has to apply to a Miss Valetta, of 9, Duke Street, Adelphi, W.C. If Scotland Yard were to seize the list of these members I have no doubt they would secure the names of several of the first 47,000 ... All the horrors of shells and gas and pestilence introduced by the Germans in their open warfare would have but a fraction of the effect of exterminating the manhood of Britain as the plan by which they have already destroyed the first 47,000. (58)

Evoking the logic of specularity, or "watching," where sexual and national ontologies are supposedly evident on the surface of the body, Billing juxtaposed the colonial with a heteronormative gaze when he deliberately libelled Allan in order to create a public forum within which to expose the German "Black Book" containing the names of 47,000 English men and women who were supposedly sexual perverts. Specular economies are both anxious and paradoxical, however, because the entire existence of the Black Book is predicated on the hysterical and panicked spectre of racial and sexual passing. In other words, these anxieties derive power from the anxieties and contradictions of a racially, sexually, and gender stratified society, where ontological borders are permeable and where the visible is no longer the ground for knowledge (Ginsberg 1996, 4). Amy Robinson (1994, 716) names this crisis more productively: "The 'problem' of identity, a problem to which passing owes the very possibility of its practice, is predicated on the false promise of the visible as an epistemological guarantee."

Billing was undone by the fear that so-called German perverts were passing as English heterosexual patriots. The trope of passing signifies movement from a time and place where true identity is known to a time and place where it is unknown. That movement, as suggested by Billing's claims, is at once geographical, metaphysical, and ontological, and it produces passing as a trope of modernity that will reappear as both time and space in later twentieth-century butch and female-to-male trans-sexual fiction (which, I argue, cites this historical moment as its temporal frame of reference and this national identity as its spatial framework). Billing's ultimate goal can only be the incitement of a public morality crusade, or the production of a moral panic, that would fire up English morale during a particularly brutal and politically volatile year of the "Great War." Billing was successful in creating that forum, which began and ran for five days in the Old Bailey courthouse in May 1918.

Of all the numerous ways that Pemberton Billing might possibly be remembered, the surest has to be that of "sensationalist showman." After entering his Plea of Justification in that courthouse (his legal statement of defence, in which he enters a plea of not guilty to the charge of criminal libel), and despite neither knowing nor following evidentiary rules, Billing refused a defence attorney and chose to defend himself in court. Why he chose to do that becomes clear very early in both his Plea of Justification (where he speaks about himself in the third person) and his subsequent performance in the courtroom: "Noel Pemberton-Billing says he is not guilty ... and for a further plea he says that all the defamatory matters alleged in the Indictment are true" (Hoare 1997, 109). Oscar Wilde, according to that Plea, was a "moral pervert," *Salomé* an "open representation of degenerated sexual lust, sexual crime, and unnatural passions and an evil and mischievous travesty of a biblical story," and Billing "the Saviour, Christ the King, come to redeem them in this moment of national peril" (109).

The trial itself, presided over by Mr. Justice Charles John Darling, whose own name, or so Billing claimed in front of a press-filled gallery, appeared in the Black Book, clustered around several related themes: German sexology and the specificity of its always already and, indeed, performative ("guilty") language; Oscar Wilde's *Salomé*, its coded (or, so Billing claimed, not so coded) perversions, and the self-evident guilt of Oscar Wilde apologists; and the implications of the so-called Black Book for British national security. Like other sex trials, this one was structured by a paradox, staging in public, as nationalist spectacle, what it rendered criminally deviant outside its domain (McClintock 1995, 219). By ordering the unspeakable spoken in public, the Billing trial took shape around the very things it imagined itself isolating and punishing. Billing claimed that, if agents of German perversion were passing within England's gates, then they would be detectable by their knowledge of medical discourse. In the 16 February excerpt from the *Vigilante* quoted above, Billing acknowledges in court that he chose the term "clitoris" quite carefully. The trial transcripts reveal bizarre and overdetermined skirmishes over the meaning of the term. When questioned about its medical specificities, Billing and his witnesses argued that, while the clitoris was a natural part of the female body, it was, more important, an excessive and "superficial" part that "did nothing to help the race," was "what remains of the male organ in the female," and, thus, was profoundly dangerous (Hoare 1997, 141). In fact, when stimulated, it "possessed the most dreadful influence on any woman [so] that she would do the most extraordinary things" (126). Wilde's *Salomé* staged this female state of frenetic hyper-stimulation, and the word "clitoris" itself, argued Billing, came to signify a group of perverse individuals of any gender who would "gather together to see a representation of a diseased mad little girl" (141).

Billing's assertions became increasingly hysterical and performative. Not only was the clitoris dangerous to both nation and hearth but even the mere mention of the word was treason.[12] Billing claimed that, because "clitoris" was such an obscure medical term, only oversexualized and perverse women and German sexologists would know its precise meaning. After questioning Maud Allan, for instance, about whether or not she knew the term, Billing claimed that it was so obscure that only a handful of professional medical men knew what it meant (115). Allan was supposedly capable of such degeneracies because these were the product of her genetic make-up. Her brother, William Henry Theodore Durrant, had been executed for committing a sensational sex crime in San Francisco ten years earlier, and Billing argued that, given that such degeneracies were inherited, Allan must be guilty of the charges against her. Allan's training similarly implicated her (she had taken her dance training in Berlin), and she was thus guilty of leading both the Cult of the Clitoris and what was left of Wilde's Cult of the Beautiful. What was not uttered during this performance of entrapment was that, at the very least, Allan knew the term because her name had become publicly associated with it in Billing's own newspaper.

The fact that this manufactured national crisis was scripted to include Oscar Wilde was no accident. Wilde's trial, held in the same courtroom and also involving a charge of public libel, permanently imbricated homosexuals, Wilde, and a particular form of aesthetic pleasure. British homosexual men were taunted with cries of "Oscar, Oscar!" up to the beginning of the First World War (David 1997, 5). And, as the transcripts of the Billing trial reveal, an attentiveness to poetic language, extended similes, and "the beautiful" were enough to betray one's secret predilection for perversion. Moreover, the text of *Salomé* was as much on trial as was Maud

Allan's reputation. In one particularly telling moment, Judge Darling, who had already been accused of treasonous perversion when Billing suggested his name appeared in the Black Book, reads aloud from *Salomé* and then performatively disavows what has been labelled as incriminating comprehension.

> Darling: [quoting from *Salomé*] "She is like a dove that has strayed. She is like a narcissus trembling in the wind. She is like a silver flower ..." I do not see where the Art is. Of course, I cannot understand it. (Laughter in Court.). (Hoare 1997, 116)

Judge Darling's protest aside, both *Salomé* and Wilde were impossibly guilty. Wilde's reputation as a "sodomite" was well known, and *Salome*, the play that had made its author's name "a household word wherever the English language was not spoken," was still banned in England (116). Billing chose his props and his witnesses very carefully.

The transcripts show that the actual text of *Salomé* became as incriminating as German (or, indeed, Wildean) sympathies might have been. Billing capitalized on the feud between Robert Ross (Wilde supporter and friend) and Lord Alfred (Bosie) Douglas (by now Wilde denouncer), the latter appearing in court as a translator of *Salomé* to support Billing's claim that it was perverse and designed to appeal to sadists, homosexuals and lesbians, and other assorted perverted individuals. Bosie also claimed that *Salomé* had been written after Wilde had read *Psychopathia Sexualis* by Krafft-Ebing, one of the German sexologists whose scientific theories were supposedly weakening England (146-7). Billing's own key medical witness was Dr. Serell Cooke, who presented a detailed medical analysis of the play, which argued that it was a text that would appeal to perverts precisely because it was filled with "the extraordinary ... language that is usually employed by homosexuals." Such language is used, Cooke assured the spellbound courtroom, "to describe as beautiful and glorious all their perversions [and] for them to read into the distinctly physical acts of sex something spiritual" (145).

Where Billing read Wilde and *Salomé* as homosexual, Cooke read them as further evidence of sadism. Testifying that sadism was the most monstrous of all the sexual perversions, combining lust and sexual excitement with cruelty and violence, Cooke went on to suggest that *Salomé* and, by implication, all who would attend its production were similarly monstrous. When, at the end of the play, Salome kisses Jokanaan's decapitated head – a moment of "pure Sadism" – all those persons of perverted instincts would "probably have sexual excitation, and even orgasm" asserted Cooke (146-7). Later, when Bosie took the stand, he helped establish the supposed link between perversion and Germanness, and hence treason, when he was unable to contextualize Billing's reminder that the most successful production of *Salomé* occurred in Berlin. Moreover, one of Billing's most important witnesses furthered what was being constructed as self-evident: "Sadism [is] the lust for dead bodies ... that [is] from a medical treatise by a German ... the Germans were clever in advocating this as a means of corrupting people by means of Sadism as they have [been] ... in advertising *Salomé*" (132).

As incredible and sensational as these claims seem, the anxieties investing this event become even more vexed as the frame shifts from the text of *Salomé* to the threats that it and the Black Book pose to war-time national security. From the second day of the trial, when the public gallery was packed with wounded soldiers in pyjama-like blue hospital uniforms whom Billing had persuaded to attend (117), through pages and pages of transcripts with questions like "Were there German agents using these public houses and baths and massage establishments?" (122), to Billing's closing statement to the judge (who did exonerate him of all charges), "I ask you to send me away from this place with the confidence that a verdict ... will give me to carry on the very heavy task which, in the interests of my country, I have seen fit to commence" (172), the entire trial was steeped in discourses of nationalism. If Prosser (1998) is correct in arguing that sexology medicalized the inverted body, then the 1918 Billing trial suggests that sexology quite inadvertently racialized, indeed nationalized, that body long before Judge Biron banned *The Well* in a similar kind of hysteria. Or, perhaps to frame this assertion slightly askew, from this vantage point these early twentieth-century anxieties over sexuality, gender, and nation pose a series of questions that could not have been asked at that time: What was the role that sexuality played in the construction of nationality? Conversely, is nationness overdetermined by the gendered and sexualized discourses of empire? What role does the notion of nationness play in the production of not just sexual identities but also in/within larger "imaginary" sexual communities?

Radclyffe Hall built her novel upon the previous articulations accomplished by the work of the Billing trial both in terms of the sexual and national Otherness of the invert and the supposedly natural ontological status of British heterosexual masculinity. I return to this legacy in the next chapter. For the moment, however, it is crucial to situate this judicial imbrication of nation and sexuality within the context of the sedimented anxieties fermenting in and around the First World War. By 1918, the last year of the war, Britain begins to think of itself and its enemies differently: the British nation becomes the protectorate of the more helpless Belgium, which has been feminized and brutalized by Germany.[13] Germany, however, remains simultaneously hypermasculine (bullying, raping, and violating the innocent Belgium) and queerly effeminized (the Pemberton Billing trial), oversexualized, and completely degenerate, invading and corrupting the otherwise pure citizens of the British Empire by luring them into deviant sexual desires. Indeed, as both a "system of ordered procedures for the production of Truth" and a disciplinary, performative, and liturgical site that paradoxically stages as a public spectacle what it renders criminally deviant, these British courtrooms remain haunted by fictions of desire (McClintock 1993, 234).

Fed by British war hysteria, the Billing trial was fundamental to Britain reassuring itself during the First World War, which brought about a "destabilizing paroxysm of nationalism" (Anderson 1983, 81). Benedict Anderson's choice of words is not without a kind of fruitful irony, given the *Oxford English Dictionary* definition of paroxysm: "fit of disease." On the one hand, the British Empire itself remains entirely imaginary or fictional. "It is nice [sic] that what eventually became the late British Empire has not been ruled by an 'English' dynasty since the early eleventh century: since then a motley parade of Normans (Plantagenets), Welsh (Tudors), Scots (Stuarts), Dutch (House of Orange) and Germans (Hanovers) have squatted on the imperial throne" (81). It is the latter member of the "motley parade" that, early in 1918, initiated the interpellative hailing of the Royal family from its former existence as the German "Hanovers" to the British "Windsors." Such a nominal connection to the abjected enemy that British sons were dying in trenches to defeat could only have been a source of profound national embarrassment and dis-ease. On the other hand, and contrary to Gilbert and Gubar's (1988) assertion that the Great War was a form of sex warfare, a climactic episode in a battle of the sexes, the First World War remains a historical event that produced particularly gendered and traumatized subjects as well as discourses of gender and citizenship at the same moment that it profoundly contested all of them.

With its metaphors of German perversion as contamination and disease supposedly infesting the otherwise pure British nation, the Billing trial heaps heteronormativity upon biological essentialism upon nationalism to insist upon – indeed, to centralize – a fictional imperative of heterosexuality, masculinity, and British nationalism, despite evidence to the contrary. Then again, as Raitt and Tate (1997, 4) note, the war brought about new levels of policing, internal surveillance, and coercion via the British Defence of the Realm Acts, the likes of which Britain has not seen since. Finally, new and prophetically discomforting discourses of nationalism remained in Europe and were to explode again in a few years' time. What becomes undeniably clear during the period between 1914 and 1945, which historians are now beginning to describe as the second Thirty Years War, are the ways in which the obsessively hygienic discourses of nation, gender, sexuality, and war imagine themselves lining up to centre whiteness, Britishness, and heteronormativity as the subjects of modernity. The

Billing trial, during the last year of that paroxysm, staged this aligning-abjection process as a sensational and regulative public spectacle.

The suggestion that sexual identities map onto those of nation is not particularly novel. In his oft-cited and still influential treatise on nationalism, *Imagined Communities: Reflections on the Origin and Spread of Nationalism*, Anderson (1983) deploys naturalized, and naturalizing, discourses of sexuality and gender to demarcate nationness as cultural and psychic artefact. Refusing the suggestion that nationness is only ideological or merely an effect of false consciousness, Anderson instead argues that it is a product with profound emotional legitimacy. Nationness, Anderson posits, is an "imagined political community ... imagined as both inherently limited and sovereign," which comes into being by aligning itself with "the large cultural systems that preceded it, out of which – as well as against which – it came into being" (15-19). "Nation-ness," he continues, "is not the awakening of a nation to self-consciousness, but rather the invention of a nation where [one does] not exist" (15).

Anderson's reworking of definitions of nationhood bears interesting, if not paradoxical, fruit. "Nation" shifts from actually being a universal, pre-existing culture to something that is the temporal and performative effect of cultural and juridical work, constructed as universal after the fact (cf. "In the modern world everyone can, should, will 'have' a nationality, as he or she 'has' a gender" [14]). Nation is not transhistorical but, rather, is a spontaneous distillation of discrete historical forces that produces national identities as unmistakably particular. To reiterate the example Anderson uses, to be Greek – or indeed, in Billing's case, to be British – is to manifest a national essence as a very precise, unique ontology. A nation is spatially limited, marked by finite, if elastic boundaries, beyond which lie all other nations; yet, a nation remains an effect of an unlimited fantasy or set of imaginings because "the members of even the smallest nation will never know most of their fellow-members, yet in the minds of each lives the image" of their commonality, communion, or "deep, horizontal comradeship" (15). Anderson's tropes bear repetition: "Ultimately, it is this fraternity that makes it possible, over the past two centuries, for so many millions of people, not so much to kill, as willingly die for such limited imaginings" (16).

Undeniably, Anderson's use of terms like "fraternity" and "fellow-member," as well as his assumption that everyone "has" a nationality just as they "have" a gender, is built upon some rather interesting assumptions about sexuality and gender – assumptions that the Billing event shared and mobilized. In their introduction to *Nationalisms and Sexualities* Parker et al. (1992) argue that Anderson's form of nationalism distinctly favours a homosocial form of male bonding. But, as Sedgwick (1985) notes, the term "homosocial" is marked by both discriminations and paradoxes. On the one hand, it merely describes social bonds between persons of the same sex; on the other hand, it is a neologism formed analogously to, yet differentially from, "homosexual." In many ways, then, for Anderson to characterize nationhood as a passionately felt brotherhood is, to quote Sedgwick, "to draw the "'homosocial' back into the orbit of 'desire'" and to dangerously "hypothesize the potential unbrokenness of a continuum between homosocial and homosexual" (1). Representing nationhood in this way would require that this passionate fraternity, constituted by an excess of affect and an always already fictional national spatiality, distinguish itself from more explicitly sexualized male-male relations and posit the homosocial-homosexual continuum as radically discontinuous. Trials such as Billing's and *The Well*'s perform precisely this function. During a decidedly homosocial event such as the First World War, which has been characterized as the "greatest changer of them all," the distinction between homosocial and homosexual slips and the state stands ready to enforce clarity at all costs (MacDonald 1996, 115).

Anderson's assumption that everyone has a nationality in the same way that they have a gender suggests that each manifestation of nationality similarly functions within a system of differences, having no positivity or presence and being defined only by that which it is not. Such definitional gymnastics clearly binds nation, gender, and sexuality within economies of self/other, where the one is forever haunted by its definitional other. Thus, as Parker et al. (1992, 5) suggest, the paradoxical task of constructing and sustaining national identities involves, "on the one hand, the nation's insatiable need to administer difference through ... segregation, censorship, [etc.] ... and on the other, the nation's insatiable need for representational labour to supplement its founding ambivalence, the lack of self-presence at its origin or in its essence." Such performative, discursive, and reiterative work is not unlike that which Judith Butler identifies as crucial to the construction and regulation of gender fictions. If, as Butler (1993) suggests, it is the reiterative power of discourse that produces the phenomena that it regulates and constrains, then what appears to be the spatial and temporal "fact" of nationness can also be understood as an effect of the historical operations of power. Thus, Anderson's (1983) nationalized subject ("the members of even the smallest nation will never know most of their fellow-members, yet in the minds of each lives the image of their deep, horizontal comradeship" [15]) is produced in the same moment as is Butler's gendered subject, both being the effect of a differential system of difference (to be English is to be heterosexual and, thus, not German and not perverse) and a regulatory machinery: "the forming of a subject requires an identification with the normative phantasm of 'sex' [or 'nation'] and this identification takes place through a repudiation which produces a domain of abjections, a repudiation without which the subject cannot emerge" (Butler 1993, 3). Butler continues: "Further, the materialization of a given sex [again, read: 'nation'] will centrally concern the regulation of identificatory practices such that the identification with the abjection of sex [or nationness] will be persistently disavowed" (3).

On Sunday, 19 August 1928, when James Douglas (1928, n.p.) reviewed *The Well* and claimed that he "would rather give a healthy boy or a healthy girl a phial of prussic acid than this novel," he materialized those regulatory practices on the bodies of both the invert and Hall's novel itself. He ensured that the appropriate bodies to be rendered were British, white, heterosexual, masculine, and male.[14] The tone and scope of Douglas's review pays uncanny homage to the sentiments mobilized by Billing only ten years earlier. The task, according to Douglas and Billing before him, was for British society to clean "itself from the leprosy of these lepers" and make the "air clean and wholesome once more" (*Sunday Express*, 19 August 1928, n.p.). Manipulating what appeared to be the self-evident factuality of an England that could not lose the First World War, Douglas, like Billing, argued that the battle against such filth "had been lost in France and Germany but not in England ... The English people are slow to rise in their wrath and strike down the armies of evil, but when they are aroused they show no mercy" (n.p.). Moreover, he mapped out the aligning-abjection process with volatile and nationalistic language: "We must protect our children against their spacious fallacies and sophistries ... we must banish their propaganda from our bookshops" (n.p.) and so on. Once again, the ghost of Oscar Wilde returns to haunt Douglas as much as Billing: "Literature has not yet recovered from the harm done to it by the Oscar Wilde scandal. It should keep its house in order" (Hoare 1997, 46).

Finally, what becomes even more remarkable about Radclyffe Hall is that she both embraced and resisted that cultural legacy bequeathed her by history. As I argue in Chapter 3, Stephen Gordon's greatest lament in *The Well* is precisely his inability to perform the masculine and patriotic duties for which he had been trained by his father. He is all but excluded from the fraternal homosocial world of masculinity that he glimpses with his father before his death and then again with Martin Hallam, who later becomes his rival for Mary. At the same time, Hall deploys tropes of nation within the text to demarcate a space of resistance for those divested of official nationness – a trope that she bequeaths to her descendants and that, some seventy years later, reappears as both the "lesbian" and "queer" nation.

2
Passionate Fictions: Radclyffe Hall's *The Well of Loneliness*

> To teach ignorance is ... to teach to *un-know*, to become conscious of the fact that what one thinks is knowledge is really an array of received ideas, prejudices, and opinions – a way of *not knowing* that one does not know ... [Thus] the question of education ... is the question not of how to *transmit* but of how to *suspend* knowledge.
>
> – Barbara Johnson, *A World of Difference*

While the event of *The Well*'s publication was over-invested within economies of nationalism and sexuality, its own internal thematics, primarily questions of knowledge, self-knowledge, and "ignorance," were similarly articulated through questions of nationness, race, and sex/gender. Alison Hennegan's introduction to the 1982 Virago reprint of *The Well* begins with a brief accounting of how it has functioned since its publication and stormy reception in 1928:

> In countless novels and autobiographies schoolgirls have been expelled for reading it and mistresses sacked for discussing it. Tremulous daughters have given it to their mothers, preparing the grounds for revelations yet to come; mothers have given it to daughters to indicate that personal revelations will be sympathetically received. Close female friends have given it to each other as a delicate hint that friendship could include yet more. Since its first publication in 1928 innumerable girls and women – in fact and fiction – have turned to *The Well of Loneliness* for enlightenment and support. (Hennegan 1982, vii)

Hennegan's observations are ironic in that, while she does document the ways Hall's novel has been discursively productive circa 1982, what she cannot possibly have known is that even a cursory review of such criticism reveals that what is more accurately revealed is how *The Well* has read those seventy years of readers.

While the narrative of Hall's story of an invert has not changed, what and how that narrative is, and has been, invested within numerous pre- and post-Stonewall feminist, lesbian, lesbian-feminist, gay and lesbian, queer and trans-gender/trans-sexual economies has changed dramatically.

There can be little argument that the book exists both before and after the most recent resurgence of butch-femme in the 1990s (evidenced by Leslie Feinberg's *Stone Butch Blues*) and before and after the emergence of discourses of trans-sexuality and trans-gender during the same time. What is curious is that, more often than not, *The Well* is, at one and the same time, cited as the transcendental lesbian text, butch-femme text, and trans-sexual text. Such unproblematic constructions of history and reading accord *The Well* a stability and continuity within economies that have used it to signify discontinuities and incongruities. Given that every reading is in many ways an inaugural production of the text, the history of *The Well* criticism (including the reading by Judge Biron, which banned the novel in the same year it was published) functions to evoke a set of epistemological, political, and juridical knowledges while, at the same time, always already deferring those knowledges. Indeed, those readings emerge within an "after-logic" reading economy, a discursive reading practice wherein each reading that is supposedly produced "after," or later in time than, *The Well* appears beside or even before it (Carlson 2000, 8). My reading of *The Well* is as much a genealogy of those articulations as it is the production of yet another. What emerges when that body of criticism is read as *The Well* reading its readers is an ironic confirmation of Virginia Woolf's assessment that "No-one has read [Hall's] book" (Whitlock 1987, 560).

My own reading of Hall's novel is articulated through/with four axioms. First, that Stephen Gordon understands himself best through the language of biological essentialism as a man and that he recognizes himself as such; second, that most of the plot of *The Well* shows Stephen struggling, unsuccessfully, to perform the duties of aristocratic British masculinity and, thereby, winning the recognition of his father and country – the very process by which some forms of masculinity are accorded intelligibility; third, that Stephen is therefore evidence of the productive failure of discursive formations, especially those of nation (Britishness) and religion (Christianity), where they realize gender (masculinity); and fourth, that Stephen is white – a racial signifier that the critical analyses of *The Well* have failed to articulate. My axioms are torsions of those found in two places: Eve Kosofsky Sedgwick's (1995) essay "Gosh Boy George, You Must Be Awfully Secure in Your Masculinity!" and Richard Dyer's (1988) "White." First, Sedgwick (1995) rehearses a number of propositions about the production and consumption of masculinity, the most important being that, sometimes, masculinity has nothing to do with men. She universalizes masculinity not as an essential identity but, rather, as a cultural and discursive subject quite separate from men. "As a woman," she writes, "I am a consumer of masculinities, but I am not more so than men are; and, like men, I as a woman am also a producer of masculinities and a performer of them"

(13). Sedgwick performs a chiasmatic deconstruction of heteronormative gender regimes wherein minoritized gender identities are thought to be effects of essential bodies. She concurs with others, both inside and outside lesbian contexts, when she flips that equation onto its head and suggests that the categorical imperative of masculinity no longer be natural, or biological, male bodies. There are, in other words, and have always been, masculinities without men.[1]

Dyer (1988), on the other hand, posits that the categorical imperatives of whiteness necessitate its hypervisible invisibility. Whiteness, Dyer argues, gains its representational power by paradoxically being both "everywhere and nothing" at the same moment (45). Whiteness masks itself as a racial category by colonizing the definition of other norms (class, gender, heterosexuality, nationality, and so on) and by representing itself as the domain of the universal. In attempts to particularize that universal, whiteness is articulated best by the very things it differentially claims not to be: nation, class, ethnicity, sexuality, and so on. In ways akin to both gender and sexuality, the subject begins to fall apart when whiteness is analyzed as whiteness: "Any instance of white representation is always immediately something more specific ... the particularity of whiteness itself begins to disappear" (46). In other words, where whiteness constructs itself as self-sufficient and capable of holding power as a result, further analytical scrutiny shows that it is often physically and/or materially dependent upon differently classed and raced domestic servants. Consequently, one of the primary tasks of whiteness becomes that of demonstrating its own virtues in order to justify domination.

In a colonial context, for instance, whiteness is often associated with modernity, reason, order, and stability, while blackness stands in for backwardness, irrationality, chaos, and violence. These are fixed, impermeable, and bound, so Dyer argues, both with and as an evolutionary trajectory from backwardness to reason/modernity (49). Texts of colonial white supremacy, *The Well* included, often struggle with the importance of fixity, tradition, preservation of conventionalities and clear boundaries – all of which keep whiteness clearly distinct from everything it claims that it is not. Hence, concludes Dyer, "whites and men (especially) become characterized by 'boundariness'" (51). In *The Well* the notion of boundedness includes both a psychic (which I return to below) and a political geography referenced by the signifier "England," which is coterminous with everything Stephen believes he should be: masculine, aristocratic, patriotic, honourable, and, above all, white. The modern nation-state of England authorized particular bodies as culturally intelligible, valuable, and natural. While Stephen recognized himself as subject to that formulation, his unthinkable body – that is, a body between genders – failed to materialize as a body that mattered.

In *The Well*, white sociality is further articulated through tropes bound by fixity, order, and rigidity. The Gordon family interacts with other families principally through codes of behaviour and rules of conduct embodied in conventionally set pieces like dinner parties, balls, foxhunts, and the like. These rituals are different from the gatherings at Valerie Seymour's salons and different again from those of the working-class domestic help, to which the reader occasionally gains access through Stephen. Finally, the codes of sociality suggested by the black American brothers, Henry and Lincoln, are overdetermined by the belief that black people have more life, more body, and more emotion because they are closer to nature. As Dyer notes, these racist ideas were endemic to processes of European expansion, colonization, and nation building. Blacks, according to Hall's novel, are somehow more natural and have more life than whites. This means that the body, emotions, sensuality, and spirituality of the black is opposed to the mind and the intellect of the white and, in *The Well*, of the invert.

However, as I suggest later, Henry, Lincoln, and Collins effect a kind of embodiment that eludes Stephen. Motifs of embodiment, as both Dyer and I argue, articulate whiteness through a series of compelling paradoxes. First, those white, especially Christian, subjects are corporeal beings that most value transcendence of corporeality. As I explore further, Stephen is written by a motif of embodiment that is *of* but not necessarily *in* the body. Black and working-class subjectivities are reducible to corporeality but Stephen both is and is not. White bodies tend to stand in for all bodies – a notion whereby whiteness is seen at once as a non-race and as the entire human race. Second, whiteness is often marked by a commitment to heterosexuality, where men are supposed to fight against the dark carnality of sexual desires and women are to have no such desires at all. Stephen is no exception here either: as a child, he is bound by the baser emotions that his crush on Collins evokes. As an adult, Stephen is supposed to know better and does eventually mature into adult sexuality, which is appropriately controlled, contained, and paternal. Hall constructs a complicated set of desires for Stephen and falls into a rhetoric of transcendence wherein the very source of those desires, the body, *has* to be controlled. Such is the stoic and masochistic glory of the imperial hero.

That said, I take as my point of departure recent querulous criticisms that possessively articulate Stephen's body with singular, absolute, and definitive status: either it is definitively lesbian or it is definitively transsexual. Such arguments are grounded in what Halberstam and Hale (1998, 283) have identified as the "Butch/FTM Border Wars." The No Man's Land between female masculinity and trans-sexual masculinity has been fracturing personal, local, and national discussions in support groups, on the pages of community publications, on e-mail lists, and in special "Trans-" issues of publications like *GLQ* and *Social Text*. FTMs are accused of possessively and exclusively occupying the category of (heteronormative) masculinity, often against or in opposition to butch masculinity or "just" lesbian women "playing" with gender without identifying as trans-gendered and often without transitioning surgically (283). In some camps, such battles are often fought over the signifiers of masculinity. For instance, members of one FTM e-mail list advise each other on clothing and hairstyles that are decidedly not-butch (avoid crew cuts; wear chinos or khakis instead of faded denim; avoid waist-length motorcycle leather jackets and wear three-quarter-length leather jackets instead). Curiously enough, this semiotics of masculinity is less about a supposed authentic maleness and more about a semiotic mapping of class topographies.

These border wars have erupted most profoundly in two places: first, over the body of Brandon Teena, the white working-class Nebraska youth whom I have previously discussed and, second, over recent critical reinvestments in *The Well*. Such border wars, by focusing exclusively on gender, similarly over-invest the protagonist of *The Well*. In his recent book *Second Skins: The Body Narratives of Transsexuality*, Jay Prosser (1998) goes against seventy years of criticism by suggesting that *The Well* is not a lesbian novel at all. What is remarkable about previous critical work on the novel is how close it has come, in the same moment as claiming the novel's subject as lesbian, to performing that reading where Stephen is a woman who really would be a man: that is, where she is not lesbian but a female-to-male trans-sexual (136-7).

In his insistence on origins of trans-sexuality and his assertion that such narrative origins are to be found in *The Well* only when the lesbian subject retreats, Prosser argues that the visibility of Stephen as lesbian has necessitated the displacement of Stephen as female-to-male trans-sexual. "Rightly tracing Hall's debt to nineteenth century sexologists," Prosser argues, "critics have wrongly reduced sexual inversion to homosexuality" (137). While my own argument looks similar to Prosser's, we differ fundamentally over the knowability of Stephen's identity. Sexual inversion can be reduced exclusively neither to homosexuality nor to trans-sexuality. Prosser's textual evidence from the novel itself is slim and consists primarily of the dream Stephen has about grafting Collin's unhealthy knee onto his own healthy one. Prosser's argument that "the dream stand[s] as a transsexual fantasy of flesh grafted from one part of the body to heal the female invert's own 'afflicted member'" makes no sense within the logic of his own argument. This is because the grafting is from a female body onto what Prosser himself reads as a female body, that is, Stephen's (165). Moreover, Prosser argues that *The Well* cannot be a lesbian novel because of the repeated failure of lesbian relationships within the text itself (166). Again, he overlooks the ways in which Stephen requires those relationships (with Angela and Mary) to fail in order to confirm what he already believes about himself – that he has failed to conform to his father's definition of manhood, a failure that seems constitutive of masculinity. Such failures also function as an erotics wherein both failure and loss (femininity as the site of both thrilling pleasure and shameful humiliation), coupled with what appears on first reading as a Christ motif, construct Stephen's gender and sexual self. This trope is actually one of male masochism misread as Christian martyrdom (masculinity figured as the Christ who suffers and who takes pleasure in that suffering) and overdetermines Stephen's libidinous and (en)gendered subjectivity.

Constructing the conversations between female masculinity and trans-sexual masculinity as a war between subjects marked only by gender and resolved only by either/or resolutions disavows many other sites of contest that are equally, if not more, important. The rhetoric of war that infuses these border skirmishes, as Elaine Scarry (1985, 87-8) cautions, forces participants on each side of No Man's Land to arrange themselves into two sides, which not only formalizes the binary but does so on the condition of exclusive and eventual singularity: "In consenting to enter into war, the participants enter into a structure that is a self-canceling duality. They enter into a formal duality, but one understood by all to be temporary and intolerable, a formal duality that, by the very force of its relentless insistence on double-ness, provides the means for eliminating and replacing itself by the condition of singularity (since in the end it will have legitimatized one side's right to determine the nature of certain issues)."

In any kind of war the participants perform some activity X and, as Scarry notes, must out-X each other until one camp is the victor and one the loser, which inevitably means surrendering the power to differentiate the former from the latter (89). In the butch/FTM border war, that activity X is the exclusive claim to authentic, natural, or real masculinity constructed as the exclusive marker of subjectivity and mapped back onto a surgically produced male body. As I have suggested, both class and race are as important as masculinity in forming who Stephen Gordon is and how he may be accorded or denied the privileges of citizenship. Moreover, both sides of the border war invoke *The Well* as somehow indicative of their authenticity. Such invocations are further proof of the instability of masculinity not only in its own subject but also in that of its readers. The inverted, masculine subject of *The Well* that is Stephen Gordon cannot be reduced exclusively either to female homosexuality or to trans-sexuality. He is indeterminate and marks a moment where the histories of female masculinity, trans-sexual masculinity, and, for lack of a better term, "male" masculinity qua nation and race all collide and overlap. Thus, as Prosser (1998) and Halberstam and Hale (1998) refract my argument,

Sedgwick (1995) and Dyer (1988) illuminate it: to begin to see white masculinity we need to look for it where it references its own difference from that which is not-male, not-white, and not-middle-class, as if only non-whiteness, non-maleness, and non-classedness can give each of those its substance (Dyer 1988, 47). Stephen Gordon works very hard, and mostly unsuccessfully, to articulate himself as not-female, not-servant-class, and very much the (good) son of his father's empire.

Modernist Predilections

Few could argue with the assertion that *The Well* grapples with the oppositional imperatives of both continuity/discontinuity and knowledge/ignorance. The ambivalent movement between these dualities becomes the primary structuring trope of this modernist narrative passing as conventional realism. Where conventional *Bildungsroman*[2] and *Künstlerroman* begin at the beginning of the protagonist's life, *The Well* begins before the beginning. And where most heroes of the *Bildungsroman* and *Künstlerroman* receive an education of some sort, the hero of *The Well* learns, as I have suggested in the epigraph that introduces this chapter, that he does not know who and what he is. His quest, then, is to both recognize himself in the subject-forming "knowledges" of his time (the Bible and sexology) and to "un-learn" those ideas, prejudices, and opinions – to rearticulate those knowledge regimes in order to reconfigure himself as a differently languaged subject.

The opening page of *The Well* constructs an image that visualizes these doubled tensions and imbues them with meaning from the supposedly natural and pastoral world (Whitlock 1987, 563). "Not very far from Upton-on-Severn – between it, in fact, and the Malvern Hills – stands the country seat of the Gordons of Bramley; well-timbered, well-cottaged, well-fenced and well-watered, having, in this latter respect, a stream that forks in exactly the right position to feed two large lakes in the grounds" (Hall 1928, 11). The first gendered and naturalist trope is the convention of the Great House and its surroundings. Morton Hall welcomes the lovely Irish bride of Sir Philip, Lady Anna Gordon, and their love for each other ripens in its embrace (12). Morton Hall also comes to represent both self-order and social order as it resonates with imagery suggesting stability, certainty, and protection (Skinner 1994, 23-4). Interestingly, this image of stability and order is gendered female and its lineage is traced, to echo Woolf, back through mothers, those female "archetype[s] of the very perfect woman, whom creating God has found good" (Hall 1928, 11). The narrator genders location as idealized femininity: "It [Morton Hall] has dignity and pride without ostentation, self-assurance without arrogance, repose without inertia; and a gentle aloofness that, to those who know its spirit, but adds to its value as a home. It is indeed like certain lovely women who, now old, belong to a bygone generation – women who in youth were passionate but seemly; difficult to win but when won, all-fulfilling. They are passing away, but their homesteads remain" (11).

The narrator further binds this image of order with and through the trope of domestic temporality by situating them both within the second trope, a supposedly natural feminized landscape. Ten years into her marriage, and as a consequence of coming from "a race of devoted mothers," the Irish Lady Anna finally conceives a child who is expected to be a boy (16). Her Irishness, like her body, is enlisted into the service of reproducing the British aristocracy. Both Anna and Morton Hall become domesticated as a naturalized, pastoral refuge for her husband: "When the child stirred within her she would think it stirred strongly because of the gallant male creature she was hiding" (12). Anna, however, becomes indistinguishable from the feminized landscape around her – a landscape that mirrors the biological changes in her own body as it is situated within the natural order: "From her favourite seat underneath an old cedar, she would see these Malvern Hills in their beauty, and their swelling slopes seemed to hold a new meaning. They were like pregnant women, full bosomed, courageous ... [and] mothers of splendid sons!" (13).

Such meaning is discursive and projectional but remains that which tyrannizes Stephen: a supposedly natural congruence between body, self, and nation. Stephen later rearticulates those meanings through this naturalized alibi of essence but, as we see later, this strategic recitation reproduces similar discursive limitations.

Stephen attempts to find solace in and integration with that natural world surrounding Morton Hall, as do many *Bildungsroman* and *Künstlerroman* heroes. His efforts are eventually met with exile and alienation (Whitlock 1987, 565). As both Hennegan (1982) and Whitlock (1987) point out, Stephen's quest is represented textually by the overuse of the adverbial imperative "must," which overdetermines both the direction and the tenor of his metagendered search for meaning. What begins as an almost annoying stylistic tic evolves into an always already failed but profoundly productive raison d'être.

> The peak of the Camp stood out clearly defined by snow that had fallen lightly that morning, and as they breasted the crest of the hill, the sun shone out on the snow. Away to the right lay the valley of the Wye, a long, lovely valley of deep blue shadows; a valley of small homesteads and mothering trees, of soft undulations and wide, restful spaces leading away to a line of dim mountains – leading away to the mountains of Wales, that lay just over the border. And because she loved this kind of English valley, Stephen's sulky eyes *must* turn and rest upon it; not all her apprehension and sense of injustice could take from her eyes the joy of

> that seeing. She *must* gaze and gaze, she *must* let it possess her, the peace, the wonder that lay in such beauty; while the unwilling tears welled up under her lids – she not knowing why they had come there. (Hall 1928, 49, emphasis added)

The "must" of such ritualized and naturalizing rites of passage suggests that these do not – indeed, cannot – happen for Stephen, whose own nature disrupts the hierarchical order of social relationships at Morton. Moreover, that "must" underwrites Stephen's "gaze" – a word that is repeated in this passage as often as is "must" – suggesting that Stephen "*must* gaze and gaze" and "*must* let it possess" him, mostly because it does not "naturally" possess him in the way that it does his father. The acts of looking and gazing, as a perceptual mode and mode of desire, respectively, have been theorized by both theorists of power and of desire, and those frameworks combined have much to offer my reading of Hall's text. The practices of looking and gazing (whether they be identificatory or sexual) at oneself, at another, at oneself through the gaze of another, or through the gaze of cultural scripts about gender, sexuality, and race, map neatly onto the practices of articulation with which I am concerned. None of these practices is innocent, and all of them constitute the circuits that knowledge/ignorance take in *The Well.*

In all his works, but particularly in *Discipline and Punish,* Michel Foucault denaturalizes and theorizes what we can safely identify as the panoptic and scientific view of enlightenment that, as I argued in Chapter 1, underwrites Stephen's metatextual existence.[3] Foucault suggests that power is intricately bound with and articulated through knowledges that produce panoptic self-regulation, where prisoners and, I would argue, those subjected to power/knowledge truth regimes, internalize that continuously inspecting gaze. As a result, the subject becomes its own overseer, exercising surveillance over and against itself, disciplining its own docility. Foucault's discussion of how the panoptic gaze works may account for at least one layer of looks in *The Well,* that is, how women such as Anna and Mary learn to appraise themselves, through the male gaze, as the objects of surveillance and objectification. Their value and power lie in their capacity to be beautiful objects. Women's beauty is expected to possess men the way that, in the passage quoted above, nature's sublime beauty is supposed to possess and overwhelm its beholder.

Where Foucault's argument explains how regulative power regimes constitute the panoptic gaze, psychoanalysis and feminist theory suggest that power lies at the heart of an unequal gendering gaze directed from men towards women. Women are defined and constituted by that male gaze: "defined in terms of her visibility, she carries her own Panopticon with her wherever she goes, her self-image a function of her being for another"

(Joan Copjec, quoted in Kaplan 1997, xcii). Feminist film theorists have been especially interested in theorizing a male gaze, arguing in general that feminine subjectivity within patriarchy is inevitably bound up with the structure of the gaze and the localization of the eye as authority. Laura Mulvey and others have argued that, as such, the male gaze is totalizing and demands that women adopt a masochistic position, in effect identifying with the male gaze and participating in their own objectification (Kaplan 1997, xix). While the gaze is not the object of this work, I do draw on a distinction that Kaplan makes between the "gaze" and the "look." As these passages from *The Well* suggest, there is a contradiction within looking relations that, I think, is the same contradiction as appears at the heart of masculinity: that of being the subject who has the power to gaze while at the same time being the subject who is possessed by the object upon whom one is gazing. When Stephen, Phillip, and Martin "gaze" at women or at nature, they clearly do so with what appears to be full entitlement, and yet the spectacle is not the object gazed at but the sublime impact that object has on its subject.

Kaplan's distinction between the look and the gaze allows for a redefinition of how the gaze works. She argues that the gaze should be understood as active: "the subject bearing the gaze is not interested in the object per se, but [is] consumed with his [sic] own anxieties, which are inevitably mixed with desire" (xviii). The object cannot look back as there is little room within the gaze for a returned process. In other words, there is an anxiety produced in the subject gazing that needs to foreclose on the possibility of a return: "The object is a threat to the subject's autonomy and security and thus must be placed, rationalized and, by a circuitous route, denied" (xviii). The gaze then is not a process, nor a relation; rather, it is a one-way gaze that seeks to relieve anxiety in the one gazing. Stephen's anxieties about his ontological nature, and about his place in the natural order, are temporarily relieved as long as he is the one gazing at nature and not the one, ironically enough, mistaken for nature. I describe Stephen's anxieties as ironic because, in the long run, Stephen and his creator, Radclyffe Hall, both rationalize their own existence by articulating it to and through the same discourses that have unthought them, that is, gender essentialisms, sexology, and biblical discourse.

Exile from those naturalizing discourses is both inevitable and overdetermined, and it is most evident in Stephen's relationship with his best friend and later rival, Martin Hallam. Stephen meets Martin at a New Year's Eve dance at the neighbouring Antrim family estate. Colonel Antrim is a regular member of the local hunt, and Stephen's own participation in such hunts has become a topic of conversation. The Colonel, "small" and "henpecked," attempts to defend his horseman skills, but to no avail (Hall 1928, 91). Into this scene comes Martin Hallam, who is introduced to

Stephen and, as suddenly as Chloe liked Olivia, Stephen likes Martin (Woolf 1928, 81). "It was Stephen who explained that she danced very badly; it was Martin who suggested that they sit out their dances ... he spoke simply, as one man will speak to another ... And Stephen, the awkward, the bashful, the tongue-tied, heard herself talking in her turn, quite freely, heard herself asking him endless questions ... such as one man will ask of another" (Hall 1928, 92-3).

This chance meeting between Stephen and Martin is a tremendously important event for it sets up the most important and telling plot-points of the entire novel. Martin later becomes Stephen's rival for Mary and the person to whom he gives Mary. Almost all the critical readings of *The Well* to date, however, have misread the significance of the relationship between Stephen and Martin. I suggest that, first, we understand Martin as offering Stephen the opportunity or, at the very least, the fantasy of an opportunity, to participate in that homosocial fraternity that is constitutive of nationness; second, that Stephen likes Martin not just fraternally but homosocially, which is, as Mosse (1985), Anderson (1983), and Sedgwick (1992) suggest, always already homoerotically. Sexual desires between men are just as unintelligible to both Martin and Stephen as is Mary's desire for Stephen, and they need, if Sedgwick is correct, to be both present and simultaneously disavowed.[4] The nature of the attachment between Stephen and Martin is crucial to my argument that *The Well* is a discursive event wherein the histories of white masculinity as male-embodied, female masculinity as butch- and lesbian-embodied, and trans-sexual masculinity as meta-embodied (and failed embodiment) all overlap. In other words, if the discourses of late twentieth-century female masculinities queer the heteronormative imperative of twentieth-century sexological and medical discourses – which have already collapsed female and trans-sexual masculinities, erroneously folding the latter into the former – then it is not only important but vital to trace both that queering and folding in and through the fictional text of *The Well*.

As I argue in Chapter 1, Mosse (1985), Anderson (1983), and Parker et al. (1992, 2) agree that nationalisms and sexualities are two of the most powerful global discourses shaping contemporary notions of identity. Anderson's (1983) assertion that everyone has a nationality in the same way that they have a gender works best when neither of those identities is marked as such but, rather, functions invisibly as the norm or universal. As Anderson notes, nationness is an imaginary or identificatory set of relations predicated on an image of the commonality, communion, or deep, horizontal comradeship between members (15). For reasons that are admittedly indeterminate, Martin Hallam seeks out a friendship with Stephen – one that is built upon a homosocial commonality of shared identity. Their brotherly fraternity is one even they can recognize: "She said: 'You're the only real friend I've ever had, except Father – our friendship's so wonderful, somehow – we're like brothers, we enjoy all the same sort of things.' He nodded: 'I know, a wonderful friendship.'" (Hall 1928, 95). Stephen and Martin engage in boyish activities together: they hunt, fence, ride, care for and understand their horses, and share a fundamental sublime awe of nature. "His youth met hers," the narrator reiterates, "and [they] walked hand in hand" (95). Suddenly, Stephen's world is no longer solitary. The natural world around Stephen and Martin protects the homoeroticism they share, while the syntax of Hall's descriptions likens their friendship to that between David and Jonathan in the Old Testament.[5] "The hills must let Stephen tell [Martin] their secrets, the secrets of bypaths most cunningly hidden; the secrets of small, unsuspected green hollows; the secrets of ferns that live only by hiding. She might even reveal the secrets of birds ... [that even] '... in death they were not divided'" (95).

Although Stephen likens his friendship with Martin to that between David and Jonathan, the secrets buried in *The Well*'s symbolic spaces are not without their telltale signs. Martin is a Canadian, living in British Columbia, and is described as a solitary and "queer sensitive fellow ... with a strange love of trees and primitive forests" (94). He is as burdened as is Stephen, tormented by inarticulate passions and unspeakable regrets, emotions that surface in relation to what is perceived as the sublimity of nature.

> And [Stephen] taught him the hills whose plentiful bosoms had made Anna think of green-girdled mothers, mothers of sons, as she sat and watched them, great with the child who should have been her son. They climbed the venerable Worcestershire Beacon ... above the Wye Valley. The Valley would lie half in light, half in shadow ... then Stephen's heart would tighten a little, as it always had done because of that beauty, so that one day she said: "When I was a child, this used to make me want to cry, Martin." And he answered: "Some part of us always sheds tears when we see lovely things – they make us regretful" ... But when she [sic] asked him why this should be, he shook his head slowly, unable to tell her. (94)

Martin and Stephen form an intense attachment in and around their common love of nature as well as through their deep, horizontal, and no longer only homosocial but also homoerotic comradeship as men. Theirs is a friendship that cannot know or name its own terms. Martin wants Stephen to come to Canada with him to be a colonial companion and paternalist settler; he stays at Morton, "held fast by the charm and the strangeness of Stephen – her very strangeness it was that allured him, yet all the while he must think of their friendship, not even admitting that strangeness ... delud[ing] himself with these thoughts of friendship" (97).

Stephen, on the other hand, longs for Martin to stay at Morton permanently so he can continue to enjoy "the companionship of men, for their friendship, their good-will, their toleration, she had it all now and much more in Martin" (96).

Nature functions as a symbolic space in this text, which mirrors the sexual truth regimes of Anna and Philip (Malvern Hills as heterosexualized), the masterful hunts of the Gordon and Antrim men through that same landscape (nature as hunted and conquered prey), and the unspoken homoerotic desires between Stephen and Martin:

> Then [Martin] started to tell her about his huge forests, so vast that their greenness seemed almost eternal. Great trees he told her of, erect, towering furs, many centuries and their girth that of giants ... then there were all the humbler treefolk whom he spoke of as friends that were dear and familiar; the hemlocks that grow by the courses of rivers ... the slender white spruces that border the lakes; the red pines, that glow like copper in the sunset. Unfortunate trees these beautiful red pines, for their tough, manly wood is coveted by builders. "But I won't have my rooftree hacked." (96)

Nature in the New Country is gendered male and, like Martin and Stephen's mutual attraction, lies "somewhere beyond the horizon," outside the frame of this novel as its "space-off," or that which, by necessity, must lie outside of the frame (de Lauretis 1987, 25-6). The space-off, as de Lauretis theorizes it, is not so much a literal space off the visual field, although it is certainly that. De Lauretis borrows this term from film theory, and it refers to the space not visible in the frame but inferable from what the frame makes visible. The space-off can also be used to map a movement between the represented discursive space of the positions made available by those hegemonic discourses and the elsewhere of those discourses – the other spaces, both discursive and social – that exist in the margins of discourse or in the interstices of institutions, in counter-practices and new forms (26). They are, de Lauretis argues, not oppositional but, rather, exist in the tension of contradictions, multiplicity, heteroglossic coexistence.

Martin's New Country is not at all visible but functions as a geographic space-off, an imaginary country inferable from England's colonial practices. Rose Tremain locates Martin Ward in a similar space in the ending of *Sacred Country*. Hall locates Martin Hallam's imaginary masculinist pastoral world in the space-off. Like Philip with a feminized, domesticated landscape, it becomes Martin's job to husband the "deep, princely rivers" and "manly," "erect" trees – the not yet domesticated land – that this young man loved with "a primitive instinct" and "strange inexplicable devotion" (Hall 1928,

92-5, 99). Like Anna, who became part of that imperial landscape to be husbanded, Stephen should find it his job to be similarly husbanded. Martin's hope is that Stephen will share this task with him, although decidedly not as a female companion. "Why can't you come back to Canada with me? What rot it is, all this damned convention; we're such pals you and I ... what a fool world we live in!" (96).

As Sedgwick (1985) notes, the homosociality of Anderson's nation-as-fraternity, similar to that shared between Stephen and Martin, must be aggressively distinguished from more explicitly sexualized male-male relations, like that unspoken current of desire that also exists between these two men. If the former (homosociality) continues to be infused by the latter (homosexuality), then the idea of a continuum of, rather than a broken continuity between, homosocial and homosexual threatens the ideological and psychical foundation of nation-formation. That continuum becomes more continuous rather than discontinuous and, as both Gayle Rubin (1975) and Sedgwick (1985) show, the exchange of a woman between men allows the homosexual to be yoked back into the orbit of the homosocial. Strangely, after Stephen is clearly gendered masculine, in an instant he is mis-sexed as female and is forced, albeit always already unsuccessfully, to fulfill that function.

Stephen experiences this enforced engendering as a psychic shock. Again, many critics, Catharine Stimpson (1988) included, note that Book 1 ends with the shock of Stephen's father's death. I suggest that the gender shock that Stephen experiences after Martin's proposal of marriage is far more disruptive and is a trauma that repeats itself throughout, and indeed overdetermines, the plot, including Stephen's betrayal of Mary to Martin. Martin's "she-ing" of Stephen occur(s), predictably enough, "when winter must give place to spring" (Hall 1928, 97). Where Stephen and Martin had previously shared a masculine gaze that desired the feminized and idealized Other by projecting it onto the landscape in and around Morton Hall, Martin looks round him one day and reads Stephen as no longer looking at nature with him but as being in and of nature, being looked at by him and him alone: "suddenly [Stephen was] there as a woman" (97). These looking relations, as I have argued, are entirely less than innocent. Martin's own desires for what previously had been characterized as Stephen's strangeness are not any more intelligible than is Stephen's longing for the companionship of men. And curiously, Martin comes to this misunderstanding as he gazes at the same cedar tree where Anna had previously imagined the strong son she was carrying: "Friendship! He marveled now at his folly, at his blindness, his coldness of body and spirit. He had offered this girl the cold husks of his friendship, insulting her youth, her womanhood, her beauty" (98).

As Rubin (1975) and Sedgwick (1985) would explain, a woman needs to be exchanged between them; Mary will serve that function later in the novel as Stephen comes to master this initial "she-ing," this moment where he is wrongly read as feminine. For now, Martin's proposal of marriage to Stephen in the garden they had enjoyed as brothers is received with horror, and Stephen's ineffable reaction described from a distance by the third-person narrator.

> "Good God! What's the matter, Stephen?" She was staring at him in a kind of dumb horror ... while gradually over her colourless face there was spreading an expression of the deepest repulsion – terror and repulsion he saw on her face, and something else too, a look of outrage ... But at that she wheeled round and fled from him wildly, fled back to the house that had always protected. (Hall 1928, 98)

Stephen experiences Martin's proposal as a betrayal but also with an inverted "femaled panic"[6] as his beloved Martin performs the rituals of heteronormative masculinity. It is as though that very performance suggested that something horrible had happened to Martin: "Without so much as a word she left him, nor did she once pause in her flight to look back. Yet even in this moment of headlong panic, the girl [sic] was conscious of something like amazement, amazement at herself, and she gasped as she ran: 'It's Martin – Martin –' And again: 'It's Martin!'" (98).

Again, this first plot-point shows Stephen struggling against not only the imposition of an unnatural heterosexual and female text onto what he experiences as his natural male self but also against the imposition of the "cold husks" of conventionality and materiality over the subject. He strugges against that original "must" with an imperative of his own: "There *must* be something wrong with Martin."

Stephen retreats, as always, to Morton Hall and to nature. Given that nineteenth-century English national identity forges itself out of a rugged and romantic masculinity, Stephen returns to that same symbolic space to make sense of himself in relation to Martin. As he re-sembles himself, this journey through the woods of Malvern Hills prefigures many journeys Stephen will take later in the novel, when the setting changes to Paris. Once he is finally permanently exiled from Morton Hall, Stephen wanders as a kind of male *flâneur* in postwar Paris. That distinctly twentieth-century Stephen (325) is not this Stephen; this nineteenth-century Stephen still wanders Malvern Hills attempting to regender himself in nature while, ironically enough, still being secure as the inheritor of a degenerating aristocracy – a national heritage that seeks to rejuvenate its supposedly authentic but failing lineage (Whitlock 1987, 563).

Stephen's efforts to make sense of what happened are quite telling. He remembers the things he loved about Martin, his "strong, young body, and his honest brown face." He had felt so "contented, so natural with him" because "they had been like two men ... [and] she had wanted Martin to treat her as a man, had expected it of him" (Hall 1928, 100-1). Stephen's thoughts search for ontological explications ("But what was she?") as he rereads moments from his childhood that seem strange. He remembers an early self-awareness of gender – "She had always been trying to be someone else – that was why she had dressed herself up as young Nelson" – as well as of sexuality: "the friend [Martin] had turned lover and had wanted from her what she could not give him" but still "she could find no answers" (101).[7] Finally, as Stephen attempts unsuccessfully to find comfort in the same garden in which Martin proposed marriage and in which the pregnant Anna found congruence, he finds only memories of his first love – the female housemaid, Collins – and his own rage when he finds Collins in the garden with her male lover (102). "The garden was full of a new memory now ... and she turned abruptly, ... and walked toward the lakes that gleamed faintly in the distance ... [to which] she instinctively went for comfort" (102). Here Stephen faces the limitations of his own ability to find meaning and is exiled from the gender that this geography offered in the opening sentence of the book (Morton has "a stream that forks in exactly the right position to feed two large lakes in the grounds"). Stephen's sense of self no longer fits the temporal (in the hall of Morton "hung the funny old portraits of Gordons – men long dead and gone but still wonderfully living, since their ... loves had made children from father to son – from father to son until the advent of Stephen") and spatial epistemologies reflected in the immediate corporeal and natural world: "I shall always stand outside" (105, 103).

Curiously though, the first time the word "unnatural" appears, it is not in relation to Stephen; rather, it is articulated in relation to notions of maternity and describes Anna's inability to love Stephen. Indeed, both Stephen and Anna are almost always awkward with each other, and their relationship is constituted by a "strange shyness" and violent affect. As a seven-year-old child, Stephen is already marked by an inarticulate frustration, defiance, and rage. "To cope with it, however, she would give way at times to sudden fits of hot temper ... it relieved her to stamp and then burst into tears ... in some vague, childish way she had hit back at life" (15). Anna responds to her "turbulent offspring" with her own mix of unnatural feelings: "queer antagonism that amounted almost to anger," an aloof "distaste," and hatred (15-16); that is, Anna recognizes in Stephen an ontological kinship between him and Philip – one described as a likeness where Stephen was, in some way, "a caricature ... a blemished, unworthy, maimed reproduction" of Sir Philip, and one that filled her with a violent passion and instant disavowal (15-16). Previously, this kinship had been described in slightly different terms: "Anna, looking gravely at her daughter, noting the plentiful auburn hair, the brave hazel eyes that were so like her father's, as indeed were the child's whole expression and bearing, would be filled with a sudden antagonism that came very near to anger" (15), and "queer antagonism" that "came very near to" or "almost amounted to" anger, but seemed to stop short of full articulation. The result of Anna's antagonism is that they both held "a little aloof when they should have been drawing together" (15). Twice this recognition is reiterated, the first time as "brave" and "plentiful," the second as "blemished" and "maimed," as if the second repetition must disavow the desire that manifests itself from the first but that must not be fully articulated. Thus, what seems more unnatural about Anna and Stephen's relationship is not necessarily her unacknowledgable desire for Stephen or her "gentle aloofness"; instead, it is her antagonism, her "rageful aloofness" and abject rejection of Stephen.

While Stephen disidentifies with Anna, he compensates for that relationship by over-idealizing and eroticizing gender difference, and then projecting the sublimity of those supposedly natural differences onto nature: "Stephen, acutely responsive to beauty, would be dimly longing to find expression for a feeling almost amounting to worship, that her mother's face had awakened" (15). Martin, too, is characterized as having lost his mother, and, as a consequence, he shares that same silent worshipping and melancholic awe in the face of naturally occurring feminine beauty (92). Stephen's relationship with Philip, on the other hand, becomes an altogether different site. This second gendered and naturalist discourse constructs Philip as the rational, civilized master, indeed, husband of these feminized undulating landscapes and father of these naturalized British inheritors of aristocratic masculinity. If Anna becomes coterminous with the "perfect proportions" of Morton Hall's domesticity – the drawing room (80) and the gardens (i.e., the restrained nature surrounding the house) – then Philip's study, "menacing, prophetic," is coterminous with reason, learning, and mastery over nature, symbolized by the ritual of the hunt and by his naming of Stephen's condition (Whitlock 1987, 563). Where Anna rejects Stephen's abject disposition, Philip reads all he can in order to understand it.

Even though *The Well* is often misread as one of the originary coming-out narratives, Stephen does not know about his own inversion and thus, as Halberstam (1998a, 100) argues, is not closeted but ignorant. Philip knows long before Stephen does; thus, self-knowledge becomes one of the thematic problems of the novel. Stephen's inversion is known to most other people around him before it becomes known to him. That Stephen is first named as invert by Philip stages one of *The Well*'s primary thematic preoccupations: that of the meaning-making process itself. *The Well* is not necessarily concerned with precisely describing inversion as made or caused; rather, it functions as a parable of meaning-making, documenting how meaning is made by attending to the processes by which physical and psychological markers get made into meaning, showing how disparate signs coalesce into ontological identities. Stephen fails to understand those meanings through the reading practices bequeathed to him (i.e., the finding of one's self in nature) and thus turns to the emerging discourses of modernity, science, and medicine for answers. In that domain conventionally marked as masculine – his father's study – he finally finds them. Ironically, upon discovering those answers Stephen does not "come out" to the world; rather, he "comes in" to knowledge regimes and discourse in all their epistemological contradictions. In the end, Stephen has to suspend those knowledges from within; that is, he has to find a way to articulate himself through the same discourses that have enunciated him in order to rearticulate what the sexologists cannot yet fully know. Part of that knowledge is that service during the First World War had productively provided an epistemological space of self-knowledge. "That battalion" had formed in the "terrible" war years, our narrator tells us: "War and death had given them a right to life, and life tasted sweet ... never again would [inverts] submit to being driven back to their holes and corners. They had found themselves" (Hall 1928, 272). We see as much in the mirror scene (which I discuss below) when Stephen attempts to articulate a body that remains stubbornly inarticulate. But we also see this in Stephen's own career as a writer.

One of the more interesting places where we see Stephen and, through Stephen, Radclyffe Hall articulating a new social formation occurs when Stephen and Mary visit Paris. Here "they [make] their first real acquaintance with the garish and tragic night life of Paris that lies open to such people as Stephen Gordon" (378).

> As long as she lived Stephen never forgot her first impression of the bar known as Alec's ... that meeting-place of the most miserable of all those who comprised the miserable army ... [a]nd looking with abhorrence upon these men, drink-sodden, doped as were only too many, Stephen yet felt that some terrifying thing stalked abroad ... Alec the tempter, the vendor of dreams, the dispenser of illusions whiter than snow; Alec, who sold little packets of cocaine for large bundles of notes, was now opening wine, with a smile and a flourish, at the next-door table. (388)

Stephen himself is the one who both gazes and is undone by that gaze. Hence, his efforts rationalize and deny that which he sees. There can be no mistaking the moralizing tone with which this scene is described. Rather than completely condemning those in the bar, however, Stephen attempts to separate perversity from perversion. While Stephen himself is undoubtedly, and quite literally, inscribed with "God's mark on [her] forehead," a scar that is the result of an injury Stephen sustained, ironically enough, while serving with the ambulance unit in the war, he does make a distinction between himself – a subject of perversion for which he could not be held accountable – and the sort of perversity he describes at Alec's, "willed, immoral behavior or vice for which the subject should be held accountable" (301). Stephen, now a well known author, clearly believes he can undo the articulation of inversion with, through, and as criminality, and although he suffers from those "treacherous nerves of the invert," he spends the last sections of *The Well* trying to finish his own novel – a book, he argues, that will tell the truth, "the whole truth [as it] is known only to the normal invert" (379-90).

Almost as if Stephen is self-conscious of his own discursive context as well as function, he precipitates the metatextual and paradoxical collision between the humanitarian sexologists and the inverted subject that they articulated:

> And what doctor can know the entire truth? Many times they meet only the neurasthenics, those of us for whom life has proved too bitter. They are good, these doctors – some of them very good; they work hard trying to solve our problem, but half the time they must work in the dark – the whole truth is known only to the normal invert. The doctors cannot make the ignorant think, cannot hope to bring home the sufferings of millions; only one of ourselves can some day do that ... this is only the beginning. (390)

This moment of consciousness crystallizes for Stephen, ironically enough, in an encounter at Alec's; not only does Stephen now encompass "the meaning of herself" but he also seeks to suspend and rearticulate that meaning (187).

When Stephen receives Martin's offer of friendship as an invitation into "the companionship of men," it is more accurate to say that it is an invitation into the company of his peers. Philip has always been a tremendously important influence and companion to Stephen; clearly, Stephen's gender performance is modelled after that of his father. Significantly, we see Philip reading the sexologists and fixing Stephen's image in their accounts of inversion, something Stephen discovers in Philip's study long after his death. "Then she noticed on a shelf near the bottom was a row of books standing behind the others; the next moment she had one of these in her hand, and was looking at the name of the author: Krafft-Ebing – she had never heard of that author before. All the same she opened the battered old book, then she looked more closely, for there on its margins were notes in her father's small scholarly hand and she saw that her own name appeared in those notes" (204).

It is profoundly ironic that in *The Well* it is Stephen's father (and not his mother) who imparts such "enlightenment and support" – a torsioning of Hennegan's (1982) suggestion that the novel has functioned to articulate the unthinkable and unspeakable between women ("Tremulous daughters have given it to their mothers ... mothers have given it to daughters ... close female friends have given it to each other"). Such differing reading practices, conceptual frameworks, and modes of articulation are the core issues of *Masculinities without Men?* There are, in the late nineteenth and early twentieth centuries, profound conceptual and epistemological contradictions and instabilities that have articulated our knowledges of trans-sexual and female masculinities. Those instabilities, and the eventual yoking of female masculinity together with the sign "lesbian," are as much my subject as are the novels that house those indeterminate subjects and their shared histories. In *The Well* Philip grooms his child according to the codes of nineteenth-century British aristocratic masculinity. Where the mothers of nineteenth-century feminine heroines attended to their daughters' marriage prospects, Philip attends to Stephen's masculine rites of passage. Stephen learns to ride and care for horses, partakes in hunts with Philip and the other men in the surrounding area, learns to enjoy physical activities like fencing and weight-lifting, and is accorded the privileges of a classical education. If Anna sits in the quiet shadow of the powerful cedar tree in the garden of Morton Hall, then Philip himself is all that such an ancient tree represents. In this novel that is preoccupied with purity of origins and a humanist and panoptic confidence in the order of things, Philip appears after we've already met Anna and Morton Hall, and after we've been introduced to its aristocratic bloodline, the Gordons of Bramley. "They might look down from Heaven with raised eyebrows, and say: 'We utterly refuse to acknowledge this curious creature called Stephen.' But for all that they could not drain her of blood, and her blood was theirs also, so that do what they would they could never completely rid themselves of her nor she of them – they were one in their blood" (Hall 1928, 108).

Where Anna becomes the archetype for all women – anterior to time, projected into naturalized space as that which provides solace and comfort – Philip is the sensitive dreamer, melancholic lover, and idealized master of naturalized spaces such as Morton (12). Curiously, nature is personified in relation to Philip and Stephen, and that same personified nature, which is gently maternal with Anna and quite daring in producing Stephen (108), becomes murderous with Philip. As if weighted down by the burdens of tradition, convention, and knowledge that the imperatives of masculinity dictate he not share, Philip, like the cedar tree after a snow storm, is crushed by the weight of what he knows about Stephen's inversion after a quarrel with Anna where he "dared not speak it[s]" name (111).

> The gardens lay placidly under the snow ... only one intimate of theirs felt anxious, and that was the ancient and wide-boughed cedar, for the weight of the snow made an ache in its branches – its branches were brittle like an old man's ... but it could not cry out or shake off its torment ... it could only endure ... hoping Anna would take note ... one morning Anna noticed its plight and she called Sir Philip ... [and] because he loved Anna who loved the cedar, he must stand underneath it directing the gardeners. (114-15)

Prophetically, the tree collapses and its weight crushes Philip, who ironically looks "monstrously tall as he lay on that white" snow. Philip, whose presence continues to loom large as idealized masculinity, dies before he can tell Stephen the truth about himself (115).

Anne McClintock (1995, 357-9), citing Walter Benjamin (1992), argues that representations of nationness and national time vacillate between nostalgia for the past and the impatient progressive sloughing off of the past; she suggests further that these contradictory representations of time are produced as a natural division of gender. These competing representations of Anna (as space and as the reproduction of Empire) and of Philip (as both historical time – the end of the long line of Gordon men – and the domestic patriarch of British imperial nationalism) slide from the white universalized and transcendent aristocratic family into a metaphorical and naturalized social order. Historical time and natural time are thus configured and collapsed into familial time (38-9). Historical time, however, and natural space cease to circulate and come to an end when, as Benjamin suggests, the nostalgia for these invented images of nationness carry the most currency. In other words, "the mapping of Progress depends on systematically inventing images of archaic time to identify what is historically new about enlightened, national progress" (358). Stephen, as a contradictory national and modern Janus, comes to represent both "that [which] melts and transforms traditional attachments in favour of new identities and ... a reflection of 'authentic' cultural values culled from the depths of a presumed communal past" (358). Through metonymy, Stephen is marked as one of the last vestiges of a natural and fledgling social order – aristocratic masculinity – although he is, at the same time, exiled out of the very order that produced him. By the time Anna banishes Stephen from Morton Hall, he is at once the conservative principle of continuity and the revolutionary principle of discontinuity: the end of the Gordon bloodline.

Biblical Torsionings

> In life and death they were not divided / ... thy love to me was wonderful, / surpassing the love of women.
>
> – David's lament for Jonathan, 2 Samuel 1

When Stephen returns to his father's study long after his death, he experiences an epiphany upon reading two books. The first, as I discussed earlier, is Krafft-Ebing's treatise on sexology, in which Stephen found his name written in his father's handwriting. The second is the Bible. *The Well*'s status as a narrative of change simultaneously struggling to preserve the status quo resonates throughout its appropriation of religious discourses as well as those of naturalism, nation, and gender. Numerous critics have already mentioned sexological discourse as one of Hall's major influences. Her second major influence is the Bible, which provides imagery, tropes, narratives, names, and syntax that an attentive reader of *The Well* can no longer ignore. Two very interesting and recent essays, Ed Madden's (1997) "*The Well of Loneliness*, or The Gospel According to Radclyffe Hall," and Margaret Soenser Breen's (1997) "Narrative Inversion: The Biblical Heritage of *The Well of Loneliness* and *Desert of the Heart*," situate *The Well* firmly within biblical discourse and rhetoric. As Madden (1997, 163) notes, "there has been little sustained analysis of the biblical language of [Hall's] novel. Most feminist and lesbian critics have dismissed the biblical allusions and language as unfortunate and politically regressive; religious critics have ignored the novel." As Madden explains, however, such allusions and language are, for Hall, the very site of contest as well as one source of the vitality of her polemic. Indeed, Madden names the stakes of such a confluence: "At stake in the novel is ... what may be said about homosexual or lesbian identity, who is allowed to say it, how it may be interpreted, and what language may be used" (169).

From its figuring as "the Bible of lesbian literature" in Jane Rule's seminal *Lesbian Images*, to its reliance on biblical allusions, characters, and narratives, *The Well* functions as a textbook example of how to turn a language of condemnation into a language of validation (Rule 1975). Madden notes in great detail *The Well*'s proliferating biblical figures, tropes, allusions, and narrative patterns. For instance, Stephen's maidservant and later friend, Puddle, evokes Job in her lament of a God who abandons the very thing it creates: "[Puddle] speaks those words on behalf of Stephen: 'Thine hands have made me and fashioned me together round about; Yet thou dost destroy me'" (Hall 1928, 183). Puddle, who is also an invert, is extremely loyal and follows Stephen after he is exiled from Morton. Puddle's loyalty is like that which Ruth pledged to Naomi: "Where you go, I go,

Stephen ... All that you're suffering at this moment I've suffered" (205). Promises of endurance, deliverance, and freedom are evoked when Stephen and fellow members of the expatriate artist community listen to two African-American singers, Henry and Lincoln, sing black spirituals at a party in Paris. Stephen transforms their song of deliverance into his own when he asks God, again echoing Psalm 6:3, "Yes, but how long, O Lord, how long" (364). (I will return to the racial politics of this scene later in this chapter.)

Stephen's name is the same as that of the first Christian evangelistic martyr, who appears in the Book of Acts. But Stephen is also a Christ figure; born on Christmas Eve, he supposedly sacrifices himself for his lover Mary and finds himself a "stranger within the gates" when he returns home to Morton (Hall 1928, 212). The speaking spirits who seem to possess Stephen in the final scene of the novel cry out "Our name is legion" and "We have asked for bread; will you give us a stone?" alluding to the man possessed by many demons in Luke 8 and Matthew 8. He, too, calls himself "Legion" (Madden 1997, 170-3). Moreover, Hall reiterates a characteristically modernist motif – that of fathers betraying their sons – when she references Christ's assurances to his followers that their father (God) will not betray them: "What man is there of you whom if his son ask bread, will he give him a stone?" (Matthew 7). Finally, if Madden is correct in suggesting that Stephen is a Christ figure, then he is a figure of both exile and deliverance/suffering. In a moment of exasperation in Philip's study, when Stephen discovers his name in Krafft-Ebing's book, Stephen tosses the Bible across the room and demands a sign from heaven. Where the book falls open, Stephen reads: "And the Lord set a mark upon Cain" (Hall 1928, 205). This moment foreshadows Stephen's wounding as an ambulance driver in the First World War – a wound that leaves him with a tremendous scar on his face. Hall resignifies inversion as the mark of Cain and metonymically links inversion, the "stigmata of the abnormal," the scarring of Stephen in the First World War, and, later, the crucifixion of Christ, overdetermining an Invert/Cain/Christ trope (Madden 1997, 169). Predictably enough, this chain of signifiers tells us from the beginning of the twentieth century what we think we've discovered at its end – that is, that outcast and messiah, normal and invert, queer and straight are inextricably bound to/with/through each other.

Hall's pillaging of biblical discourse dovetails effectively with theories of articulation that are the central objects of this study. As Stuart Hall reminds us, theories of articulation do not posit that a subject is formed, and, by implication, reformed *new*. Since subjects are "languaged" by discourse, in this case the discourse of sexology or popular religion, so they must use and reconfigure those same discourses to, as Stuart Hall (1996a, 143) puts it, "construct some narrative, however impoverished and impure, to connect the past and the present: where they came from with where they are" and indeed where they are bound. In turning these texts, discourses, and dialogic languaging processes upside-down, subjects remake themselves, becoming and exceeding what they are in order to find a meaning that fits. Previously ignored biblical analyses, especially Madden's argument that Stephen functions as a Christ figure, are remarkably productive when we expose the internal workings of the articulations that work through the (inverted) gender politics of Hall's novel. Where Madden asks how Hall appropriates a Christian discourse and incorporates or transforms it into a liberatory discourse, however, I want to question what it is about the figure of Christ that makes this articulation work so well. In other words, I do not necessarily want to pursue the question of whether or not *The Well* is "Christian," whether or not Stephen is a Christ figure, and whether or not such a queering is a good or a bad thing; rather, I am more interested in pursuing how fantasies about masculinity embedded in the figure of Christ are reiterated in and by the men in *The Well* and then function to produce, or perhaps inflect, contemporary notions of female and trans-sexual masculinities. Simply put: I am less interested in the direct correspondences between Stephen and Christ, or in the facts of religiosity in the text, and more interested in raising questions about how "Christ" functions as one trope of male subjectivity. The Stephen-as-Christ motif is often misread as Stephen-as-martyr; the motif has far more currency if, instead, we read it as male masochism and understand it to function as the privileged trope of masculinity in this text.

Judith Halberstam (1998a) is partially right when she suggests that, in order to best answer the question "What is masculinity?" we should not look directly at male masculinity but, rather, look askew at female masculinity. This is because "many other lines of identification traverse the terrain of masculinity, dividing its power into complicated differentials of class, race, sexuality and gender ... masculinity ... [best] becomes legible as masculinity where and when it leaves the white male middle-class body." However, and as many butches know but rarely admit, the opposite is also true: in order to best understand and, indeed, fashion female masculinity one always looks askew at male masculinity. For my purposes here, I want to look directly at one particular view of masculinity. As a productive trope, Stephen-as-Christ-as-masochist fixes two not altogether unrelated narrative motifs and imperatives that follow *The Well* in late twentieth-century fictions and autobiographies about butch and trans-sexual masculinities: first, that of renunciation, where stone butch masculinity must renounce the flesh in a performative disidentification with the female body and aggressively reidentify with wounded masculinity; and second, that of an imperative of transcendence, where trans-sexual masculinity must transcend the limitations of the body as the ground of identity and, whether non-, pre-, or post-operative, must live by a "faith" in the ability to privilege spirit, or subjectivity, over materiality.

Sigmund Freud (1984) theorized three kinds of masochism: (1) erotogenic, a primary instinct or corporeal pleasure in pain that is constitutive of the other two types; (2) feminine, which positions its presumably male sufferer as a woman whose desires are to be placed in characteristically female situations like being treated as a small, helpless, naughty child, being castrated, being copulated with, or giving birth to a child; and (3) moral, in which "an unconscious sense of guilt" gives way to a need for punishment (192-7). Freud focuses particularly on moral masochism, which, he argues, begins when "the ego reacts with feelings of anxiety ... to the perception that it has failed to perform the behests of its ideal, the super-ego" (197). As Freud himself argued, many of his own patients who were diagnosed as masochists were either men or effeminized men who sought to be punished by the symbolic father and to have a passive (feminine) sexual relation to him. For the moral masochist, the ego reacts with feelings of anxiety to the perception that it has not lived up to the demands of either the super-ego (the introjected representative of the parents) or the influences of the past or traditions of teachers, publicly recognized heroes as authorities, or self-chosen models (421-2). This introjected super-ego may become harsh, cruel, and inexorable against the ego that is in its charge. So it becomes a representative of the external world and a model for the endeavours of the ego. The result is that those suffering as moral masochists are suffering under the domination of an especially sensitive conscience and an unconscious ultramorality that "provoke[s] punishment from this last representative of the parents [i.e., a monstrously large and harsh, indeed, titanic super-ego], [and] must do what is inexpedient, must act against his own interest, must ruin the prospects which open out to him in the real world and, must perhaps, destroy his own real existence" (424-5).

Theodore Reik's (1941) study of masochism warrants critical attention as he posits a subject that is both male and masochistic. Where Freud's moral masochist seeks punishment from the external world for adverse incidents, Reik's Christian masochist is both the victim and the victimizer and thus seeks punishment from within (304). There is something of the public spectacle – indeed, one might even argue something of the exhibitionist – that is constitutive of the pleasurable punishments for Reik's masochist (72). Whereas Freud's subject might skillfully manipulate external events to solicit punishment, Reik's subject manipulates public events to solicit both reward and punishment (314). Reik identifies four primary features of his masochist, all of which have special significance for Stephen Gordon. First, the Christian masochist, like Christ himself, seeks out the gaze of those who can either reward his deeds or witness his suffering (351).

Reik argues that the social, or Christian, masochist requires an external audience, the central display of the body (as this references Christ's suffering on the cross), and a master tableau or fantasy where what is beaten is not so much the body as the flesh and, beyond that, sin itself (351).[8] Within the Christian masochist lies the desire to remake the world in another image altogether, to forge a different cultural order. Failing that, the "nobility of the martyr is proved by his defeat" (352). Hence, the remaining three features of the Christian masochist are his reiteration of the need for fantasy, the suspension of punishment (or reward) for as long as possible, and the orchestration of a punishment imperative where the masochist aggressively demands punishment to relieve the accumulating anxiety. Ultimately, or perhaps penultimately, the moral masochist seeks to be raised on an invisible pedestal and, eventually, to assume his place within a divine family in the same way that Christ himself came to be installed in a suffering and castrated position as the living promise of redemption (Silverman 1993, 45).

One of the reasons I prefer Reik's Christian masochist to Freud's is that the former allows me to analyze the content of Stephen's masochistic fantasies as particularly Christian rather than just their structure. The content is far more historically specific and foregrounds the heroics of Nelson; the courtly love rituals and ethos of Stephen's father, Philip; and suffering as it was embedded in the spiritual cultures around Stephen. Gayle Rubin (1994, 79) argues for the historical specificity and social content of meanings when she suggests that neither can be reduced to castration or the Oedipus complex: "Fetishism raises all sorts of issues concerning shifts in the manufacture of objects, the historical and social specificities of control and skin and social etiquette, or ambiguously experienced body invasions and minutely graduated hierarchies. If all of this complex social information is reduced to castration or the Oedipus complex ... I think something important has been lost."

Simultaneously, as a set of desires and as a gendered/gendering fantasy, masochism first emerges for Stephen during his pre-adolescent libidinous crush on the housemaid Collins. His attraction to Collins is, interestingly enough, constituted by the same commingling emotions of guilty pleasure, brooding ambivalence, and thrilling shame that mark Stephen's relationship with Anna – although, unlike that relationship, this one cuts across important class and age differences. Yet it has been all but summarily dismissed by both the courts and critics alike. The section in which Stephen obsesses over Collins and languishes in powerlessness is sandwiched between two very important sections in which he attempts to materialize his phantasmic masculine identity as impossible-real and in which he seeks that impossible-real in desire (Hart 1998, 91). In the previous section, Anna tries to come to terms with both her offspring and her rageful, bitter hatred of that child. Her "unnatural" and "monstrous" anti-maternal instincts are likened to a thing that had "crept upon her like a foe in the dark" and remain the one secret she keeps from Philip: "Now there were times when the child's soft flesh would be almost distasteful to her; when she hated the way Stephen moved or stood still, hated a certain largeness about her, a certain crude lack of grace in her movements, a certain unconscious defiance" (Hall 1928, 16). Stephen responds to his mother's beauty by sensing her feelings, and he replies with aloofness or volatile fits of inarticulate rage. By the conclusion of the Collins episode, the gulf between Anna and Stephen has both widened ("They had gazed at each other as though asking for something, as though seeking for something, the one from the other; then the moment had passed – they had walked on in silence, no nearer in spirit than before" [32]) and become gendered. Anna and Stephen share a ride into Great Malvern to shop, and the formerly tempestuous child performs the semaphoric rituals of aristocratic masculinity. "Stephen would suddenly spring to attention, especially if they were crossing the street. She would look right and left for imaginary traffic, [and] slip a hand under Anna's elbow ... Anna would feel the small hand ... and would think that the fingers were ... strong and efficient ... like Sir Philip's ... and [she] would [try] to keep that displeasure from her voice" (33). Stephen's crush on Collins and the fantasies, narrative scenarios, and dreams that that crush articulates transform the former Stephen into the latter.

The Collins crush is activated by two psychic events: Stephen's identification with his father ("she adored her father ... he was part of herself, he had always been there, she could not envisage the world without him" [16]) and his introjection of masculinity (his recognition of his "urgent necessity to love" [16]). The latter compels him to focus his desires onto the housemaid Collins, and a shared but entirely insignificant deceit between them (Collins oversteps her duties as a maid by telling Stephen to wash his hands; Stephen's nursemaid censures them both and Stephen then witnesses Collins's denial) binds them in a moment of guilty collusion. Stephen's love for Collins is inseparable from his contempt for the lie ("this very injustice seemed to draw her to Collins, since despising, she could still love her" [18]), in a move designed to display Stephen's developing outrage at injustice and his emerging belief in the redemptive power of (aristocratic) honour in the face of the less worthy. Hall foregrounds the emerging overlap of desire and shame, suffering and satisfaction: "Stephen brooded darkly over Collins' unworthiness; and yet ... she still wanted Collins ... thinking about her made Stephen go hot down her spine" (18). Witnessing Collins, kneeling and vulnerable, knowing she was a member of the servant class who was being chastised by the nurse, then seeing her lie to protect her job, was enough to activate Stephen's empathy, hatred, and desire. Realizing that she needs Stephen's complicity, Collins then kisses him. The result for Stephen is a bond between them that is a complicated mix of identification and desire, suffering and pleasure: "Stephen stood speechless from a sheer sense of joy, all her doubts swept completely away. At that moment she knew nothing but beauty and Collins, and the two were as one, and the one was Stephen – and yet not Stephen either, but something more vast, that the mind of seven years found no name for" (18).

Such an epiphany initiates an identificatory chain of possible masculine subject positions – fantasies made available to him in different kinds of narratives – that Stephen tries on until he finds the one that fits. Interestingly, the private moment that initiates the search for an identity is converted into a search through public narratives of heroics and suffering, a public spectacle anticipated by Reik.

> [Stephen] had very much liked being read to, especially stories from books that were all about heroes; but now such stories so stirred her ambition, that she longed intensely to live them. She, Stephen, now longed to be William Tell, or Nelson, or the whole Charge of Balaclava ... And [she] would say gravely: "Yes, of course I'm a boy. I'm young Nelson, and I'm saying: 'What is fear?' ... I must be a boy, 'cause I feel exactly like one, I feel like young Nelson in the picture upstairs." (20)

Stephen dresses the part of his chosen hero,[9] stalks about Morton in search of Collins, and performs until Collins shoos him back to his nursery.

Stephen's performances are not limited to secular heroes. One evening he discovers two things: first, that Collins suffers daily with a painful knee injury and, two, upon reading the *Child's Book of Scripture Stories,* that Jesus had chosen to bear pain – to suffer – for those he loved. "That evening," the narrator suggests, "[Stephen] studied the picture of the Lord on His Cross, and she felt that she understood Him" (21). Stephen prays frenetically for God to give him the same affliction that Collins has and, once he finally falls asleep, dreams that "in some queer way she was Jesus" (22). In that dream Collins kneels and kisses his hand because Stephen had cured her knee by grafting part of his healthy one onto Collins' damaged one. From that night on, Stephen no longer dresses as Nelson or William Tell; instead, he spends all of his time kneeling on the floors to damage his own knees, both to prove his devotion to Collins and to enact an identification with her suffering, thus complicating the supposed distinction between identification with (Collins, Christ, those suffering from injustice) and desire for (Collins, those suffering from injustice): "It was really rather fine to be suffering," asserts Stephen, "it certainly seemed to bring Collins much nearer; it seemed to make Stephen feel that she owned her by right of this diligent pain" (23).

Stephen's suffering fantasies not only foreground ambiguities and contradictions but also imbrications of class, gender, and desire. They reveal how Stephen's gender identity is articulated in and through disavowed class identifications. (That this classed and gendered subject is also racialized is an argument I return to in the final part of this chapter.) In *The Well*, secularized and aristocratic masculinity knows itself and its desires best through a threshold figure, in this case not the figure of the Victorian nurse but of a housemaid. In *Imperial Leather*, McClintock (1995, 83-98) makes a convincing argument when she suggests that the "men on the cusp of modernism" first encountered knowledge and self-discovery through the bodies of two differentially classed "mothers": that of the biological but absented mother and that of the ever-present nurse. Beginning with an analysis of class relations, McClintock goes on to read the diaries and papers of Arthur Munby, a well-known Victorian barrister and man of letters who had a compulsive infatuation with the spectacle of working women. She argues that Munby's class fetish facilitates an analysis of the ways that domestic servants function in the psychosexual development of the young men in their care. For Stephen, that threshold figure shifts from the nurse (who later becomes loyal companion Puddle, the non-object who is not lost) to the housemaid Collins, with whom he learns (and eroticizes) both the social scripts of class difference and his conceptions of gendered erotic difference. Collins was Stephen's first erotic arousal as well as his first sexual humiliation and rejection; this combination condenses and fixes for Stephen a masochistic and doubled erotics of loss (loss of his first object, Anna, as well as Collins) and a split, abjected, and complexly layered somatic identification (with Philip, an almost anachronistic form of masculinity, but also with Christ, who suffers for those he loves, as well as with Collins, who is abjected in terms of class and suffers as a result).

This moment that consolidates desire, gender, and class is also a productive moment of orthogonal disidentification for Stephen. As a spectacle where the injurious contrasts of femininity are on display but controlled (i.e., where some women are valued precisely for their ability to endure menial work in contrast with other women who are valued because they cannot), Collins is able to furnish Stephen with the recognition he needs when he is dressed up as a boy. As that which is not-(recognizably)-feminine but classed, Collins then becomes the means by which Stephen similarly becomes not classed but aristocratically gendered. In other words, neither Collins nor Stephen is Anna, the domestic but abjected and Cruel Angel in the House. At one point, Collins chastizes Stephen for always being underfoot as "Nelson," and Stephen, dejected, slinks back to his room, replaces his boy-clothing with those chosen by Anna, and, in a fit of abject rage, beats the dolls that look most like her (but also like Stephen as a miniature of Anna) in those clothes in that moment. "Because she so longed to be someone quite real, instead of just Stephen pretending to be Nelson ... she would go to the cupboard, and getting out her dolls would begin to torment them. She had always despised the idiotic creatures which, however, arrived with each Christmas and birthday. 'I hate you! I hate you! I hate you!' she would mutter, thumping their innocuous faces" (Hall 1928, 20). Stephen does not rage directly at either Anna or Collins but, rather, at a projection of that which he is expected to, but cannot, perform. The most public and spectacular feature of Stephen's grotesque body is its wrongness in time, space, and knowledge as it makes the impression of a man in a woman's clothing.

> She stood there an enraged and ridiculous figure in her Liberty smock, with her hard, boyish forearms. Her long hair had partly escaped from its ribbon, and the bow sagged down limply, crooked and foolish. All that was heavy in her face sprang into view, the strong line of the jaw, the square, massive brow, the eyebrows, too thick and wide for beauty. And yet there was a kind of large splendour about her – absurd though she was, she was splendid at that moment – grotesque and splendid, like some primitive thing conceived in a turbulent age of transition. (52)

An important part of that turbulence for Stephen occurs when he is banished from Morton after a disastrous affair with a married American woman named Angela Crossby. It is possible to trace both the doubled erotics of loss (femininity as the site of both thrilling pleasure and shameful humiliation) and the masochism motif (masculinity as both the Christ who suffers and the Christ who saves) through all of Stephen's libidinous affairs. Stephen's banishment from the pastoral Morton functions as the second most important plot-point of the novel. After discovering Collins in the arms of a footman, the ever rageful Stephen eschews sociality altogether. But long after his father's death, and after the beginning of the "breaking up of the stables at Morton," a fortuitous motorcar drive into Upton to purchase new gloves affords him a chance meeting with the American Angela Crossby (128). It is no accident that Stephen's first adult affair is with an American woman. From our first glimpse of Angela to the moment when Stephen is exiled from Morton, both Angela and her husband, Ralph, are constructed as somewhat crude, suspect, "aggressively new," and almost of an entirely different race (150).

Like many of the men in *The Well*, Ralph Crossby is characterized as a "mean-spirited" man – someone who is small, vile, petty, and yet, still entirely ineffectual and a failure as a man (150-1): "What Ralph lacks in virility, he tries to make up for by being revengeful" (181). Angela, on the other hand, seems like a hybrid Henry James/F.S. Fitzgerald heroine in her

Americanness: when Stephen first sees her, two dogs are engaged in a vicious dog fight. Angela charges towards the dogs with her parasol "as though it were a lance" and as though she intended to enter into battle (130). Stephen finally rescues Angela's dog and stops to look at its distraught owner: "Her hair was ... cut short like a mediaeval page; it was straight, and came just to the lobes of her ears ... her skin was very white ... all the colour that she had seemed to lie in her eyes, which were ... of rather an unusual blue that almost seemed to be tinted with purple, and their candid expression was that of a child" (131). Stephen looks, and listens, to Angela, who, as it turns out, speaks with "the drawl of the South," and it dawns on him that "this woman was lovely – she was like some queer flower that had grown up in darkness, like some rare, pale flower without blemish or stain" (132).

Like all of Stephen's love affairs, the trajectory of his relationship with Angela is one in which his longing for public recognition and reward penultimately fails and culminates in public humiliation. Nevertheless, Angela's existence is crucial in that she functions, albeit temporarily, as a rediscovered libidinous object that may be possessed. Paradoxically, Angela's absent-presence both consolidates Stephen's gendered class position (Angela recounts for Stephen her own biographical history, which is filled with poverty, abuses, and injustices) and conflates the previous loss of Anna and Collins with the loss of his ancestral home and, hence, status. Ralph discovers their affair and, after conferring with Anna, insists that Stephen not see Angela again. In a confrontation with Anna, and in the honourable manner bequeathed to him by his father, Stephen protects his mother's reputation by renouncing his newly refound object to masculinity qua masculinity; that is, to Ralph as well as to Roger Antrim, Angela's lover and Stephen's childhood rival (who also discovers their affair). The body of the feminine continues to function as a site of thrilling masochistic desire and public shame for Stephen, who experiences this most recent humiliation as both the fruition and limitation of his identity as his father's son.

After Philip discovers Stephen's disastrous crush on Collins, he teaches him to "be a man" by taking loss "like a man":

> "And now I'm going to treat you like a boy, and a boy must always be brave, remember. I'm not going to pretend as though you were a coward; why should I, when I know that you're brave? I'm going to send Collins away. (29)

> You're all the son that I've got ... You're brave and strong-limbed, but I want you to be wise ... Stephen, come here – look me straight in the eyes – what is honour, my daughter?" She looked into his anxious, questioning eye: "You are honour," she said quite simply. (61-2)

Stephen's sense of self is profoundly divided and split, but he nevertheless introjects his father, which he experiences henceforth and paradoxically as a non-corporeal body (of laws), anachronistic, idealized as almost divinely transcendent and yet always already failed, dead: "Always she had the sense of a dead thing that lay close against her heart ... A corpse – she was carrying a corpse about with her" (195). However, this corpse, or body, "that lay close to her heart" is also, simultaneously, the introjected body of Christ with whom he so profoundly identifies.

Peggy Phelan (1997) notes in her reading of Caravaggio's painting, *The Incredulity of St. Thomas* (hereafter *The Incredulity*), that both it and the biblical story from which Caravaggio took his drama stage a paradoxical proposition in the story of redemption. In the Bible, after Christ has been crucified, his body is entombed with the cave entrance blocked by a large rock. The prostitute Mary of Magdalene goes to Christ's tomb and finds that the large rock has been rolled away and that his body is no longer inside. She returns later with Peter and Simon to find an empty shroud that previously wrapped Christ's dead body. The men leave, but Mary, bewildered, stands outside the empty sepulcher, weeping. Two angels appear and tell Mary that the body that died lives again. Christ himself then appears to Mary and says, "Touch me not." He tells her to tell the disciples that she has seen him and, a week later, Christ appears to them as well. Thomas is not among them, but when he hears the report he does not believe it. He believes his friends have seen a phantom and says he will believe Christ is resurrected only when he puts his hand in the wound of Christ's living body. Eight days later, Jesus meets Thomas. Thomas now claims he does believe since he can see him. But Christ now doubts, too, and needs Thomas's validation almost more than Thomas needs Christ's. Jesus takes Thomas's hand and pilots Thomas's fingers into the wound. This is the moment that Caravaggio paints, the plunging of Thomas's fingers into Christ's wound.

Phelan argues that Caravaggio discovers two incompatible but related propositions in the story of the redemption – propositions and problems that similarly resonate throughout *The Well* (27-30). First, the wound on Caravaggio's Christ does not bleed, and so Christ similarly doubts who he is after the resurrection, especially (like Stephen) who he is in relation to the men with whom he shared a history and with whom he had tried to forge a collective body. To quote Phelan: "Having given up all his blood for salvation, Christ, logic would indicate, should have no more blood left. If he is a bloodless body is he still 'the son of God made man?'" (30). Christ attempts to resolve the contradiction between the divine body and the fallen body by giving his body to the biblical script – a script that had him say the words, "This is my body, take and eat" (28). Thus, Caravaggio narrates a fundamental uncertainty about the ontology of Christ's body –

an ontology that both *The Well*, and the fictions of female masculinity that come after it, repeatedly rehearse. Butch masculinity, especially stone butch masculinity, spins around the same imperative to renounce the body – an imperative that manifests as a wounded imperative: "Touch me not." And yet Christ's ontological status (i.e., the viability of the self, or interiority, which is to say his awareness of himself as the son of God made flesh) must be reflected through or perhaps with the materiality of that same exterior or uncertain flesh. This particular trope, that of the imperative of the subject to transcend the limitations of the body, is rehearsed around and through the impossible but compelling injunction to the intersubjective Other to "Touch me." Thomas does appear to touch Christ; that which he touches appears in the painting as a paradoxical hole, a threshold, liminal space between a fictional *living* body and an (in)substantiated non-real, or metaphorically *dead*, body, which does not bleed.

Such transcendences, or resignifications, are a consistent trope of FTM trans-sexual fictions, which, after *The Well* (and which, given the current status of FTM surgeries), require a leap of faith to read and, hence, materialize the noncorporeal absent (male) subject as *substantial* rather than as the stand-in, or corporeal, (female) body. Christ needs Thomas to know him as real, to witness him publicly as real, as the self that transcends the body. *The Incredulity* stages the drama of intersubjectivity not only for Thomas and Christ but also for those butch and FTM masculinities. In other words, female masculinity is framed, arrested in (passionate) fictions of gender and a theatre of substantiation, where the authenticity of the most intimately *felt* self could only become "real" (i.e., of "substance") through the recognition of the Other and the masochistic renunciation of the flesh. The proof can only be provided by the object of desire for either imperative ("Touch/See Me" or "Touch/See Me Not") and cannot be authenticated by measures of corporeality (33). Undeniably, Christ's body is a fallen body that manifests its own contradictions in a wounded, suffering body. Similarly, in a moment that foreshadows Stephen's supposedly honourable love for Mary, where it finds its most profound pleasure in the pain exercised upon it by this same internalized corpus/corpse of the Father('s Laws), a corpus reflected in Hall's choice of syntax (i.e., you must be honourable like your Father), Stephen "[finds] her manhood" and wilfully relinquishes all ties to Morton Hall and to the world his father groomed him to inherit: he leaves "the grey and crumbling ruins" behind (Hall 1928, 202).

The ultimate moment in which Stephen "takes it like a man" occurs in the supposedly honourable truncation of his relationship with Mary Llewellyn (Savran 1998, 37-8). Mary poses a number of interesting and productive problems for readers of *The Well* but especially for those reading it through the middle and towards the end of the twentieth century. Mary is the subject who exposes the limitations of what Hall and Stephen could think (through sexology) within a model of inversion wherein one's performance of gender supposedly signifies the truth of one's erotic tastes. Even though, for "true" inverts (like Stephen, Wanda, and Jonathan Brockett) the problem of knowledge is one of coming into knowledge about the self by learning to read and articulate the signs so obviously worn on the body itself, for other inverts (like Valerie Seymour, Barbara, and Jamie) the problem of knowledge is not so much about recognition as it is about rereading and avoiding misrecognition: "The grades were so numerous and so fine that they often defied the most careful observation. The timbre of a voice, the build of an ankle, the texture of a hand, a movement, a gesture – since few were so pronounced as Stephen Gordon" (352-3). However, if a reader was to look askew at, or perhaps read against the grain of, this third-person limited omniscient narrative that allows us – indeed, needs us – to see Stephen so clearly, it is possible to see that Mary's existence, albeit written completely through Stephen, is the thing that lies outside of the frame and whose very invisibility conditions Stephen's hypervisibility. Hall cannot let Mary speak for herself in this text. Mary, who is marked as both feminine and lower middle-class, functions primarily as a kind of psychic projection of everything that Stephen cannot quite make sense of and yet all that he needs not to be ("she" and "working-class") in order to be "he."

Mary, a nineteen-year-old orphan, emerges out of almost nowhere to serve with the Breakspear Female Ambulance Unit in France, the same one with which Stephen serves. After the war ends, Stephen takes Mary back to his home in Paris, where servants do the work that would normally fall to Mary. Where Anna Gordon found her place as the mistress of Morton Hall, Mary lacks the necessary training to run a house of that class (340). Even though Mary actively pursues Stephen and eventually initiates their sexual relationship, Stephen mandates himself courtly keeper and builder of Mary's "refuge" (356). Where Philip's paternalism engendered Stephen through a realm of action, knowledge, and subsequent choices (including those laid out for him by sexology), Stephen's paternalism similarly overdetermines Mary's path, instructing him in the sexology he learned from his father (331). Ironically, that path is one that is quite different from his own and that can only fulfill the imperative of honouring the Father by steering Mary directly towards Martin. For Stephen, such impossibilities are, of course, constitutive of desire.

From the opening pages of the novel to the melodramatic conclusion, the erotic world in and around Malvern Hills is conditioned as a pastoral, courtly romance. Both Jacques Lacan (1991) and Slavoj Žižek (1994) theorize the world of courtly love as that constituted by *anamorphosis*, or any kind of construction that, by means of an optical transposition, allows a certain form that was not visible at first sight to transform itself into a readable image (Lacan 1991, 135). On the one hand, the primary form we think we see is Stephen's tragic suffering in a culture that refuses to recognize his competing needs to live honourably and with a partner. The form that is not immediately visible, although it is my hope that it certainly is by now, is that of Stephen trapped within the paradoxes of courtly and, according to Žižek, masochistic desires. All of Stephen's love objects are marked by inaccessibility, even the ones he "acquires." Despite the rhetoric, these women are not sublime objects, abstracted, elevated, and idealized. These women, and especially Mary, function much like the paradoxical "Lady" of courtly love; that is, they function as the space around which the subject's desire is structured. That space, as Žižek reminds us, is bent like space in the theory of relativity: "the only way to reach the Object-Lady is indirectly, in a devious, meandering way – proceeding straight on ensures that we miss the target" (94). Stephen proceeds head on with Mary, whisking her off to the idyllic and pastoral Oratova to consummate their desires. But in the long run, Stephen manipulates external circumstances to rebuild obstructions and obstacles. His introjection of an imperative to love by honour does not mix well in a culture whose message to both Stephen and Mary is that their union is essentially dishonourable. That introjected imperative compels Stephen to sabotage Mary and to end their relationship. Both Lacan and Žižek argue that, in courtly love, the Lady functions as the primary paradox: "The Object, therefore, is literally something that is created – whose place is encircled – through a network of detours, approximations and near-misses" (Žižek 1994, 95). However, it would seem evident from Stephen's performance that he himself is the paradox. His own reconstitution of artificial obstacles suggests that he functions as the retraction, as the desiring subject, but also as the force that prevents its attainment (95). The logic of courtly love defines the parameters through which Stephen enacts a drama of erotic hindrance: that same inaccessibility, holding back, and suspension that, as I suggested earlier, is constitutive of male masochism. Stephen's desires are fulfilled paradoxically by way of a public spectacle of incessant postponement.

Mary functions as a paradoxical realization and deferral of Stephen's desire; she also functions as one of the weakest characters in Hall's novel. Clare Hemmings (1999) raises intriguing questions about femininity in "Out of Sight, Out of Mind? Theorizing Femme Narrative," one of the most recent theoretical forays into thinking femme subjectivities that provides some interesting ways to rethink Mary. Hemmings revisits late nineteenth-century sexology to argue that, from its inception, the logic of sexology has failed to think the feminine invert. Either the feminine invert, who has failed in her femininity by passively receiving the attentions of the wrong object (i.e., the masculine woman), will "cure," or redeem, the blight on her femininity by returning to the "real" heterosexual male or she has always already failed in her femininity because she is in the category that Havelock Ellis suggests is made up of "women whom the average man would pass by" (quoted in Hemmings 1999, 452). In either scenario, she remains teleologically bound by suspicions: either her heterosexuality is compromised or her supposedly natural femininity is compromised. The only other option that sexology provides, Hemmings argues, is curious: "Ellis's construction [of the feminine invert] raises the possibility that, given their status as objects of masculine attention, all heterosexuality-bound women have the capacity to commit the same 'error' of mistaking the masculine invert's attention for 'the real thing'" (452). Thus, argues Hemming, rather than resolving the problem of the feminine invert, Ellis universalizes the problem as constitutive of all femininities: "While the femme may continue to be haunted by her 'inevitable return to heterosexuality,' heterosexual femininity itself is scarcely free of perversion, but remains haunted in turn by the possibility of seduction by the masculine woman" (453). Hemmings's argument elaborates on Butler's rethinking of the relations between sexuality and gender in the sex/gender system. In other words, Hemmings's reading of femininity posits that sexuality works against gender to let that which cannot fully appear in any performance of femininity – its inevitable perversion – persist in its disruptive promise (Butler 1991, 29).

These renderings leave the house of femininity in a state of disarray. Such a position, as Hemmings herself notes, leaves the feminine woman structurally positioned as object of both a heterosexual and a homosexual gaze. And while femininity is conferred and consumed in those sexualizing gazes, it is also true that one cannot tell, just by looking, which gaze she will return (Hemmings 1995, 453). Femininity, and, by implication, her "queer-ing" cousin fem(me)ininity,[10] is thus a perception of a successful naturalization of discourses of femininity, especially when those discourses are naturalized on what is also conventionally presumed to be a female body, and especially when the effect is to receive and similarly naturalize a heterosexualizing male gaze.[11]

Hemmings makes some important theoretical observations about femininity as well as the one suggested in the above quote. She suggests, for example, that "femininity is conferred upon [a woman] though the masculine gaze" (453). Hemmings is responding to the way a crisis of visuality around fem(me)ininity has been named in queer theory and performed in queer fiction and performance art. Given that many of the visual signifiers of femininity are the same for both heterosexual and queer feminine subjects, in representational contexts queer fem(me)ininity can often pass as heterosexual femininity. In narrative terms, as Hemmings argues, this means that the femme is invisible as a queer sexual subject once she is out of the sight of, or does not return, masculinity's gaze (455). Or, to phrase this as did Teresa de Lauretis in 1993 when she responded to the concerns Esther Newton raised concerning the "feminine invert": "in most representational contexts, [Stephen's lover] Mary would either be passing lesbian or passing straight, her (homo)sexuality being in the last instance what cannot be seen. Unless ... she enter the frame of vision *as* or *with* a lesbian in male body drag" (de Lauretis 1993, 155, emphasis in original). In her earlier essay, Newton (1989, 292-3) critiques Radclyffe Hall for the ways that she articulates "lesbianism" with masculinity:

> The notion of a feminine lesbian contradicted the congenital theory that many homosexuals in Hall's era espoused to counter demands that they undergo punishing "therapies." Though Stephen's lovers in *The Well* are all feminine and though Mary, in effect, seduces Stephen, Hall calls her "normal," that is, heterosexual ... As a character, Mary is forgettable and inconsistent, weakening the novel and saddling Hall with an implausible ending ... Hall was unable to publicly articulate – perhaps to believe in – the persona of a real lesbian who did not feel somehow male. If sexual desire is masculine, and if the feminine woman only wants to attract men, then the womanly lesbian cannot logically exist. Mary's real story has yet to be told.

I quote Newton at length in order to foreground the historicity of the questions that Hemmings poses about femme subjectivity. In the twentieth century lesbianism and female masculinity have been realized as gender transitive, as about movement in and across genders. But, at the same time, there have been pivotal and contradictory moments where the heterogendering of desire – where sexual systems are realized in and eroticize gender difference – has been repudiated for ideological reasons. One of the effects of that repudiation has been to render fem(me)ininity a logical impossibility. Hemmings's article, the history and trajectory of fem(me)ininities in mainstream cultures, and queer cultural productions that articulate femme suggest that moment is shifting.

The notion that femme represents an occlusion, an "articulate silence" but also a subjectivity hailed by a masculine gaze, suggests equally that femme can be refused or repudiated by that same gaze (Hall 1928, 434). Newton is decidedly right to critique Hall's strategy of producing closure by having Stephen nobly turn Mary over to Martin (293). Despite all of Mary's best efforts to articulate herself, she remains bound by that gaze – that is, by both Stephen's and Martin's gaze. Newton acknowledges some of the ways that Hall attempts to rethink Mary: it is Mary who pursues Stephen when they are both drivers in the Breakspeare Ambulance Unit, and it is Mary who continues to pursue a sexual relationship once they have left the war and have returned to Paris. Indeed, Hall attempts to allow for a femme gaze: "Stephen was busily grooming her hair with a couple of brushes that had been dipped in water ... Seeing Mary in the glass she did not turn around, but just smiled for a moment at their two reflections. Mary sat down in an arm-chair and watched her, noticing the strong thin line of her thighs; noticing too the curve of her breasts – slight and compact, of a certain beauty" (323-5).

Mary's desiring and lustful gaze can only be grafted onto and out of (i.e., can only be narratively and visually bound by) Stephen's gaze in the mirror. What follows this passage is a curious realization of desire between Stephen and Mary triangulated through a gendering of domestic objects. Mary assumes responsibility for Stephen's wardrobe, activities that "become" her: "And yet there was something quite new in [Mary's] face, a soft, wise expression ... She was at the stage of being in love when she longed to do womanly tasks for Stephen" (323). However, Mary is unable, as if "dumb," to articulate her desires outside a certain fetishization, and yet projectional personification, of objects in Stephen's bedroom. Those objects and, ironically, Mary's inarticulateness, can speak nothing other than "Stephen."

> The bed could only have been Stephen's bed ... The chairs could only have been Stephen's chairs ... The dressing table could only have been hers [sic], with its tall silver mirror and ivory brushes. And all these things had drawn into themselves a species of life derived from their own, until they seemed to be thinking of Stephen with a dumbness that made their thoughts more insistent, and their thoughts gathered strength and mingled with Mary's so that she heard herself cry out: "Stephen!" (323)

At a later moment in the narrative, Stephen is commanded home by his mother, Lady Anna, although he is instructed not to bring Mary to Morton Hall. Stephen respects his mother's wishes and returns without Mary. Upon Stephen's departure, Mary herself takes up (temporary) residence in Stephen's study to pen a letter to him that the reader never sees. Curiously though, as Leslie J. Henson (1997, 338) points out, the authority of that letter is ascribed to a pen other than Mary's: "That letter was full of many things which *a less privileged pen had best left unwritten* – loyalty, faith, consolation, devotion; all this and much more she wrote to Stephen" (emphasis added). Even though the narrator instructs the reader to understand this as a scene in which "Mary met and defeated the world's first tentative onslaught," the defeat is tenuous and, indeed, is left "unwritten" in the scene's space-off, a place unthinkable outside the text and knowable only as an occlusion (338). Thus, according to *The Well*, fem(me)ininity is guilty of passing as femininity, although in this case, Mary is unable to return a gaze at all. She is an object to be exchanged between men, or is, at best, an articulate silence that suggests the possibility of articulation and agency in a place beyond the authorial and masculine gaze.

Stephen most becomes his gender qua masochism in relation to a repudiated fem(me)ininity, a position that strangely and ironically feminizes the subject even as it appears most installed in its place as suffering and honourable. Such tensions are evident in Stephen's names. "Mary" is both Stephen's second name and the name of his lover. In the biblical context, Mary is the mother of Christ but also Mary Magdalene, the reformed prostitute who witnesses Christ's suffering and redemptive resurrection. In the end, our Messiah figure must sacrifice Mary in a homosocial exchange with Martin Hallam, a gesture that is stereotypically and simultaneously feminine (the surrendering of one's own desire in favour of the beloved's) but also masculine (the exchanging of women between men). Breen (1997, 193) argues that Stephen can "be" Mary only insofar as he cannot "have" Mary. Paradoxically, while Stephen does resemble his second namesake slightly more than his first, I would argue that, within this masochistic triangulation, Stephen ("he") could only be Stephen ("he" qua "Christ") when he is not her ("Mary"). This penultimate and masochistic act of self-sacrifice, the denial of one's own (wrongful) corporeality, is also where both trans-sexual and stone butch masculinity become most performative, somatically articulating an ambivalent and metagendered identity that otherwise haunts them: "Touch/See Me [the subject]" and "Touch/See Me [the body] Not."

The Articulations of Whiteness

> I kept losing track of the subject.
>
> – Judith Butler, *Bodies That Matter: On the Discursive Limits of "Sex"*

While the sexual politics of Stephen's gender identity map neatly onto class politics, his discontent as a suffering man bears the most interesting fruit when mapped onto the racial politics of Hall's novel. As I have suggested already, what is often not read in and through *The Well* are the ways in which it articulates a subject that is always already racialized. Much of the criticism of *The Well* cannot know the ways that it has been, and continues to be, located securely within the operations of white supremacy by misreading Stephen's unintelligible gendered corporeality as it materializes (albeit paradoxically) through colour. A close reading of what *The Well* does know about race, and what that criticism has missed, has much to tell us about the ways that whiteness articulates itself as universal through particular forms of sexual subjectivity. *The Well* reads us misreading the very paradoxes it is written through: that modern sexual subjects articulate themselves through a grammar of white supremacy and that this grammar often functions to formulate a narrative of change (the emergence of differently embodied subjects of masculinity) that simultaneously struggles to maintain, as much as to resist, continuity with the status quo when it allows whiteness to remain unmarked. Part of what is (re)produced in the readings of *The Well* when its critics read for sexual subjectivity and disregard racialized subjectivity is a performance and reiteration of whiteness. That failure, where whiteness is so hypervisible as everything that it becomes, paradoxically, invisible as nothing – that is, it becomes the norm – is one of the categorical imperatives of white supremacy.

The scene that most critics of *The Well* return to repeatedly is the mirror scene. Because of its crucial importance to their, as well as to my own, arguments, I quote it at length.

> That night she stared at herself in the glass; and even as she did so she hated her body with its muscular shoulders, its small compact breasts, and its slender flanks of an athlete. All her life she must drag this body of hers like a monstrous fetter imposed on her spirit. This strangely ardent yet sterile body that must worship yet never be worshipped in return by the creature of its adoration. She longed to maim it, for it made her feel cruel; it was so white, so strong and so self-sufficient; yet withal so poor and unhappy a thing that her eyes filled with tears and her hate turned to pity. She began to grieve over it, touching her breasts with pitiful fingers, stroking her shoulders, letting her hands slip along her straight thighs – Oh, poor and most desolate body! Then, she, for whom Puddle was actually praying at that moment, must now pray also, but blindly; finding few words that seemed worthy of prayer, few words that seemed to encompass her meaning – for she did not know the meaning of herself. But she loved, and loving groped for the God who had fashioned her, even unto this bitter loving. (Hall 1928, 186-7)

Any reading of this scene must include a rethinking of the materiality of the body itself. In *Bodies That Matter*, Butler (1993) takes issue with the assumptions of social constructionist theory, arguing, in part, that the notion that gender is imprinted onto sex is no longer adequate. Questions such as "How is gender constituted as and through a certain interpretation of sex?" no longer deal with the sophistications of regulatory power regimes whose success is measured by the very assumptions of that question, that is, un- and undertheorization of "sex" itself. Butler rephrases the question to account for the limitations of prying gender apart from sex, arguing that our question should now be "How is it that treating the materiality of sex as a given presupposes and consolidates the normative conditions of its own emergence?" (10). In other words, there can be no reference to a pure body that is not at the same time a further formation of that body.

Butler's insight into the performativity of discourse, not *on* materiality but *as* materiality, provides insight into the commentary that reads Stephen reading his body in the mirror scene. If Butler is correct in suggesting that analytical interrogations should not accept the body, or "sex," as a given but should, instead, foreground the normative conditions under which the materiality of the body itself is framed and formed through the differential categories of sex, then the differential categories of these critics (trans-sexual man rather than butch, lesbian rather than straight woman) produce the body they need *The Well* to articulate. In other words, the ideological investments of each overdetermine not only what kind of body materializes in that mirror but also which kind of body cannot materialize. As I have noted a number of times already, Butler argues that it is "as important to think about how and to what end bodies are constructed as is it [sic] will be to think about how and to what end bodies are not constructed and, further, to ask after how bodies which fail to materialize provide the necessary 'outside,' if not the necessary support, for the bodies which, in materializing the norm, qualify as bodies that matter" (16). There are multiple bodies constructed in *The Well*, bodies gendered, sexed, classed, and racialized. According to Newton (1989), Prosser (1998), and Halberstam (1998a), the only body that Stephen can see in the mirror is inevitably female, even when the language of the passage fails to articulate it as such. These critics fail to see that a racialized body, a white body, has also materialized, although for whiteness to function most effectively as a marker of white supremacy that whiteness cannot be marked and must always be trumped or cloaked by gender. These critics all read, and by reading articulate, Stephen's body as female in order to build a functional polemic around it, even though that is not what the language of the passage tells us. Moreover, the fact that Stephen's white body has gone unremarked suggests that, in Butler's terms, the white body is hypermaterialized and articulated as/with the norm, the unnoticed, the unmarked in order for the gendered body to be materialized. Unmarked whiteness provides the necessary support for gender just as gender provides the necessary support for the materialization of that racial norm.

Both Jay Prosser (1998) and Judith Halberstam (1998a) have theorized the processes of somatic materialization in *The Well*, offering productive (mis-)readings of its articulations of gender and whiteness. In *Second Skins: The Body Narratives of Transsexuality*, Prosser explores the dialogic relations between trans-sexuality and narrative, arguing that, because trans-sexuality is not self-evident on the body, trans-sexual identities emerge as an effect of autobiography. He suggests that trans-sexuality takes autobiographical narrative as its primary symptom by manifesting that which is not immediately obvious: the body's misrepresentation of the subject's "authentic" self (Prosser 1998, 142). Prosser rightly argues that there is a kind of vacillation between rage and pity in *The Well* that marks Stephen's relationship to "her" female body – a body that misrepresents who he actually is. Arguing that Stephen unequivocally sees a female body in the mirror – a body marked by lack, inadequacy, and ontological failure – Prosser makes the somewhat questionable argument that, because there are no scenes of "integration" in the novel, Stephen is forever trapped in that "mirror phase" (163). The result, according to Prosser (who does not specify what he means by "mirror phase"), is that, despite the moments of compassion and healing evidenced by the transition from rage to pity in the mirror scene, Stephen's bodily alienation remains frozen in the plot: "The female body is alien, horribly dislocated from self, in the gap between the morphology of her masculine body image and her duplicitous material female body, Stephen's alienation is engendered, and transgendered" (163). Without access to technology (presumably hormones and surgery), Stephen never transcends or transforms "physicality." The whiteness of Stephen's body, and its subsequent qualities of strength, self-sufficiency, and leadership, are built around the phrase "so white," and yet that logic seems to stand without attracting any notice.

Prosser's assertion that trans-sexual subjectivity is an effect of narrative warrants rethinking. While narrative is indispensable in articulating what otherwise might not be entirely self-evident, *The Well* stages the self-evident and self-knowledge as a crisis of certainties and a crisis of language. As I have suggested, Stephen's gender difference was evident to all but him. His coming into knowledge regimes, not his coming out of a metaphorical closet, is the primary thematic of the novel. The process that allows, or perhaps facilitates, one's own knowledge of one's self is precisely what is at stake in *The Well*. Indeed, it seems much more plausible to argue that, in *The Well,* bodies are the effect of both reading and rearticulation practices. As Prosser himself notes, Stephen's father comes into knowledge about Stephen through reading. In his study, Philip is surrounded by books, including those by sexologists, and by portraits of his family, Stephen having been painted with matriarch Lady Anna. Philip's gaze travels between text and image as he learns to read what he notices in Stephen as an "indefinable quality ... that made her look wrong in the clothes she was wearing" (Hall 1928, 27). Stephen's difference is evident on his body as Philip rereads it through Ulrichs. Philip writes in the margins of Ulrichs's text what he understands to be the truth about Stephen – notes that Stephen later finds and uses to articulate himself into and through language.

Prosser offers an interesting reading of the relationship between Stephen and the housemaid Collins. Where I read this relationship as overdetermined by class differences, Prosser sees it as structured primarily by gender difference. He reads the dream that Stephen has in which "she" – and Prosser insists on reading Stephen as female – grafts part of Collins's wounded knee onto his own in an effort to be just like his beloved. Prosser argues that this moment of identification functions to mark Stephen's gender difference. In other words, he argues that, when Stephen grafts Collins's knee onto his own, his "own body is displaced onto and rescued through the beloved's. In rescuing the woman and establishing her difference, Stephen effectively rescues herself from her own womanhood" (Prosser 1998, 165). This, in other words, is a moment of pre–sex reassignment surgery somatic transformation. What Prosser seems to miss are the class differences between Stephen and Collins and how, despite his youth, Stephen manifests the aristocratic and masculine rituals of courtship as a complex and masochistic rescue fantasy. These class differences between Stephen and his phantasmic lover (in this case, Collins) stand in, as it were, for a kind of courtly gender difference and for an imaginary courtly love that Stephen longs for but cannot quite materialize in the flesh and so materializes in fantasy – that is, the (both gendered and erotic) pleasures of suffering. The difference in social standing between Stephen and Collins functions to exaggerate Collins's need to be rescued (at least what Stephen perceives as such) and then Stephen's rightfulness as her rescuer.

This motif repeats itself incessantly throughout *The Well*. Stephen rescues wounded animals, befriends the domestic servants Collins and Old William, cares for and then grieves the deaths of social misfits Barbara and Jamie, pays for the wedding of his servants' daughter. These behaviours can be securely located within the domain of the charitable and paternal aristocratic patriarch. By fetishizing surgery and complete physical transformation as the only way to accomplish the trans-sexual quest for corporeal selfhood, Prosser disavows the ways that bodies are signified as masculine and the way that Stephen, in particular, resignifies what is always misread as "her" and "she" to a body that he himself suggests is indeterminate. When the narrator describes Stephen looking at the body in the mirror scene, what is certain is the colour of the body (not its sex) and, more important, what that colour stands for: "So white, so strong and so self-sufficient."

Critics continue to read Stephen through a sex/gender system structured by dualities. What is transformed or transcended in the mirror scene are binaristic genders: Stephen is neither one gender nor the other but, rather, is figuratively intersexed – not "either/or" but "and/both" (Pratt 1995, 104). The language of the passage is structured by oppositional and bounded contradictions. These are not necessarily resolved but stand as productive and articulate discourses that produce limits and that bind subjects within those limits. What appears to pass as a reversal, where one emotion simply stands in for another, functions instead as a kind of carnivalesque site marked entirely by excess, surplus, and supplementarity (S. Hall 1996b, 300). That which is inevitably repressed, refused, disavowed surreptitiously returns. Stephen both hates and loves what he sees: muscular shoulders, small compact breasts, and slender athletic flanks. Only the word "breasts" signifies as a foundational minimum constitutive of femaleness; the remaining terms speak against those resonances, especially when compared with the ways that Anna, Collins, and Mary, the women who are prototypically female, are described. Stephen rages against and then pities that same body. With the change in emotion comes another reiterative and performative articulation: this time, she began to touch "her" breasts, stroke "her" shoulders, let "her" hands slip along "her" thighs. The imprecisions and failed circumlocutions of language mediate these meta-articulations: "Few words ... seemed to encompass her meaning – for she did not know the meaning" (Hall 1928, 187). Prosser's privileging of twentieth-century surgical interventions is interesting and ironic given that, like Stephen's image in the mirror, surgery for FTMs is neither functional nor visible within the sex/gender system. As I argue in more detail in Section 4, the bodies that many FTMs imagine themselves to have cannot materialize outside the body of discursive, psychic, and linguistic contradictions that not only articulate but also contain them. The body that appears is, in many ways, constituted as "grotesque," an "unnatural" or aberrant body outside the conditions of intelligibility in the sex/gender system – a body that is both genders and neither. This same intersexed[12] body is rearticulated in the fictions that comprise the fourth and final chapter of this book.

Despite the limitations of his thinking, Prosser (1998, 168) raises the penultimate question about *The Well:* "Dogged attempts to read [*The Well*] as lesbian in spite of its narrative have been a case of trying to fit a square peg into a round hole. But in this failure to reconcile *The Well* to a lesbian context lies the novel's value for a transsexual canon: for it is those narratives that don't quite fit, which exceed or resist their homosexual location that (perhaps like transsexuals themselves) might find belonging in a transsexual context." Even though Prosser opens his chapter on *The Well* with the erroneous assertion that "its critics have generally agreed on one thing: that the sexual subject at the center of Hall's novel is lesbianism," he does raise the question of why so many of its critics (himself included) insist on investing it with definitive currency at all (135). In fact, whether or not the subject of Hall's novel is lesbian is the one thing over which the critics most vehemently quarrel. When Prosser asks this question, he answers it by positing category B (trans-sexuality) for category A (lesbianism) and ignores how both are racialized as white. In other words, where he refutes the label "lesbian" he does so by replacing it with another – the label "trans-sexual."[13] *The Well*, its subject, and, for that matter, its author cannot be categorized or conceptualized other than as indeterminate. Trans-sexual narratives evoke the novel as lesbian in order to refuse it; lesbian-feminism has evoked it (and its subject) as internalized misogyny in order to posit lesbianism as "woman" identification and eroticism; Athena Douris (1998) evokes it in order to talk about gender rather than sexuality; here, Prosser evokes it as trans-sexual in order to refuse an imbrication of FTM trans-sexuality and female masculinity; *Stone Butch Blues*, as I argue in Chapter 3, rewrites it in order to refuse the binary sex/gender system completely. *The Well* functions as a kind of polemical blank slate that is read and written only to be refused and rewritten as the thing its readers need it not to be. Its critics, or so it seems to me, agree on nothing.

Judith Halberstam's *Female Masculinity* promises one of the most interesting readings of these contradictions in Hall's novel. Arguing that *The Well* presents "the best record we have of masculine inversion in women" (by which she means a masculine identity expressed through a female self and perceived by society as unnatural and wrong), Halberstam argues that a sartorial aesthetic (i.e., of tailoring, or men's clothes or costume) works in *The Well* to actively oppose the notion of a "true sex" by equating gender and costume (Halberstam 1998a, 90). Halberstam argues that relations between the invert and his male costume provide the site where nakedness can only signify essentially within the sex/gender system, in contrast to clothing, which actually defines the contours of gender. In other words, masculine clothing does for female masculinity what the penis does for male masculinity: it "bears the subject's desire in a masculine mode" (104). "Stephen literally redresses the wrongs of her embodiment by taking on male clothing, meticulously tailored and fashioned to fit her masculine spirit" (106).

Halberstam is certainly right in suggesting that Stephen marks his body as male through his identifications as well as his clothing. However, she herself permits an essentialism to creep back into her argument when she suggests that what appears in the mirror is Stephen's "secret female body" (99). In other words, Halberstam reads the body in Stephen's mirror as undeniably female – a reading that works against the ambivalent language of the passage as I have read it as well as against Halberstam's own assertion that we not read Stephen's body as the definitive site of all meaning. Halberstam warns against the violence of misreading Stephen as "lesbian." Stephen was clearly an invert, which is reducible neither to lesbian nor to trans-sexual: "When modern lesbian critics, historians, and theorists try to read an idealized lesbian history of lesbian identification into and out of the bodies ... of masculine women, a great violence is done to the meaning of those lives" (109). Halberstam grounds her readings of the materiality of Stephen's body itself within the normative and differential categories of the sex/gender system. In other words, "reading" for these critics seems to be the process where discourse functions not *on* materiality but, rather, *as* materiality. For both Prosser and Halberstam, what emerges as hypermateriality through the cracks of the sex/gender system is whiteness.

Despite the best efforts of critics like Prosser and Halberstam, who are armed with theories of performativity, queer theory, parody and irony, and postfeminist queer redeployments of gender performances, Esther Newton's 1984 essay, "The Mythic Mannish Lesbian: Radclyffe Hall and the New Woman," remains one of the most sophisticated and complex studies of both *The Well* and female masculinity. Where Halberstam argues that *The Well* does not mark a point of departure from nineteenth-century notions of female friendship, Newton argues that Stephen Gordon functions as a kind of double and indeterminate trope, simultaneously referencing a new political identity for women generally and a new sexual and gender identity for lesbians. The "lesbian" (i.e., Stephen) in *The Well* asserted a new sexual identity distinct from that associated with the world of female friendship or the two generations of "New Women" who preceded Hall and who are the subject of Hall's earlier novel, *The Unlit Lamp* (1924). Newton's essay does a brilliant job of surveying the discursive background of *The Well* by situating it within its multiple and dialogic contexts. Newton is one of the first critics to reclaim *The Well*, and she argues that an entire battery of camps hover over it, waiting for its eventual and long overdue death. Heterosexual culture condemned it, according to Newton, because it argued for the lesbian's right to existence. Lesbian feminism, on the other hand, treated it like the embarrassing cousin, hated the mannish lesbian, and entirely willed it away. That said, "mannish lesbians," or that gender orientation with which an important minority of lesbians still actively identify and "toward which another minority is erotically attracted," embraced the image and writings about inversion as a way to break out of the asexual model of romantic friendship (Newton 1989, 283). Masculinity, in other words, signifies active sexual desire in a way that, in women's homosocial and gender-segregated world, femininity cannot. "Unlike Orlando," Newton argues, "Stephen is trapped in history [and] cannot declare gender an irrelevant game" (290).

Despite Newton's best efforts to rescue Stephen's gender performance, she inevitably reads the mirror scene as evidence of Stephen's perpetual and agonizing estrangements. Continuing to read Stephen as female and lesbian, Newton does acknowledge that Stephen has learned that "her body [should] be cherished ... since its strength could rejoice her" (Newton 1989, 289; Hall 1928, 58). However, Newton reads against *The Well* by suggesting that, "in one of Hall's most moving passages Stephen expresses this hatred [of her body] as alienation" from his mother, from women, and from his own body. The irony of Newton's argument lies in what she does not or, perhaps, cannot read. When she cites the mirror scene, she elides the words "so white, so strong and so self-sufficient," allowing the metonymous and synonymous relationship(s) to operate. Newton's is a reading practice that pushes the suffering and butch body forward and forces the aristocratic and white body into the background. While Newton wrote her essay at a time when neither the former nor the latter were completely thinkable as such, her elisions, which are not hers alone, continue to cloak, and ultimately, reproduce, whiteness as universal, unmarked, and invisible.

Despite its limitations, Newton's essay stands as one of the earliest and most important interventions into, and articulations of, the functionality of the sex/gender system. Noting that, for Stephen, "crossing-dressing is not a masquerade," Newton acknowledges that female masculinity is one effect of the complex processes of identification and social construction. Prosser, on the other hand, suggests that narrative manifests the body, while Halberstam argues that gender's physicality is made in the masquerade. All three argue that the mirror scene is the moment in which ontological and essentialist truths, passing as the real, return to fix, or stabilize, the meaning of that body. I suggest instead that, for Stephen, the body is destabilized, unmade, and remade in constructions of nakedness itself. The image of Stephen naked in the mirror does not reveal ontological truth but, rather, reads a kind of intersexed self that is, as I have been suggesting, an effect of invested and stabilizing reading and representational practices. Post-Butler critiques of essentialist constructions of identities and bodies posit gender as drag or parody, where identities (as the foreground) are read against the signifiable limitations of the body (as the ground). What happens if we assume a different definition of drag or parody, where the body itself is the performance, the foreground, the thing dragged beyond identity, and that functions as the ground? If, as Krafft-Ebing noted in his reading, the physical signs of "viraginity," or inversion, in a "woman" are a "deep voice, manly gait [and] small mammae" (in other words, how the invert "makes the impression of a man in woman's clothes"), then what are the discourses of reading that continue to produce this figure as a woman making the impression of a man and not a man's body making the impression of a woman's? In other words, what makes it possible to hear "drag" and think "cross-gender performance" and not "corporeal instabilities"?

Part of an answer lies in Butler's interrogation of the limitations of "sex." In her introduction to *Bodies That Matter*, Butler calls for a reformulation, indeed, an entire rethinking, of the terms of corporeal materialization as an effect of power. The production of bodily norms, argues

Butler (1993, 3), is governed by an exclusionary matrix that simultaneously produces a domain of abject bodies that are not yet subjects but that form the outside to the domain of the subject. Thus, as Butler theorizes it, the formation of the subject requires an identification with the normative idea, or phantasm, of "sex," an identification that takes place through a repudiation of that which is made abject. What Stephen sees in the mirror constitutes that domain of abjection, or a body outside of many of the cultural norms that govern the materialization of bodies. Stephen has yet to assume a sex and so, accordingly, is in the state of becoming a subject. One of the primary thematics of Hall's novel is the abject, or that zone of subjectness that is designated "unlivable," "uninhabitable," and "inarticulate" by virtue of being outside the status of subjectivity. In the mirror scene, what happens when clothes come off? When Stephen looks in the mirror and sees a body, the only gendered descriptors of that body that warrant articulation are breasts. No other feature of the body will perform gender as quickly as the presence or absence of breasts.

In Chapter 3, both of the contemporary novels that I examine foreground breasts and their removal as the beginning of reassignment surgeries. For the characters of *Sacred Country* and *Stone Butch Blues*, gender identity is signified by the absence or presence of breasts. The author photograph of Leslie Feinberg, for instance, portrays her with what appears to be a completely reconstructed chest. For Stephen, the smallness and compactness of his "breasts," combined with "the muscular shoulders" and "the slender flanks of an athlete," work to emphasize his masculinity rather than his femininity. Where Prosser (1998) reads Stephen reading and hating this body as female, I find Stephen reading this body as male: "That night she stared at herself in the glass; and even as she did so she hated her body with its *muscular shoulders*, its *small compact breasts*, and its *slender flanks* of an *athlete*." None of these emphasized words suggests that Stephen is reading a feminized body. What Stephen finds "monstrous," "sterile," and "impositional" is decidedly not a female body but the impression or form of a male body that the body in the mirror is beginning to drag, perform, imitate: "It made her feel cruel; so white, so strong and so self-sufficient." What Stephen grieves, therefore, is not so much the "inadequate," or "incomplete," female body but the fiction that his is a female body at all.

Interestingly, the narrative gaze ceases to travel with Stephen's to describe what must exist below Stephen's waist. The first long paragraph of the passage ends as Stephen "begins to grieve" his body, and his hands travel down over breasts, shoulders, and down "along her straight thighs –." Despite the fact that what lies below Stephen's waist remains productively inarticulable, grotesque, and monstrous (a portrait that both Feinberg and Tremain revisit), Stephen nevertheless makes, reads, and eventually learns to become the "impression of the man" he himself sees in the mirror. That man is not coterminous with the impression left behind by Stephen's father (Philip). Stephen is discursively unable to narrate the body he sees in the mirror as it stands outside the phallic economy; that is, it is a man's body and yet it is, at the same moment, masculinity without a penis. This contradictory image is one that Jess Goldberg (*Stone Butch Blues*) and Mary Martin Ward (*Sacred Country*) return to and are able to articulate differently. Despite its phallic masculinity, where social standing and class accomplish the work that the penis does not, the contents of that indeterminate "–" are continually filled in as female to grant Stephen legitimacy, functionality, and intelligibility; Stephen refuses such (dys-)functionality by remaining partially inside of language and its interpellative imperatives in terms of race and nation (but inside/out in terms of gender).

As I have shown, while critics contest the sex of Stephen's body in the mirror, they neither materialize nor contest that body as white. In the moment in which Stephen looks into the mirror and attempts to pass into subjectivity, "languaging" himself from object to subject, his self-articulation(s) mirror those of white critics when all neither notice nor mark whiteness as a constitutive performance of white supremacy. Even though Stephen productively fails to pass completely as/into gendered subjectivity, he also fails to notice that the white body does not exist outside of discourse, meaning, or ideology. The racialization of bodies by white supremacy – or those technologies that similarly link bodies, identity, and power – works to naturalize arrangements of power that are, instead, socially constructed and historically variable. In other words, the white body does not just exist: it is as much put on, as it were, as is any other cultural identity. It, too, is a product of discourse, power-knowledge regimes, and representational practices; and it is those technologies of white supremacy that are most successful when we fail to notice them. In *The Well* they function to naturalize Stephen's whiteness and articulate it to/with gender variance in a number of veiled ways.

It is precisely Stephen's (and indeed John Radclyffe Hall's) currency as white aristocrats that affords them, both inside the text for Stephen as a novelist and in Hall's own writing of *The Well*, authorial intelligibility and power. Stephen publishes his first book, *The Furrow*, and becomes, as a result, something of a celebrity, which functions to increase his status amongst the artists at Valerie Seymour's salon. One particular event at that salon is worthy of scrutiny: the gathering that features two "Negro" American brothers, Lincoln and Henry Jones, who provide the entertainment by singing an old black spiritual. All of those misfits – Brockett, Jamie, Adolphe, Barbara, "even Valerie Seymour" – who gather regularly under Valerie's tutelage are moved to the epiphanic affective sublime by the Jones brothers' suffering. The language of the passage rises to new biblical registers as the suffering Jones brothers sing a song of salvation: "And all the hope of the utterly hopeless of this world, who must live by their ultimate salvation, all the terrible, aching, homesick hope that is born of the infinite pain of the spirit, seemed to break from this man and shake those who listened, so that they sat with bent heads and clasped hands – they who were also among the hopeless sat with bent heads and clasped hands as they listened" (363).

The result of the performance by blackness for whiteness is that Stephen finds a vehicle in which to manifest his own gender discomfitures by identifying with those suffering from race and economic injustices. All the subjects in attendance are lifted, as it were, to a kind of spiritual plane that supposedly transcends the limitations of that suffering body. The performance of suffering allows – indeed, necessitates – that race (as racism, injustice, suffering) stand in not only for sex and gender variance (homophobia, gender variant discrimination, punishment) but also for those injustices caused by class and wealth. But the former (sex) is never trumped by the latter (race) and always already stands in as a particular, the specificities of which disappear against the injuries of the universal, which, by the end of the novel, Stephen represents. As a figure that emerges from a specific positionality (aristocratic, white, almost male), Stephen, like Christ, suffers the afflictions of all who endure injustice even though, paradoxically, Stephen's sufferings are most representable as the suffering of those less privileged than he. The universal is represented as all particulars; and the particulars disappear, indeed, are colonized by the universal. Invisible and universal whiteness, as Dyer (1988, 46) notes, colonizes the categorical substances of other norms (in this case, racial specificity) until its own particularity disappears. Because Stephen is disarticulated from, and disentitled to, all that other men of his class are entitled to, he functions metonymically for all injustice, this being evident in the repetitions of the last sentence in the passage quoted above. The Jones brothers sing with "bent heads and clasped hands," which becomes all the white listeners sitting with bent heads and clasped hands. In the suffering of the particular, Stephen finds his own suffering and the promise of his own redemption: "And now there rang out a kind of challenge; imperious, loud, almost terrifying. They sang it together, those two black brethren, and their voices suggested a multitude shouting ... shouting a challenge to the world on behalf of themselves and of all the afflicted" (Hall 1928, 363). By the end of the novel that multitude has changed from the particular "black brethren" to the universal and transcendent "marred and reproachful faces with the haunted, melancholy eyes of the invert[s]," subjects no longer marked by race (436).

Stephen's transcendent whiteness either remains unmarked or has no substance qua whiteness other than as the particulars of Henry and Lincoln's suffering. In addition, his suffering as a man who has lost the privileges of masculinity is representable as the suffering of racial and class oppressions. In other words, what Stephen laments, grieves, and mourns is the loss of what a white classed male body can do: he loses his right to protect England during the First World War; he loses Morton and the comforts of the traditions that come with it; he, in fact, loses access to embodiment; and, finally, he loses other women, including his mother (there was that "indefinable quality in Stephen that made her look wrong in the clothes she was wearing, as though she and they had no right to each other, but above all no right to Anna" [27]). To be precise, he's denied masculine currency, especially when compared to biological men like Roger Antrim. The price of his ticket into whiteness is far more than Roger's – hence the nostalgic, melancholic, and mournful tone of the entire novel. He loses community, history, place – things to which he is entitled by virtue of his class, gender, and race. That loss is reinforced in readings of the novel that allow it and Stephen's white body to stand unnoticed. Butler (1991, 10) is helpful when she argues that matter, including bodies, should be read not as fixed sites or surfaces but, rather, as processes that stabilize over time to produce the effect of a boundary, fixity, and surface. My next chapter interrogates how that "monstrously" articulated and disarticulated white body in Stephen's mirror has "materialized" in two contemporary narratives both to contest and to consolidate, to de(re)-construct, the articular conditions of its own emergence.

3
Impressions of the Man: Sacred Countries and the Stone Butch Blues

> We have a story that by definition cannot be self-present to us, a story that, in other words, is not a story, but *must become* a story. And it cannot *become* a story except through the *bond of reading*.
>
> – Shoshana Felman, *What Does a Woman Want?*

> Thank-you for reading this journal entry in class – it puts you into a complex history of reading and re-reading this text and suggests what is at stake for you in elaborating your history of reading it ... can you be more discursive ... Be prolix? Verbose?
>
> – Kathleen Martindale, notes on a journal entry

This chapter tells stories about reading. The first occurs in the mid-1970s, in an otherwise unremarkable high school in southern Ontario where I read my first queer book, Del Martin and Phyllis Lyon's (1972) *Lesbian/Woman*.[1] I had searched the school library for books that might help me come to terms with, or find a name for, that elusive difference that seemed so obvious to me but that defied "languaging."

I do not remember how I found the book, but I am quite certain I did not find it in my high school library. Published in 1972, two years after the first appearance of the Radicalesbians' (1972) manifesto "The Woman-Identified Woman," and ten years *before* Adrienne Rich's (1983) "Compulsory Heterosexuality and Lesbian Existence," *Lesbian/Woman* was marketed as "the most complete and revealing book ever written about women who love other women" (front cover). Part conduct manual, part autobiography, part apologia, and certainly an exciting read at the time, *Lesbian/Woman* articulated not only the term "lesbian" but also a Foucauldian game of truth, an ensemble of rules and procedures with which I came to recognize myself as subject of a certain kind of sexual practice (Foucault 1985, 26).

What I thought *Lesbian/Woman* and other texts, including *Sappho Was a Right-On Woman* (Abbott and Love 1972), gave me *then* was an identity and the language to name what seemed to be the core truth of who "I" was.[2] These texts could be read as lesbian autobiography, collocating an identity dispersed throughout psychoanalytic, medical, heterosexual feminist, and gay liberatory discourses, reversing that dispersion so that any lesbian could speak using that "I" as it was represented. The "I's" of these numerous discourses were now one entity and spoke as that, empowered by a form of nationalism that, so the story goes, came to be known as the "lesbian nation." "Lesbians really did exist," the text told me, "and this book, written by Lesbians, proves it." In case there were any lingering doubts, the back cover assured me of its "truth":

> The authors of this book are lesbians. They have been "married" for over 20 years. They will tell *you* what it's like to grow up gay, to "come out," to share a life with another woman, and to be a lesbian mother. They will tell *you* how they – *and thousands of women like them* – live, love and survive in a male-dominated society. Intimate, candid, filled with fascinating personal and social history, packed with true stories, here is the most complete and revealing book ever written about women who love other women. (back cover, emphasis added)

Interpellated by the "you," I began to "language" myself differently. Even though, as Jess Goldberg in *Stone Butch Blues* corroborates, these books were the product of a political movement that disparaged female masculinity as a capitulation to conservative patriarchal culture, they remained entirely productive of new subjectivities.

I tell this story of reading, and include the lengthy publisher's blurb from *Lesbian/Woman,* for several reasons. First, since this chapter represents a series of questions about the relationship between reading, identity, and identification as well as a genealogy of reading practices vis-à-vis the portraits of female masculinity in *The Well* and selected contemporary texts (i.e., *Stone Butch Blues* by Leslie Feinberg [1993] and *Sacred Country* by Rose Tremain [1992]), it is necessary to locate those readings within one specific, although inevitably always already fictional, story about my own reading practices. Indeed, "people tell their stories (which they do not know or cannot speak) through others' stories"; thus, this chapter inevitably elaborates not only a particular story told through my own reading of Feinberg and Tremain but also the stories told by Feinberg and Tremain reading their predecessor, Radclyffe Hall, who, as we know, was herself rereading the sexologists (Felman 1993, 18). I suggest that the contemporary prose narratives rearticulate the story of a sexual subject quite different from that produced by the games of truth in *Lesbian/Woman*. My current texts reread and renarrate, or animate, one story of female masculinity as it was told in sexology and was then rewritten by Hall in *The Well of Loneliness*. In doing so they cumulatively foreground and problematize the representational history of female masculinity, "rummaging through the image reserves of the past in such a way as to show the history of representation"

(Hutcheon 1988, 93). Stephen Gordon lurks around the edges of the portraits of female masculinity in these two novels, portraits bound by but simultaneously rearticulating the limitations of the "invert" produced by sexology at the end of the nineteenth century.

I argue that *Stone Butch Blues* (hereafter *SBB*) and *Sacred Country* (hereafter *SC*) are most productively read as a rearticulation of the discourses producing female masculinity in *The Well* in order to foreground a particular problem in a genealogy of reading practices and to undo, or reread, my own story as I have told it here. In previous chapters I argue that the discursive technologies producing the "invert" as "species" (i.e., as both the lesbian of Martin and Lyon's text and the trans-sexual subject of Tremain's and Feinberg's) coalesce around the publication and subsequent banning of Hall's *The Well*. Hall's novel fictionalizes the late nineteenth- and early twentieth-century notions of female "inversion" as theorized in the writings of sexologists. The obscenity trials in Britain stabilize the medical and legal discursive practices of a power/knowledge regime, in effect producing that which it attempted to "know" and regulate. The effect of this particular episteme was, and remains, the subject positions opened in and across the texts under discussion here.[3]

The story of identity formation that I am interested in telling concerns subjects as much written by the reading of these texts as those that are rewriting and rearticulating their own sense of self. In other words, in languaging themselves differently and, thereby, activating new social relations, these subjects are also performing an inevitable epistemological problematic that structures this and, perhaps, any theoretical exercise. Racevskis (1991, 22) names that problematic: "thought contains that which contains *it* as well; it is shaped by that to which it can only tentatively, gropingly attempt to give shape in turn. Thought and thought-of-self thus partake of the same paradox." José Esteban Muñoz (1999, 7) calls this problematic "disidentification" and defines it as a productive moment where "identities-in-difference emerge from a failed interpellation within the dominant sphere. Their emergence is predicated on their ability to disidentify with the mass public and instead, through this disidentification, contribute to the function of a counterpublic sphere." Muñoz theorizes the differential consciousness as it emerges in the "minoritarian subject," or queers of colour; I also reference a Bakhtinian set of operations when I discuss how female masculinity articulates and rearticulates itself through the same languages by which it was produced, permanently transforming both (7). The two prose narratives under discussion here, as well as my own desire to read and reread them, reproduce and work against the limitations of that epistemological problematic; that is, I believe my own reading practice is at stake in these texts as much as is each author's. I find myself in the unusual position of reading across both supposed geographical and temporal differences to once again "language" disparate parts of myself in each of these texts.

The commencement of my graduate student career overlapped with the death of two of the primary men in my family – men very different from each other but with whom I identified: my grandfather and my father. My parents divorced when I was around four years of age, and my relationship with my father continued in fits and starts. It ended completely several years after the divorce. As an adult I had little contact with my father, although my early years with him remained precious memories. At one point in my adult life I had the great pleasure of exchanging letters with him. In one set of letters we did an odd thing. We actually "came out" to each other. My working-class father, who had driven city buses for most of his adult life, disclosed to me that his marriage with my mother had failed because he "had always had sexual feelings about men." I told him that I had always had sexual feelings about women, along with a great deal of confusion about my own gender identity. This curious exchange was interrupted with the news that my maternal grandfather, who lived in the same city as my father, on the other side of the country from where I resided, died, and I returned for the funeral, not quite ready to visit my father. At my grandfather's funeral, I discovered details about his past.

My grandfather was, according to the family narrative, one of the "Little Immigrants." I soon discovered that this phrase referred to the white, working-class orphaned children shipped to Canada from the homes of Thomas John Barnardo, a philanthropist in nineteenth-century London, England. Thomas Barnardo, along with other humanitarians – Annie Macpherson, Ellen Billbrough, Dr. Guthier, and Mary Carpenter – were deeply moved and troubled by the numbers of poor children and "orphans" living on the streets of London (Bagnall 1980, 91). They established a series of reformatory and industrial schools known as "ragged schools" (because of the ragged clothing of the attendees) for homeless and abandoned children; in the nineteenth century, they struck a deal with the Canadian government whereby they would export large numbers of these children to Canada to work as "farm" help and "mother's helpers" in Canadian homes and farms. In 1833, between them the Children's Friend Society and the West Kirk Workhouse took over 200 children to Canada and placed them out as apprentices (Wagner 1979, 309).[4] The workhouses had been sending young men and women abroad for many years, and the prisons, reformatories, and even the ragged schools had been sending prisoners, released prisoners, and students to the colonies for some time. Thus it was that in 1869 Maria Susan Rye, who started her work by helping young women to emigrate, turned her attentions in a different direction and took her first group of children to Canada.

At its peak this emigration was responsible for shipping anywhere between

80,000 (Bagnall 1980, 9) and 100,000 (orphaned or abandoned) children to Canada. These children were a ready-made, exploitable "working" class. Most of them, now known as the Barnardo kids, would end up working as indentured domestic servants. My grandfather was one of those boys who came to Canada via Montreal in 1916 to work as farm help. My grandfather stayed on in this particular situation, living in the barn, ill fed, beaten, and overworked, until he was old enough to run away. He then set up a life for himself in Canada as a labourer, eventually marrying my grandmother in northern Ontario. One of the inhabitants of a ragged school, my grandfather was still unable to read and write when he died in 1992.

Six weeks after I returned home from my grandfather's funeral, on Thanksgiving, I received a phone call telling me that my father had died. I once again returned east for a funeral. I said goodbye to my father at the funeral and visited his home. In my father's home I discovered that, while it was unlikely that he ever acted on his feelings for men, he certainly did act on what I could only read as a cross-gender identification. My father's home read like the home of an old woman: thanksgiving pies remained freshly baked on the kitchen table; half-knit sweaters dangled on knitting needles beside his favourite chair; all tables were covered with lace doilies; and I found on the wall a very old photograph of him as a young boy wearing a dress standing beside his own mother, who treated him as the daughter she never had. After a vertiginous flight home, I dove back into my first year of a master's program and have been attempting to make sense of my relationships with these two men ever since.

About one thing I felt certain: these were the primary influences on my gender. My grandfather had an entirely ambivalent relationship with England: I suspect he had always felt abandoned and banished from it, although, as a young boy from a very poor family, he had already lived the life of an exile on the streets of London. He remained vehemently class-identified and anti-British for his entire life, continuously evoking cultural traces of England while, at the same time, constantly disparaging them. He worked as a labourer and was a rough, hard-drinking, and, at times, physically abusive man. He was also, however, a sweet, charming storyteller, and I spent much of my time as a child listening to his stories and longing to be just like him when I grew up.

My youngest years were similarly marked by an intense relationship with my father. He was also a working-class man, a hard-drinking labourer who taught me all the best parts of being a boy right up to the time of my parents' divorce: riding my bike, playing baseball, going skating, and playing street-hockey. There was always, though, that "something a wee bit different" about my father – a softness that I certainly could not name at the time but that seemed to make so much sense when he named it much later in a letter and when I saw it in the text that was his home. Strangely, I find traces of both of these men in the novels I read here and, in finding these traces, find traces of myself. The rough, smoking, hard-drinking yet somehow vulnerable masculinity of the butches and FTMs in *SBB* brings my father back to me, while, in some kind of temporal and geographical displacement, I find traces of a repudiated white Britishness in *SC* and *The Well*. If the temporality of the (reading) subject is neither clock time nor the temporality of living beings but, rather, the temporality of the unconscious, then, time and time again, I find myself in the "I don't know yet" and the "Oh yes, I already knew that" of masculinity as it is performed in these texts (Stoler 1995, 64). In other words, my own performance of masculinity is shaped by these temporal and epistemological distortions and, ultimately, losses (retroaction: "I already knew I identified with them"). Each time I read one of these texts, I come closer to memories that are entirely allusive, ineffable, and, despite my own hopes, nonrepresentable (anticipation: "I can't and never will know either of them and so can't know I've lost them"). Perhaps both retroaction and anticipation are the very reasons why my own narrative is "after"[5] rearticulation in/as Hall's, Tremain's, and Feinberg's?

Distanced Cousins

> She held up an object. I understood I was supposed to accept the realness of this object ... She pointed to the circle the ring cast on the ground. I nodded, acknowledging that the shadow was as real as the ring. She smiled and waved her hand in the space between the ring and its shadow. Isn't this distance also real?
>
> – Leslie Feinberg, *Stone Butch Blues: A Novel*

> Between the idea
> And the reality
> Between the motion
> And the act
> Falls the Shadow.
>
> – T.S. Eliot, "The Hollow Men," epigraph to
> Rose Tremain, *Sacred Country*

The texts that I consider here are all written in a tradition of realism, with little of the parodic or self-reflexive language play or experimentation often characteristic of contemporary texts. Indeed, the "worlds" of the texts are represented, or rendered, in such a way as to give the reader the illusion of "actual," or "ordinary," experience. While there is little or no direct poaching of actual citations between texts such as "Sexual Inversion in Women" and *The Well* – and none between *The Well* and the contemporary texts – there is, nonetheless, productive discursive conversations between texts as well as a shared structure of signs, features, and a common stock of literary procedures and conventions.

Taken individually, *The Well* and *SBB* seem as though they are worlds apart. However, when read side by side they seem like the inverted mirror image of each other, sharing stock features, metaphors and tropes, characters and conventions, yet separated by history, geography, and class. *The Well* opens with a "Commentary" by its own discursive "mentor," Havelock Ellis, while *SBB* opens with an acknowledgment of the Stonewall "butches, passing women, drag kings and drag queens, FTM brothers and MTF sisters – transsexual and transvestite –" a taxonomy similar to those categories found in sexology only now authorized by the signature "Stonewall" (Feinberg 1993, 5). *The Well* also opens with a genealogy of Stephen's family name and place; *SBB* opens with an account of two working-class and "already bitterly disappointed people," Jess's parents (13).[6] In *The Well*, Stephen roams the pastoral family estate at Malvern Hills; Jess roams the unpaved streets of the "projects," Buffalo, New York. Stephen identifies with the portrait of "young Nelson" as well as "the funny old portraits of the Gordons," while Jess queers narratives of masculinity such as "Captain Midnight," "The Fugitive," striking union men, and the leading men of adult movies during the Saturday matinees at the local theatre. In their home, Mary attends to the intimate details of Stephen's wardrobe. Likewise, in *SBB*, a heterogendered eroticism is signified not only by the performative details of Jess's wardrobe but also by the femmes' recognition of those details: "Jackie smoothed my lapels and nodded in approval"; "Peaches fussed with my lapels"; "Edna held my eyes as she walked over to me and smoothed my lapels"; "The femmes just kind of smoothed the lapels of my suit coat and held me in their gaze" (30, 58, 103, 108). Stephen's body does not fit his gender identification and he is taunted with the question "What is it?" Jess's does not fit, and s/he is similarly taunted with the same refrain, "How the hell should I know what it is?" Stephen characterizes himself as "never ... worshipped in return by the creature of [his] adoration," while Jess, too, is a "stone" butch. Stephen's world revolves around the strength of masculine figures – Stephen himself, Philip, even Stephen's rival for Mary, Martin Hallam – while Jess's world evolves around Theresa, Jacqueline, Angie, Edna, and Ruth, figures of femininity to whom Jess returns, and by whom s/he is tended, after every beating.

Even though sixty years separate *The Well* and *SBB*, both received popular but not critical acclaim upon publication. It is precisely this popular context that interests me, along with the ways in which the reading of these narratives within that context stages an ironic reassertion of subjectivity at the moment of its derision – a devaluing that, as I argue in Chapter 1, began with late nineteenth-century sexology. Where *The Well* incited legal action and obscenity trials everywhere it surfaced, *SBB* both incited and ignited "discourse." Published originally in March 1993, its first two press runs were doubled. By the end of 1994 it was in its third printing and has not slowed since. Feinberg he/rself punctuates its success: "I've gotten hundreds of letters, not only from all over this country [United States] but from England, India, Australia, Sweden, Canada, all kinds of places ... and I don't think it's done yet" (author interview). In 1994 *SBB* won both the prestigious American Library Association Gay and Lesbian Literature Award (Fiction) and the Lambda Literary Award (Small Press Book). To date, *SBB* has been translated into German and Dutch, with book tours following fast on the heels of both translations. There are at least two Internet listservs solely devoted to discussing *SBB*; there has been at least one documentary[7] about Feinberg and, in a recent interview, s/he confesses that s/he still receives letters addressed to Jess Goldberg, the "fictional protagonist of her novel" (Lee 1998, 31). One reader review at the huge on-line book retailer, Amazon.com (an indicator of popular acclaim if ever there was one), named what many of the writers of hundreds of Web sites argue about Feinberg and he/r novel, making a claim that anyone who reads lesbian or trans-sexual fiction will recognize: "This powerful [and] deftly-told story is a 'fiction so that it could tell the truth' [and has] captured the imaginations of a generation of young gender-transgressive or questioning women. It coaxed out of the closet a community of FTM (female-to-male) persons, and popularized Leslie Feinberg as a leading gender warrior" ("NYC").

In early 1994 I co-wrote an article about Feinberg and had occasion to interview he/r about the success of he/r novel (Noble and Taylor 1994). One of the first questions I asked h/er concerned the status of *SBB* as autobiography. "Is it true?" I asked h/er over the phone. "Did it really happen the way you wrote it?" I was to discover then, and in every subsequent article about Feinberg or the novel, that he/r answer to this most frequently asked question is always the same: "I always answer that question with another question: 'What's at stake for you in that question?'" Like Radclyffe Hall, Leslie Feinberg, the author, is constantly confused with Jess Goldberg, the character – so much so that *SBB* continues to appear on reading lists of English department courses on life-writing and autobiography. In part, the novel's form and narrative voice encourages such misrecognitions. Written in the first person, *SBB* is characterized by a narrative style that is as gritty, abrupt, and blunt as are many of its working-class butches. As Kate Bornstein (1993, 28) quipped in a review: "*Stone*

Butch Blues is not an easy read. Then again, anyone who's ever known a butch knows they're never easy to read."

But it is the subject matter of *SBB* that continues to contribute to the collapse of the distinction between the author and main character. Echoing previous *Bildungsroman* like *The Well, SBB* passes as a fairly conventional coming-out novel.[8] Published by a small alternative press, its author photograph occupies over 25 percent of the cover space (and, like *The Well, SBB* is rarely mentioned in reviews without a photograph of the author), while the author biography gives permission and credence to those misreadings: "Leslie Feinberg came of age as a young butch in Buffalo, New York, before the Stonewall Rebellion. She is a journalist and typesetter by trade" (back cover). The cover design itself seems to welcome the confusion between author and subject. The back cover is split with a diagonal line running from the top left corner down through the bottom right corner. One side (the right side) is black and shows a photograph of Feinberg, flat-chested and dressed in a man's suit and tie, standing at a podium, with the author biographical information under the image. The other side is a pale blue and implicitly asks (and answers) the question evoked by the author photograph: "Woman or Man?" It continues: "That's the question that rages like a storm around Jess Goldberg, clouding her life and identity. Growing up differently gendered in a blue-collar town in the 1950s. Coming out as a butch in the bars and factories of the prefeminist '60s. Deciding to pass as a man in order to survive when she is left without work or a community in the early '70s" (back cover). The publishing machinery itself draws specific parallels between author and character: both are marked by unreadable genders; both grew up working class; and both "came of age" in a blue-collar town "before Stonewall."

The stakes of my question to Feinberg in 1994 are much clearer to me now than they were when I first asked it. At stake in both Feinberg's and Hall's text were questions produced by their form – the relation between reality, realism, and readers – questions that remained *articulate* as the direct result of Judge Biron's banning Hall's text in 1928 as obscene moral poison. E.J. Graff (1993, 25), in a review of *Stone Butch Blues* for *The Women's Review of Books*, describes the physicality of the relationship between the reader, the novel, and the realism of these texts – a triangulated relation that provokes disbelief and denial as much as identification and catharsis.

> *Stone Butch Blues* shows us a world that was lived. Even when the writing was simple, the insights and details are authentic and powerful. For instance, there's the never-ending anxiety about bathrooms: will Jess and the other butch women be harassed if they go into the women's room – or the men's? There's the shit floating in the jail toilet in a scene that will turn your hair white. There's Jess's jaw clicking when she tries to talk,

> after cutting the wires that held it in place for weeks after a beating. *You believe: this happened. So how do you keep reading? At times I had to stop and look at the picture on the back of the book to remind myself: This woman is still alive. She wrote a book. It's okay.* (emphasis added)

Where Biron disagrees and eventually disavows the "It's okay" imperative of Graff's reading strategy, readers of *SBB* require it in order to keep reading. Graff's need to physically handle the book is one familiar to many readers of Feinberg's first-person narrative. It functions to distance oneself from a painful narrative that is both unbearable and compelling, and whose very materiality deflects repression, grounds incredulity, and allows the reader to sift through the denial that acts as a mechanism against pain. Hence, the logic of Graff's trauma (and, indeed, of Biron's fear) in response to painful realism: "You believe: this happened. So how do you keep reading? At times, I had to stop and look at the picture" and so on. The materiality of the *book* allows the reader to work through the trauma of reading such a painfully realistic *text* ("You believe: this happened ... I had to stop and look at the picture on the back of the book"). As we saw in Chapter 2, it was the success of the verisimilitude of Hall's text that compelled Judge Biron to remove it from circulation for almost forty years.

The fact of *SBB*'s translation into German and Dutch is fascinating given the distinctly American flavour of the text. In opposition to *The Well*, whose context and content are far more European, *SBB* is set in American cities (Buffalo and New York). Both its historical frame of reference and its internal time-frame are littered with the events of American history – events that have a direct impact on the characters and the emergence of the novel's axiomatic commitment to social justice: an injury to one is an injury to all. The constructions of these events, in conjunction with the slippage between reality and fiction (which I discuss below) foreground *SBB* as, above all, a history of the present (Foucault 1977b, 31). Many of these events – the shooting of President Kennedy and Martin Luther King Jr.; the emergence but also the decline of American factories and unions; the communist panic of the late 1950s; the Stonewall Rebellion of 1968; the student uprisings in universities; the aftermath of slavery and increase of racial tension; the rise of lesbian-feminism; and the emergence, at the end of the novel, of contemporary gay, lesbian, bisexual, and trans-gender liberation movements – function as metatextual plot lines compelling the call for justice that underwrites this text.

Structured by three stages, or movements – Jess's coming out in the bars of Buffalo; he/r passing as a man in New York City; and he/r eventual and paradoxical return to queer communities that stand in for he/r former butch-femme community – Jess Goldberg's is a homecoming quest narrative that succeeds where it fails. In other words, Jess does not return to the communities from which s/he had been exiled, but s/he does become part of a metatextual rearticulation of a new community that, ironically and extratextually, receives both he/r and he/r narrative. The context of reception for *SBB* is precisely the same "trans-gendered or questioning community of ftm (female-to-male) subjects" coaxed out of the closet by Feinberg and he/r text ("NYC," Amazon.com). It is this very community *in* the novel that receives Jess Goldberg as s/he exits from the subway into the middle of a gay and lesbian protest where s/he is coaxed onto the stage to speak. At this closing moment of Feinberg's text, the distinction between the external production and reception contexts of the novel and its internal time-frame and world entirely collapses ("You believe: this happened"). Both Jess Goldberg and Leslie Feinberg function as metonymic signifiers and "gender warriors leading the community of the transgendered" ("NYC," Amazon.com).

Sacred Country was published in the same year as was *SBB,* and yet its author has not emerged as a gender warrior. While its subjects are rural, poor, and British, as opposed to the American urban labouring class represented by the subjects of *SBB,* they have a great deal in common with those in Feinberg's novel; indeed, read together, in many important ways the books function as disparate echoes of *The Well.* Where Stephen Gordon mourns the inability to serve and protect his country as one of its sons, Jess Goldberg (*SBB*) and Mary Martin[9] Ward (*SC*) articulate their positions between homes, between metaphorical countries, and between "real" (qua thinkable) genders in No Man's Land. Even though both Mary Martin and Jess seek out medical interventions in order to alter their bodies (especially through chest reconstruction surgeries), they both retreat from that process and choose to reside permanently in No Man's Land, neither one gender nor the other but *both.* In addition, each text, like *The Well,* narrativizes temporality and spatiality in order to demonstrate the assertion I made earlier: the subject's time is not linear but, rather, is articulated through tropes of retroaction ("I always already knew I was a boy") and anticipation ("I can't wait until I am a boy"). In *SC* tropes of "country" and "nation" further complicate those of time, where the knowable past – Swaithey, England – is home to "Mary," and, until at least the penultimate moment of the novel, "Martin" is the future, located differentially in another place: not-Swaithey.

Published in Great Britain in 1992, and in North America during 1993, *SC* has been utterly eclipsed by the popularity of *SBB* and has received less popular, but slightly more critical, attention. *SC* is the sixth novel by the British novelist Rose Tremain, who is married and lives in England, and who received widespread kudos for her earlier novel *Restoration.* Although mostly written from an omniscient point of view, *SC* has many first-person sections in which its many characters tell those same events from their own points of view. Seemingly less interested in wide narrative brush strokes, Tremain's novel does tell stories of subjects who exist across three generations, many of whom remember England during the wars, and many more who, like those who pause to remember the dead King George the Sixth, mourn the passing of time and the inevitability of change that brings about the end of "glorious" England.

This novel, which is full of people sorting out their identities, moves through thirty years of Mary's life after that painful two minutes of silence as she tries to transform both herself and the image others have of her. Elegiac and melancholic in tone, *SC*, a novel obsessed with transformations, is still unable to, as a whole, adapt or fully mourn the effects of changes. Walter Loomis, an heir to the Loomis & Son Family Butchers, wants desperately to transform himself from a butcher's son into a country-and-western singer and eventually does by moving to his sacred country: Nashville, Tennessee. He fails to become the singer of whom he had always dreamt. Edward Harker, surrogate father to Mary and famous for his cricket bats, marries his housekeeper, Irène, and waits for the day when his soul will transcend his current body and transmigrate into another time and place. England itself, as an imaginary landscape that this novel shares with Hall's, continues on a trajectory mapped earlier by Hall, only now it turns its back on all its inhabitants (Tremain 1992, 286). Mary's mother, Estelle Ward, whose own mother died in a glider crash, keeps checking herself into Mountview Rest Home, where her best friend is Alice the Chicken Woman, a person who feels herself happier as a hen than as a human.

Referring to rooms or divisions in a prison or hospital (as in "psychiatric ward") and the act of guarding or defending a place (to avert something) but also suggesting confinement, custody, and a guardian's control (a ward of the state or court), the "Ward" family name overdetermines the potentialities of its charges. Mary's brother, Timmy Ward, sees himself at the intersection of a ninety-degree angle that cuts across the family: the horizontal line of his swimming career and the vertical line of his calling into God's service as a minister. His desire is to see both lines stretch across space into infinity. Patriarch Sonny Ward remains bound by physical and psychological injuries from his service in the Second World War and chooses to kill himself rather than see his farm taken over by the large industrial farming practices sweeping across England. "All I wish," he tells his son when Timmy refuses to husband the land Sonny fought to protect, "is that the fucking Germans had shot away my heart" (256). Estelle Ward, too, seems bound by that war. She often lies beside her husband hoping to kill herself in his wake: "I put my face close to his mouth, and breathed his breath, like *mustard gas*. For I had often thought, the breath of a person you no longer love or respect could be a poison to kill you" (42, emphasis added). As Mary herself tells us, she is not only trapped in the No Man's Land between genders but also in the No Man's Land between her warring parents, neither of whom, by the end, is able to fully transform enough to parent their children. While *SC* does end with Estelle's overture to Martin, the novel as a whole, with its individualist explanation of Mary Martin's distress and without a larger cultural interrogation of the sex/gender system that necessitates the existence of No Man's Land, is unable to move beyond the limits of its self-imposed wards and confinements.

Despite the depth of its narrative, the richly woven texture of its language, and the breathtaking crispness of its voice, *SC* has failed to draw the popular success that follows *SBB*. Tremain's novel was reviewed in a number of venues: *The New York Times Book Review; The Women's Review of Books; New Statesman and Society;* and *The Antioch Review.* While almost all of the critics highly praised its narrative style and voice, not one hailed it as an overall success. Graff reviewed it for *The Women's Review of Books* alongside *SBB,* and while she praised its content and form, she criticized it on a number of counts. The most curious criticism Graff levels against *SC* is the exact opposite of the praise that she heaps on *SBB*; that is, the latter is a success because it references a reality outside of itself – butch-femme histories actually lived by its author. *SC*, on the other hand, fails for precisely the same reason. Tremain is a "married writer," Graff tells us, who researched (read: "did not live") the lives of trans-sexuals in order to write this book. Hence, its "outside-in method shows in the novel's missing heart" (Graff 1993, 26). In other words, some sixty years after Radclyffe Hall's novel was published and banned, critics continue to measure the verity of a novel against the supposedly self-evident truth of the author's sexual essence. Graff argues that the result of the outside-in method is that Mary's trans-sexual surgery feels like a maiming, a terribly sad mistake, even though, as I argue later in this chapter, the success of both Mary Martin's and Jess Goldberg's characters is that both follow the exact same path and end their transitions before they have completed them. In other words, both acquire power in what I identified earlier as a mamillian economy by removing the signifiers of objectification within a phallic economy – breasts – without adding the requisite penis. Both acquire a particular kind of currency by completing the narrative articulated by Stephen at his mirror. In *The Well* Stephen attempts but is unable to articulate himself and his body into being; his is a productive failure. Martin and Jess begin where Stephen failed: they articulate themselves and their bodies into being through what I have been calling "onto-performative" speech acts.

The socio-cultural impact of this articulation process is, as the "NYC" reader on Amazon.com alluded, the rearticulation of larger communities that remained bound by the same constraints that bound Stephen Gordon, albeit in different locations and in different moments in history. Both of these texts, as distant cousins of Hall's *The Well,* show the characters ambivalently subjected to and by the discourses of the sex/gender system but especially by legal, medical, and psychiatric discourses. Stephen knows that sympathetic doctors can be important allies but that, ultimately, one of the inverts themselves must write the novel that Stephen produces as a writer. Jess Goldberg is continuously mistreated and misdiagnosed by doctors; s/he, however, remains misread until s/he is able to pay one enough money to physically aid he/r transition using male hormones and surgery. Similarly, Mary is both helped and hindered by psychiatrists and surgeons but continues to feel "like a horse, trying to pull along the idea that a surgeon could transform me" into Martin (Tremain 1992, 204). By necessity, all of these narratives, including my own, articulate subjectivity through the discourses and diagnoses made available by medicine and as the benefactor of sexology and clinical psychiatry; however, all three also rearticulate resistance to those discourses, evidenced by, among other things, Martin's resounding "No" (295).

As I argue in more detail below, that "No" is also a repudiation of very particular losses and constraints in these texts. If, as I suggested earlier in my own narrative, these identifications are also disidentifications, then these four narratives together elaborate not only a genealogy of present onto-performative identifications and disidentifications with masculinity but also with masculinity in the (F)/fathers. At the same time that Martin's "No" produces disidentifications with the Father, it also facilitates the onto-performative rearticulation of masculinity and inverts/perverts the temporal and linear logic of that phallic economy from No Man's Land in order to render it dysfunctional. In other words, such men do not find a secure place in the patriarchal order; rather, they reconfigure it from No Man's Land. In one particularly pregnant scene, we see Martin, as a speech act, languaged into action after Mary is attacked by Sonny who, in a fit of rage, violently cuts off the bandages that have been binding her breasts. "'You're an abomination,' [Sonny] said ... He held her breasts in his hands. He pushed them up, showing them to her. He said: 'Look at them. Go on. You look at them!'" (117). Martin refuses that interpellating gaze, and his reply could be Stephen's at the mirror, or it could be Jess's in front of many mirrors, or it could even be my own act/ion as a language effect, the onto-performative rearticulation of the differently gendered and counter-discursive speaking body: "Now it's over. Except that it isn't. It's now that it all begins" (118).

Scenes of (In)utterability

> This is probably best. This is the future, but it's a future without words. Things will be done and never spoken about.
>
> – Rose Tremain, *Sacred Country*

SC begins with the performance of both terms of its title: Mary Ward, *daughter* of Sonny and Estelle, enters into two minutes of silence on 15 February 1952 somewhere around two o'clock in the afternoon to mourn the dead King George, and she emerges from it with the realization that she is, in fact, a boy.[10] As we will see, that gendered space that will become Martin will also become Mary's sacred place. Because the second hand had fallen off Sonny's cheap watch, the impoverished Ward family knows neither when to begin nor when to end the vigil and are dramatically out of synchronicity with the two minutes of silence that they imagine the rest of England is observing. What begins as an unsynchronized two minutes evolves into thirty minutes and, for Mary, into a lifetime. While many people across England wept during the "silence that was heavy with eternity," weeping "not merely for the King ... but for the long, ghastly passing of time," the Ward family gathers in their potato field looking "pathetic and poor," out of time with "that of the nation as a whole" (Tremain 1992, 3-4).

What is supposed to be a shared ritual of grief becomes a moment of punitive tyranny as Sonny insists on absolute silence. Ironically, Timmy (Mary's brother), Estelle, and Mary herself live out noisy and dialogic dramas as those thirty minutes pass. Estelle begins speaking her thoughts aloud while Mary chides Timmy for pulling his boots off. Sonny insists on starting the "two minutes" over, and it is during this second repetition that Mary feels history changing the way time was changing: "And then the idea of them waiting there in the field, the snow little by little settling on them and whitening them over, gave Mary a strange feeling of exaltation, as if something were about to happen to her that had never happened to anybody in the history of Suffolk or the world" (5). That repetition is as much about being subjected to and by both the national and temporal periodizations signified by British "Royalty" as it is about subjection to Sonny's violent, paternal masculinity. It is also a repetition that productively fails to condition and enable national and gender identifications; instead, these identities are disrupted and reconfigured in the same moment that they are constituted (Butler 1991, 29). Mary silently utters that newness, and Martin is born in the space of that metaspeech act. Martin functions as a new kind of space born out of a silent temporality and grief, a silence (national) within a silence (a quiet farmer's field) that was already there: "[Mary] stared at her family, took them in, one, two, three, quiet at last but not as still as they were meant to be, not still like the plumed men guarding the King's coffin" (Tremain 1992, 6). Nobody but Mary knew that the memory of that silence would last a lifetime: "I have a secret to tell you," Mary utters to herself during these silence(s), "and this is it: I am not Mary. That is a mistake. I am not a girl. I'm a boy" (6).

Silence functions as the primary trope through which crises are revealed and "countries," other than the supposed real ones, are produced in this novel.[11] Repeatedly, silence and its communicative functions fill in spaces where language fails. All of the moments of silence in *SC* function to mark the limits of language; instead, bodies communicate things that are unintelligible and repeatedly circumscribed in language. When Mary asks Miss McRae, her teacher, to let her move in, silence is the vehicle through which the details of Mary's life are acknowledged: "She continued to look out Miss McRae's front garden. Silence came again" (121). Later, after Sonny assaults Miss McRae: "I sat in silence by Miss McRae's fire ... She said, 'Time changes everything.'" (150). Eventually, Mary confides her secret to Edward, who becomes her surrogate father: "Neither of us spoke for quite a while and the silence marked the passing of something" (154). Gilbert, the town dentist who seduces one of his patients, Walter, can live with his mother only by "allowing himself to imagine the silence that would arrive when he finally left the house" (193). During their affair, Gilbert tells Walter: "Things will be done and never spoken about" (162). Later, when Gilbert leaves Walter and moves to London, Walter's pain is ineffable: "Gilbert was far beyond the reach of his words" (194). Finally, when Mary contacts Dr. Beales, the psychiatrist in London who will authorize her sex reassignment interventions, she communicates the truth of her life in silences between the fabrications: "they sit in silence" (231).

Butler (1997b, 1) makes a strong case for ascribing an agency to language, recognizing in it "a power to injure" or wound. Part of the reason why, or so she argues, language can injure is because, "in some sense, we are linguistic beings, beings who require language in order to be" (1-2). My project, like Butler's, argues that names are powerful imperatives that have the ability to injure because they have the potential to authorize being. "The name holds out another possibility as well," Butler argues: "by being called a name, one is also, paradoxically, given a certain possibility for social existence, initiated into a temporal life of language that exceeds the prior purposes that animate that call" (2). Louis Althusser (1971) theorized one relation between speech and social being by elaborating the interpellative function of speech. According to him, the speech act brings the subject into linguistic existence by hailing the passerby with "hey, you there." The one who recognizes himself and turns around to answer the call is a subject (of the call) animated into existence. Thus, the act of recognition in language becomes an act of constitution.

The hailing of Mary Martin, however, occurs in a national moment of silence, not language. While in this moment national identification, or hailing, achieves successful recognition (the working-class Ward family observes the two minutes of silence, albeit painfully out of synchronicity with the public rituals of what is represented as the rest of England and, hence, outside a shared and naturalized fiction: time), it also remains unsuccessful in that Mary fails to fully recognize herself and her body as something that is like that of the rest of the nation. Even though Sonny's fully authorized performative, "Shut you up, girl," accomplishes the linguistic silence, it fails to silence, or still, or gender that body (Tremain 1992, 5). The grammar of Mary's observation of their silence bears this out: "[Mary] stared at her family, took them in, one, two, three of them, quiet at last but *not as still* as they were meant to be, *not still like* the plumed men guarding the King's coffin, *not still like* the bulrushes in a lake" (6, emphasis added).

The "like" of these similes foregrounds the ways that "England," and indeed any national identity, signifies in representations (the plumed guards) but also in pictorial images of its boundaried geographical matter (lakes, marsh land, and moors) not "as" but always already "like" something quite different from itself. A simile is, after all, a self-conscious comparison between two unlike things, a fiction and, in the case of national identity, a hegemonic and discursive one. If, as Benedict Anderson (1983) suggests, nationness is an imagined fraternity that is produced in moments like the death of a king, then in this instance, for the Ward family, that imaginary relation fails. Not only is masculinity depicted as dissembling but Britishness continues the trajectory of ruin mapped by Hall's novel. Tremain's novel is set on the same soil. Performing as a "good citizen of England" means participating in public rituals, protecting the vulnerable, husbanding the land, and imagining oneself as part of what Anderson describes as a "deep, horizontal comradeship" that constitutes a national psyche (15). Like Hall, Tremain shows that fraternity very much in crisis. By definition, England is outdated, dissembled, imploding, and no longer viable. Both Martin and Walter find their *sacred* in Nashville, Tennessee, but that discovery necessitates the fall of England: "'England!' he said through the smile. 'You mean to tell me England's still there?'" (Tremain 1992, 304).

If Mary fails to recognize herself properly – that is, if she succeeds in misrecognizing herself as quite unlike the thing she is supposed to be, a silent British girl subject of England and subject to gender – then we must concur that something of the body is evident both inside and outside of the speech act. In *Excitable Speech*, Butler cites Shoshana Felman's work on the literary speech act to make two useful points: first, that, while there are often distinctions made between the domain of the "mental" and the domain of the "physical," the acts of languaging are themselves physical acts, that is, "speaking itself is a bodily act" (Butler 1997b, 10-11). Second, the fact that speaking is itself a physical act does not imply a simple unity of these terms. It does suggest, though, that the speaking body signifies in ways that are not reducible to what such a body "says." In other words, to quote Felman, "the body becomes a sign of unknowingness precisely because its actions are never fully consciously directed or volitional" (10). That unknowing body marks the limit of intentionality in the speech act, where the speech act says more, or says differently, than it means to say (Felman 1987, 84-5). In speaking, the act that the body performs is never fully understood, thus Felman and Butler can argue that "the body is the blindspot of speech, that which acts in excess of what is said, but which also acts in and through what is said" (Butler 1997b, 11). The body, then, is redoubled in the speech act: there is what is said, and there is a kind of saying that the bodily instrument of the utterance performs. For Mary Martin, silence is the body tripled: there is what is (un)said, then a kind of not saying of which the body is the instrument, then (re)saying when the body rearticulates itself differently. In other words, gender changes have their own agenda, and that agenda in *SC* is to articulate a corporeality (and its failures) not self-evident in language outside of performative tropes of silence (Cromwell 1999, 3). Martin's body speaks in the silence of that two minutes and, by doing so, performs a kind of reversal of effects, where naming enables the process that I have called an onto-performative articulation: disidentification, rearticulation, and materialization.

My argument collapses J.L. Austin's (1975) supposed clear-cut distinctions between different kinds of speech acts. According to those distinctions, locutionary speech acts are those that merely say something; "illocutionary" speech acts are those that, in saying, do what they say and do it in the moment of that saying (as opposed to performing an act of saying); finally, "perlocutionary" speech acts are those that produce certain effects as their consequence. As Austin himself realized, these are distinctions that cannot hold: "There can hardly be any longer a possibility of not seeing that stating is performing an act" (138).

Austin's work privileges moments of speech rather than performative acts of silence. Such speech acts require correspondences between language, such as "he" or "she," and their referents – a correspondence that the texts under discussion clearly trouble. Stephen begins the work of articulation but is unsuccessful. Jess and Martin begin where Stephen's work ends ("it's now that it all begins") and materialize themselves and their bodies as things that language says cannot exist by finding themselves in the auditory and linguistic space-offs of/in speech acts, or in the occlusional spaces where regimes of knowledge name that which supposedly cannot exist in order to disavow it. "I'm a boy," Mary utters in an onto-performative moment of silence, birthing Martin as a direct effect of the non-saying. The longer-term consequence of the non-speech act is the materialization of Martin's body, which, prior to the two minutes of silence, does not exist but which certainly will eventually exist in the future (following hormonal and surgical interventions). The morphology of Martin's body already exists and is every bit as "real" (i.e., it exists as an effect of discourse) as is Mary's. It seems not to exist because there is, as yet, no language with which it can be hailed as a body that matters.

In *SBB* Jess Goldberg articulates he/rself through the same trio of onto-performative acts. What is significant about the way that this onto-performative articular trio works – disidentification, rearticulation, and materialization – is that it, too, functions as a kind of auditory space-off where both Jess and Jesse find themselves. For Martin materialization is the product of silence; for Jess it is the product of labour. Jess does the "work" of "making" and "remaking" identity as a process that resists the price of whiteness; that is, as a commodity purchased in a (white supremacist) economy of singularity, where identity must be reduced to its lowest common singular denominator. Where silence is the productive trope of *SC* that allows Mary to disidentify with Sonny's "Shut you up, girl" and Martin to find himself in the auditory "elsewhere" of a degrading Englishness, labour is the trope of *SBB*. Jess *labours* to rearticulate identity at the meeting point of many different discourses – a point where the union[12] call of "an injury to one is an injury to all" challenges an economy whose power invests its subject as singular and essential (i.e., you are your gender or your race or your class, but you are certainly never all of them at the same moment). For Jess, the process of "unioning," however contingent, is precisely the moment where she arrives in representation, articulates, and re-cognizes he/rself into perception and, to return to Muñoz (1999, 6), is the same moment when "the social order receives a jolt that may reverberate loudly and widely, or in less dramatic, yet locally indispensable, ways."

Like *SC*, *SBB* dramatizes the failures of both interpellation and identification. Its opening pages articulate those linguistic and discursive failures and Jess, unlike Stephen, possesses self-knowledge differentially, that is, Jess knows what s/he is not: "No one ever offered a name for what was wrong with me. I only came to recognize its melody through this constant refrain: 'Is that a boy or a girl?'" (Feinberg 1993, 13). Throughout he/r life, Jess hears this refrain repeatedly and feels the physicality of its enforcement when s/he is constantly attacked and beaten. The scenes that follow that refrain and those beatings show Jess engaged in a drama of recognition ("re-cognition" and "re-cognate"), the mental work by which the mind attempts to look again at a thing and, when necessary, to make revisions and amendments until it thinks it is seeing the thing as it really is. In other words, Jess's life's "work" is to make revisions and amendments both *on* he/r body and/or *in* language in order to make one or the other fit. Indeed, part of the erotic intensity in Jess's affairs with femmes comes from the pleasures of recognition, where Jess's lovers *know he/r again as similar to them* and provide a mirror in which Jess sees that he/r labour has been successful (or not).

One of the strategies of survival that Jess chooses – a strategy that eventually works both with and against the conditions of (un)intelligibility mandated by the sex/gender system – is that of passing. Where Martin emerges to enable Mary's *becoming more himself*, especially once Mary leaves Swaithey for London, Jess's passing enables self-alienation and almost virtual erasure. Again, whereas there are no mirror scenes in *SC* (a point I return to later), *SBB* repeatedly rewrites Stephen's scene at the mirror in order to stage the failures of passing and the failure of interpellation. The first time Jess looks into a mirror, s/he has just entered into the forbidden zone of he/r parent's bedroom:

> I went directly to my father's closet door. His blue suit was there ... it took even more nerve to open my father's dresser drawer. His white shirts were folded and starched stiff as a board ... it was too late. Too late. I stripped down to my cotton panties and T-shirt and slid on his shirt. It was so starched my eleven-year-old fingers could hardly get the collar buttoned. I pulled down a tie from the rack. For years I had watched my father deftly twist and flop his ties in a complicated series of moves ... I tied it in a clumsy knot. I climbed upon a footstool to lift the suit from the hanger. Its weight surprised me. It fell in a heap. I put on the suit coat and looked in the mirror. A sound came from my throat, sort of a gasp. I liked the little girl looking back at me ... I stared in the big mirror over my mother's dresser, trying to see far in the future when the clothing would fit, to catch a glimpse of the woman I would become ... I wondered if I was brave enough to grow up and be her. (20-1)

More than any other scene in *SBB*, this one invites us to see Stephen lurking on the other side of that mirror. Like Stephen's, Jess's scene at the mirror initiates he/r into subjectivity. Unlike Stephen, however, s/he recognizes he/rself as conventionally female, although female with a twist; that is, s/he is part he/rself and part he/r father. S/he is neither one nor the other but both. If Stephen's scene at the mirror fixes female masculinity within the limitations set by sexology, then Jess's scene(s) at the mirror troubles and proliferates female masculinity beyond those limitations. In other words, if *The Well* wrestles the subject's portrait away from sexology, then *SBB* languages and rearticulates that subject position somewhat differently.

Gayle Rubin (1992, 469-70) emphasizes the torsional relationship between discourses of masculinity and female masculinity.

> Forms of masculinity are molded by the experiences and expectations of class, race, ethnicity, religion, occupation, age, subculture ... [N]national racial, and ethnic groups differ widely in what constitutes masculinity, and each has its own system for communicating ... "manhood" ... There are many different ways to be masculine ... and there are at least as many ways to be butch as there are ways for men to be masculine; actually, there are more ways to be butch, because when women appropriate masculine styles the element of travesty produces new significance and meaning. Butches adopt and transmute the many available codes of masculinity.

In the moments in *SBB* when we see Jess at the mirror, we see he/r "labouring" to transform those codes in relation to he/r identity, and "working" to make he/r body fit in relation to he/r gender identification. In he/r search for the "how" of female masculinity, we see Jess alternately emphasizing either "female" or "masculine"; that painful oscillation does not end until Jess resolves to transcend the two terms altogether. Where masculinity for Martin meant not *being* lack, female masculinity for Jess is a subject position that emerges precisely in the gap between "female" and "masculine." Jess, too, refuses lack and the gaze by having he/r breasts removed; s/he, too (eventually), challenges, that economy by removing breasts – in an equation where an empowered subject is masculine, which means a lack of (obvious) breasts but without the addition of a penis.

One of the early mirror scenes in *SBB* occurs when Jess, just at the onset of the feminist movement, lives with Theresa. Feinberg painstakingly documents the violent relationship in the early 1960s between gay/lesbian cultures and the police; in this scene, Jess has just been arrested in a bar raid and is, once again, beaten by police. S/he looks into the mirror and sees a different "Jess" looking back at he/r – someone who is unlike the very young "Jess" dressed in he/r father's suit. This Jess seems to be well on he/r way to becoming the "woman" s/he wondered if s/he would grow up to be. "I drifted in and out of consciousness. I remember Theresa propping me up against a brick wall ... [chewing] her lower lip and [fingering] the bloody places on my shirt. 'I'll never get these stains out.' She held my head on her lap all the way back ... And then I found myself in our home again ... As I looked in the mirror I felt sorry for the reflection – bloody, bruised, lumpy" (Feinberg 1993, 136-7). This portrait occurs when Jess considers passing as male through hormone injections. He/r world is changing. Lesbian-feminism is making it harder for the butch-femme culture of Buffalo to sustain itself. A recession is closing down factories, eliminating vital jobs for butches. And Jess sees he/rself in a dream about Rocco, am FTM trans-sexual s/he met much earlier in he/r life. Sex reassignment surgery emerges in the historical moment in which *SBB* opens. It is an option Jess has chosen: "She reached forward and stroked my cheek. I touched my own face. I felt the stubble of beard" (142).

We do not see Jess in a mirror again until after he/r body responds to testosterone injections. In an image that resonates with Stephen's scene at the mirror, we see Jess as s/he begins to read this slowly emerging portrait of the masculine body.

> As I brushed my teeth, I glanced in the mirror and had to look a second time. Beard stubble roughed my cheeks. My face looked slimmer and more angular. I stripped off my T-shirt and BVD's. My body was lean and hard. My hips had melted away. I could actually see muscles in my thighs I never knew I had ... this is almost the body I'd expected before puberty confounded me. Almost ... I took a hot, soapy shower, enjoying the feel of my hands on my skin. It had been so long since I'd been at home in my body. (171)

Later, we see Jess at a barbershop, looking at he/rself in the barber's mirror, seeing he/rself reflected back through his eyes.

> I looked at myself in the mirror. "Well, maybe something different. Maybe it's time for a change." The barber smiled ... "What about a flat top?" "Yeah! That would be a change" ... With a flourish he pulled away the red cloth that covered me and gave me a hand mirror so I could see the back of my hair. "What do you think, my friend?" This time I didn't try to hide my excitement. I was passing. (172)

Once more, we see Jess in the bathroom mirror at Annie's house. Jess, now passing as male, is known as "Jesse." The addition of the "e" on the end of the name is curious; while evoking (but not definitively) "Jessie," the "e" functions to add the absented feminine back on to Jess, who is now completely passing as male. The addition of the diminutive letter functions as a performative not only to signify masculinity (Jess's passing) but also to signify what cannot be revealed in that passing but what nevertheless remains fundamental to it (Jess's resignified male body). Jesse's name, as a form, mirrors the transformation of Jess into Jesse; that is, it is a performative imitation of cutting off the breasts and adding a scar. It is Jesse whom Annie, who is heterosexual, meets and with whom she becomes lovers. The sex scene between them is described with careful irony as the reader continues to read Jesse as both he and s/he, while

Annie reads Jesse only as he. At the end of the scene Jesse tucks his dildo into his briefs and heads into the bathroom in darkness: "I locked the door, pulled my bag out from behind the tub, replaced my dildo with a sock in my briefs. I looked in the mirror as I splashed cold water on my face. Still me looking back at me ... the light was on when I returned to the bedroom. I clicked it off ... Annie came into my arms and nestled against my shoulder. 'You are one strange man.'" (192).

Ironically, Jesse's strangeness relative to he/r body is the least obvious when s/he is with Annie. Much earlier, the butches of Jess's world are asked to honour Butch Ro by wearing dresses to her funeral, which was to be attended by her family. All of the butches show up wearing women's clothes and look, as did Stephen, monstrously and grotesquely wrong:

> These were burly, big-shouldered he-shes who carried their womanhood in work-roughened hands. They could playfully slap you on the back and send you halfway across the room. Their forearms and biceps were covered with tattoos. These powerful butch women were comfortable in work chinos. Their spirit roared to life when they wore double-breasted suits. Wearing dresses was an excruciating humiliation for them. Many of their dresses were old, from another era when occasional retreats were still necessary. The dresses were outdated, white, frilly, lace, low-cut, plain. The shoes were old or borrowed: patent leather, loafers, sandals. This clothing degraded their spirit, ridiculed who they were. Yet it was in this painful drag they were forced to say their last goodbye. (117)

This painful and grotesque drag is donned once again when Jess and some other butches are shut out of factories and consider dressing as female in order to find employment: "'This is a real crisis,' Grant stressed. 'We either got to change how we look or we're gonna starve to death! Katie got some wigs'" (143). The butches try the wigs on, hoping to find temporary work in department stores until the plants reopen: "Four stone butches trying on fashion wigs. It was like Halloween, only it was creepy and painful. The wigs made us look like we were making fun of ourselves. Grant told me, 'I put one on, now it's your turn, Jess.' Edwin shook her head while she held up a mirror for me to see. I threw the wig on the floor. 'I look more like a he-she with the wig on" (143).

The *Oxford English Dictionary* defines "grotesque" as "strangely or fantastically distorted." As such, the grotesque is a useful trope for thinking about the meanings attributed to female masculinity made abject. The label of "grotesque," which implies "deviance" in its opposition to normative femininity and masculinity, signifies beyond "unattractive"; it suggests a kind of surreal inversion of a well-ordered state. Grotesquerie is associated not only with the ironic parody typical of the carnival but also with the external public expression of a disordered inner state (Russo 1995, 8). The grotesque draws attention to heteronormativity in its mockery of it. In *The Female Grotesque*, Mary Russo writes: "The images of the grotesque body are precisely those which are abjected from the bodily canons of classical aesthetics" (8). The grotesque exists in a dialectical relationship with the classical. Like the mutual dependence between the perverse and the normal, the grotesque requires a category of "beautiful," against which it is contrasted, in order to be intelligible: "The classical [beautiful] body is ... closed, static, self-contained, symmetrical and sleek ... the grotesque body is ... multiple and changing ... it is identified with ... social transformation" (8). In other words, the grotesque body crosses boundaries; it pries apart overdetermined distinctions and articulates new forms. It becomes clear that the grotesque body is that which interrupts normative repetitions of gender.

Bakhtin's (1968) work on the grotesque body also warrants mention here. In his work on Rabelais, Bakhtin elaborates a theory of the grotesque body in order to conceptualize social formations, social conflict, and one particular means of carnivalesque resistance. He suggests that the grotesque is a system of material imagery, created by folk humour, that builds upon associations of feasts and the body to degrade and parody high culture. Bakhtin's ideas about degradation are particularly interesting in that degradation is essentially an ambivalent act that is linked with the body's lower stratum: "To degrade also means to concern oneself with the lower stratum of the body, the life of the belly and the reproductive organs; it therefore relates to acts of defecation and copulation, conception, pregnancy, and birth. Degradation digs a bodily grave for a new birth" (24).

Bakhtin's grotesque body, like his notion of dialogism, privileges the duality of the supposedly singular unit; that is, the grotesque body, degraded or brought back down to earth, is a body that is constantly productive of its Other. "It is not a closed, completed unit; it is unfinished, outgrows itself, transgresses its own limits ... [T]he body discloses its essence as a principle of growth which exceeds its own limits ... From one body a new body always emerges in some form or other" (26). The grotesquely gendered body, like those displayed in these scenes, is that which calls attention to normative gender roles while it distorts and inverts them. These grotesque bodies – like Stephen Gordon's – always exceed their own limitations and suggest the opposite gender even when fully displayed and costumed as the supposedly "correct" gender. What is mocked in these scenes is not femininity per se but the thought that somehow these he-she's were women. Their bodies are not closed units but produce a new body; that is, they produce the impression of a male body, especially when contrasted with the clothing conventionally associated with femininity. Krafft-Ebing (1965, 410) identified this contradiction when he noted that female inverts "make the impression of a man in women's clothes." The contradiction between butch masculinity and the female wigs marks these bodies as grotesquely degrading the sex/gender system that, in turn, has so violently misread them.

One of the last times we see Jess in a mirror s/he is at a gym working out. By now, the constitutive contradiction between "female" and "masculine" is completely erased, as is the contradiction between the "Jess" the reader knows and the "Jesse" of the mirror image. Without that frame, Jess's subjectivity threatens to foreclose on itself by reaching its logical end, that is, Jesse completely passing as a man.

> I thought about my body a lot as I pressed against the resistance of cold iron. I enjoyed getting leaner and harder. I thought of my femme lovers who cursed each thickness and fold in their bodies – beautiful flesh I loved. But as I watched myself clench my muscles while I pumped, I found the weight and shape of my own body pleased me. I concentrated on my discipline and endurance ... I learned that strength, like height, is measured by who you're standing next to. I was considered a scrawny guy in the gym. (210)

When all traces of Jesse's former self are erased after Edna, one of the "femmes from the old days," has left he/r, Jesse finally realizes s/he is just as isolated and trapped passing as male as s/he had been living as a butch in a lesbian-feminist cityscape.

> I took my time in the shower, trying to scrub away the grime of isolation with hot, soapy water. Loneliness had become an environment – the air I breathed, the spatial dimension in which I was trapped ... I ... looked in the bathroom mirror. The depth of sadness in my eyes frightened me ... As much as I loved my beard as part of my body, I felt trapped behind it. What I saw in the mirror was not a man, but I couldn't recognize the he-she ... I simply became a he – a man without a past ... I could see my passing self, but even I could no longer see the more complicated me beneath my surface. (221-2)

The need for that constitutive tension between "female" and "masculine" has returned. Jess has quit injecting hormones and wonders if s/he can return to the past and to the first portrait of he/rself in he/r father's suit: "I ... remembered the child who couldn't be catalogued ... I saw her standing in front of her *own* mirror" (222, emphasis added). Yet Jess knows that is impossible: "I thought how brave she was to have begun this ... I wasn't traveling backward ... who was I *now*?" (222-3, emphasis added). This "now" produces one of the final and lasting images of Jess in the text (265). Jess and Ruth – a trans-sexual MTF/femme "whose voice is as complicated" as is Jess's – spend a Christmas together and exchange gifts (265). Jess gives Ruth a sewing machine: "I could tell by the way her fingers trailed across the machine how happy it made her. 'I'll make you a suit,' she whispered" (266). In return, Ruth gives Jess two gifts: the first is a copy of *Gay American History*; the second is a gift of re-cognition and visibility in representation.

> "Look," Ruth took the book from my hands and turned to the index ... "This whole part is about women like you who lived as men." ... She handed me a package wrapped in red tissue paper. "Open this." Inside was a watercolor of a face filled with emotion, looking up at a host of stars. It was a beautiful face, a face I'd never seen before. It was *my* face. (266-7, emphasis added)

Unlike all the other portraits in *SBB*, that face is not described for the reader. The indeterminacy of the final portrait of Jess functions, in many ways, to leave that question not just unanswered but also unanswerable, and it is a strategy that Tremain also uses, although to different ends. Where Martin finds himself by answering the question "are you a man or a woman?" Jess rearticulates the question itself: "it could never be answered if it had to be asked" (222). "All my life I'd been told everything about me was really twisted and sick. But if I was a man, I was 'cute.' Acceptance of me as a he felt like an ongoing indictment of me as a he-she" (178). With Ruth, a potential femme lover, Jess negotiates the question and knowledge materializes in the gap left by unknowing: "I laughed and picked at my salad. 'Do you know if I'm a man or a woman?' 'No,' Ruth said, 'That's why I know so much about you'" (254). Like *The Well*, *SBB* opens as a quest narrative in which Jess struggles to find he/rself in language. However, unlike *The Well*, *SBB* ends by deconstructing and rearticulating the terms of the search that is its own imperative.

"Between the Motion and the Act"

Jess's and Martin's crises of embodiment are rearticulations of that which Stephen Gordon represents through a disidentification with Christ. Given the importance of mirrors in both *The Well* and *SBB*, it is curious that there is not one scene in *SC* in which Martin sees himself in a literal mirror. In the former novels Stephen and Jess struggle to articulate themselves within a system of representation and signification that has languaged them out of existence. Martin, on the other hand, refuses the discursive anxieties of embodiment vis-à-vis language. His method of articulation is less bound by language and more constrained by imbrications of masculinity and suffering. Where Martin does exist in language, his body paradoxically exists outside of the reality-effects of language; that is, his body is not so simply materialized or hailed into being by language. In this sense, *SC* functions as a kind of anti-coming-out narrative. Whereas Stephen and Jess quest to come into, unlearn, and rearticulate (somewhat different) knowledges, histories, and languages, Martin seeks to emerge as the teleological end of Mary's suffering.

Elaine Scarry (1985, 54) argues that pain shatters, or "unmakes" subjectivity precisely because it is an experience that is fundamentally unrepresentable and destructive of the ability to language: "The tendency of pain not simply to resist expression but to destroy the capacity for speech is in torture reenacted in overt, exaggerated form. Even where the torturers do not permanently eliminate the voice through mutilation or murder, they mime the work of pain by temporarily breaking off the voice, making it their own, making it speak their words, making it cry out when they want it to cry, be silent when they want its silence, turning it on and off, using its sound to abuse the one whose voice it is."

Not only can pain shatter the ability to articulate but it also culminates in what Scarry calls an "unseen sense of self-betrayal" (47). In torture, the subject's own body is experienced as an active agent in the production of pain. Torture that forces the body into one position for hours at a time, for instance, transforms the subject's body into yet another agent of pain for the torturer. Bodies that formerly may have been the agent of pleasure are now replaced with a body that is made a weapon against itself. As Scarry so emphatically argues:

> What the process of torture does is to split the human being into two, to make emphatic the ever present but, except in the extremity of sickness and death, only latent distinction between a self and a body, between a "me" and "my body." The "self" or "me," which is experienced on the one hand as more private, more essentially at the center, and on the other hand as participating across the bridge of the body in the world, is "embodied" only in the voice, in language. The goal of the torturer is to make the one, the body, emphatically crushingly *present* by destroying it, and to make the other, the voice, *absent* by destroying it. (49, emphasis in original)

For Mary and Jess, subjects of a kind of domestic daily torture both as children and as adults, resistance to pain means reversing the process. In particular, Mary becomes silent during pain, and in that silence Martin's voice emerges to refuse obliteration by claiming a body that must be his, a body that emerges *after* pain. Pain paradoxically shatters and consolidates subjectivity as a different gender both spatialized and temporalized in another frame of reference. Mary's preoccupation with inventions and inventors mirrors the failure of embodiment as survival strategy and the need to articulate gender beyond those categories recognized within the sex/gender system. Her reconfigurations of time, given that Martin emerges in the gaps between time, also allow her to think outside the nationalized terms of "history," to conceptualize a time she calls "pre-invention," which is especially interesting given that she imagines herself as the teleological pre-invention space of Martin (Tremain 1992, 33). She is able to – in fact, needs to – think of the world in a state of becoming, where daily items such as Estelle's sewing machine, farm equipment, the revolver and thermometer are things that, once upon a time, did not exist. "I always thought the world was finished," Mary says to Miss McRae, who had just given her a *Dictionary of Inventions* (30). "'Well, that's perfectly true, Mary'" Miss McRae responds, 'and this also means, of course, that there is a great deal yet to come, things we might not be able to imagine now'" (30). One of those things not yet invented is Martin: "Before, no one had dreamed of a boat with wheels, just as now, no one could dream of Mary Ward not being a girl ... one day, she would be in a dictionary" (31). Someday Mary would be credited in a similar dictionary for creating something new. That "new" thing will be the product of an inverted ritual of transubstantiation, where new substances interjected into Mary's body, including the filling of a cavity, become the building materials of Martin. As Mary explains: "As Gilbert began to drill into her decaying tooth, she felt Mary annihilated a little more each second, Mary becoming fragments, pulp ... behind him ... she could hear the nurse grinding some substance ... mortar and she thought, this substance is new and is part of Martin Ward" (70).

The new substance that is constitutive of Martin is the product of suffering. One of the things that Mary Martin shares with Stephen Gordon and Jess Goldberg is the belief that masculinity is somehow coterminous or metonymic with suffering. Just before Gilbert drills Mary's tooth, he probes it; in that moment, Mary finds Martin, and more: "The probing, for Mary, was like an electrocution and all memory of no-pain vanished and became the past, to which there was no return ... beyond the two faces and beyond the light, beyond the lost past ... Mary rediscovered her old ally – suffering. She had forgotten its power ... but now, once again in its company, she let herself yield to its transforming properties ... Her thoughts were clear and hard" (70).

Mary Martin sees transformation, change, and "re-invention" all around her. The first love of her life, Lindsey Stevens, becomes Mrs. Ranulf Morrit (170); Cord's face is partially paralyzed from reactive palsy but then changes back again (135); Sonny favoured Mary until Timmy was born (12-13). Sonny wants Timmy to take over the family farm, but Timmy refuses (284-5); kings die, epochs come to an end, presidents are assassinated (157); a missile crisis threatens the world (139); revolutions threaten national stability in France (221); and an American female tennis star beats a British male player (337), confirming that even "the Empire [itself] *had* a lifespan" (284, emphasis added). But Mary Martin's construction of masculinity as suffering is the most consistent trope of the novel. Mary equates suffering, silent suffering, with the mortar of masculinity and, by extension, with the body of Martin.

Mary's father, Sonny, is a paragon of suffering masculinity. Sonny was one of many British subjects injured during the Second World War when part of his left ear was shot off, and he watched a "small piece of himself floating away" (6). His own suffering makes him revisit that moment, only during these times the wounds are self-inflicted: "In his deaf rages, Sonny would gouge at [his ear] with his thumb, making blood run down his neck" (6). Throughout the trajectory of Sonny's life he becomes increasingly silent, as if he were functioning like a trapped animal. While Sonny is very different from Stephen's father, Philip, both men fail as the subjects of England. Philip is crushed by the weight of the tradition he is forced to carry; Sonny and his broken watch signify the end of time as he and men like him have known it. If England's time as a nation ends with the death of King George ("they wept not merely for the King but for themselves and for England: for the long, ghastly passing of time" [3]), then Sonny's watch, as a symbol of patriarchal time, marks its dissolution and breakdown.

It is important to note that the broken watch is not passed on to Timmy, who, despite Sonny's best efforts, refuses to carry on in his father's footsteps: neither time nor his home/land remain "sacred" to him. Sonny's own thoughts betray his sense of himself as the image of the end of Empire, defeated, wounded, broken, powerless, unrelenting, self-destructive, dying off: "He'd lost half an ear for England. England owed him something, a few glasses of something every night. 'Darn right,' as John Wayne would say" (162). Sonny retreats into his mind, identifying with the increasingly more phallic bearers of masculinity – that is, an idealized "American" cowboy – and attempting (albeit unsuccessfully) to fulfill the requisites of adult, rural masculinity: he lives to pass on his own corner of England to Timmy, who eventually refuses the family farm. While Timmy does not challenge his father, he "successfully" lives without resolving the contradictions that mark him, by his father's standards, as a failure: "His mind emptied itself of his old and present life and filled up with the life to come" (256). Sonny's powerlessness comes to its logical conclusion when, after Timmy's final refusal of the farm, Sonny shoots himself with his own rifle.

It is just after Sonny kills her pet bird, Marguerite (Mary's silent interlocutor), that Mary first decides: "if I suffer a lot, I will grow a man's skin" (34). Again, in school: "She reminded herself of a pupa, suspended by a thread in its interim life. She imagined that as she grew, her man's skin was *hardening* on her" (95, emphasis added). Even after Mary is beaten by her father, and her breast bindings[13] are violently torn away, she believes her vengeance will come from being just like him: "Without speaking, she said to her father: When I'm a man, I will kill you" (50). Even in this particularly violent attack by Sonny, Mary equates emotionality and the release of pain with the end of hope and the death of Martin: "She hauled her neck free of [Sonny's] choking wrist ... She felt a sickly sorrow, like a dose of poison going into her and spreading all through her. She started to cry. This was a thing she never wanted to do and never wanted him to see as long as she lived. Not crying was what had given her hope" (117). Mary directly correlates phallic masculinity with suffering and with hegemonic constructions of a male body in a relation in which one could easily stand in for the other: "If I suffer and refuse to cry, a penis will grow out of all that is locked away inside. It needs only time" (34).

In a move that allegorizes the constitutive impasses of masculinity and its failures to acquire the phallic power of the father, time passes and Mary's male skin fails to appear: "She was fifteen and she could see and feel damage all around. It had begun in her. Her flesh had refused to harden as she believed it would. It had disobeyed her mind. In her mind, she was Martin Ward, a lean boy ... she hoped that, with the bandages on, it would be her mind that showed" (112). Where Stephen Gordon's suffering was Christ-like, Mary's seems truer to her gender(ed name) when the product of her pain is a new entity named Martin. For both Mary and Stephen, to be "Mary" means to be possessed by men, to be powerless, to exist as a "crime against herself" (5). On the other hand, to be Martin means to occupy – indeed, embody – hardness and physicality; it means to "take possession of things," not to be possessed; finally, to be Martin means to no longer be objectified as feminine nor to be identified with the female body through breasts (179). Mary realizes that Martin is no longer "little Martin" when he has sexual fantasies about Lindsey. In her sexual scenario, Mary's breasts are Lindsey's, who "begged me to go deeper into her, to hurt her. She said: 'Destroy me, Martin.' ... I wasn't little Martin anymore. I was a young man" (150).

Like Stephen Gordon, both Jess and Mary learn that to "be a man" means to suffer silently and bravely within impossible contradictions. One of those contradictions in *SBB* is that between race and gender. Within a white supremacist economy, whiteness functions by violently marking its *differences from* those supposedly marked by race rather than by interrogating *differences within*, or the ways those marked by whiteness are different from each other. In other words, one of the ways that white supremacy works is by privileging and regulating singularity of subjectivity, binding the subject to whiteness through its appeals to universality. As a Jewish child, Jess learned that to be he/rself meant to be possessed by others, to endure violence, anti-Semitism, rape, institutional violence and discipline, parental abandonment, and daily terror.

One of Jess's first lessons in gender as racial enforcement occurs long before s/he is even ten years old, when s/he is attacked by a group of neighbourhood children. Although, even then, Jess is unintelligibly different, he/r gender difference could not be articulated on its own terms. Jess is chased, tied up, beaten, and locked into a neighbour's coal bin. The terms of he/r emergence are telling: "I don't know what [Mrs. Jefferson] thought when she heard all the thumping and kicking in her coal bin. But when she opened the little trap door on the coal bin and I squirmed out onto her kitchen floor, she looked scared enough to fall down dead. There I stood, *covered with coal soot* and blood, tied up and half-naked in her kitchen" (18, emphasis added).

Significantly, Jess emerges from this first experience of alienation and violence at the hands of white children marked not only as different but also as *racially different;* that is, he/r difference is only intelligible through the primary tropes of difference that have currency in the United States during the 1960s – racial difference. While Jess's last name marks he/r as Jewish and, therefore, racially different, s/he visually passes as, and identifies as, white (Britzman 1989, 109). As Deborah Britzman rightly argues, the supposed fact of Jess's whiteness is not enough to effect "public normalization" (109). The image of Jess standing in a neighbour's kitchen, bleeding and covered in black soot, functions metonymically to foreground he/r difference; that is, Jess's gender difference is one still unthinkable, and this scene functions almost allegorically to allow racial difference to stand in, as it were, for gender difference.

Jess's history as a stranger does not begin with this incident. When Jess was an infant he/r mother was entirely indifferent to her. In the absence of maternal and paternal care, she was nurtured and raised by the Dineh women who lived across the hall from he/r and he/r family. As long as someone else was doing the work of raising Jess, the proximity of the Dineh women seemed insignificant. But when Jess answers he/r father's question one day "with words he'd never heard before," Jess's father "rescues" he/r from maternal neglect (Feinberg 1993, 14). That rescue reveals a racial panic: "He said later he couldn't stand by and watch his own flesh and blood be kidnapped by Indians" (14). Within economies of white supremacy, this is an instance in which a white-appearing subject is so utterly alienated from mainstream white culture that it is as though s/he begins to pass as another race. While Jess's Jewishness does not mark he/r as visually different (the one instance of it marking he/r as different occurs when s/he is outed by he/r last name), he/r gender difference most certainly does; that visual difference, in this scene, registers on a *racialized* scale. Of course, Jess's appearance on a racialized scale of difference does not exempt he/r from the histories of racism within which s/he matures. One of the more painful lessons of that maturation occurs when Jess's interracial friendship with Ed ends with the latter's suicide. It is not until years later that Jess finally reads the book that Ed gave he/r – W.E.B. DuBois's *The Souls of Black Folks* – which forces he/r to think of the differences, rather than the similarities, between them. Ed leaves Jess a final message underlined in DuBois's book: "It is a peculiar sensation, this double-consciouness, this sense of always looking at one's self through the eyes of others, of measuring one's soul by the tape of a world that looks on in amused contempt and pity. One ever feels his twoness – ... two souls, two thoughts, two unreconciled strivings; two strivings" (178).

As Jess matures and finds he/r way to the butch-femme community in Buffalo, s/he is taken in, as it were, by Butch Al and her lover, Jacqueline. From early on in he/r childhood, Jess learned that to survive s/he had to "toughen up," and it is with Butch Al that s/he learns to "take it like a man" (30). The result is that Jess(e)'s strategies of survival materialize as "stone hardness," an identity similar to that which built Martin from a substance as tough as "mortar."[14] Al eventually becomes a significant father-figure to Jess, teaching he/r everything s/he needs to know about surviving as a young butch: "It was always the same lesson: toughen up. Al never said exactly what was coming. It was never spelled out. But I got the feeling it was awful. I knew she was worried about my surviving it. I wondered if I was ready. Al's message was: *You're not!"* (30).

Al teaches Jess the mechanics of making love to women as a stone butch and teaches Jess how to survive bar fights, rapes, beatings, and eventual institutionalizations. "Toughen up" was the message, and, for Jess, 'toughen up' functioned not only as a symptom of but also as a syllogistic triangulation of masculinity. In other words, to be a butch meant to be tough and emotionally invulnerable, to be granite hard, impenetrable, unemotional, and manly. Therefore, butchness came to be synonymous with "stone" hardness. Jess represents it this way: "Deep down, my insides seethed. I knew I was stone, too. It was a home alarm system that didn't seem to have an on-off switch. Once installed, the sirens went off and the gates shut, even if the intruder was loving" (94).

Despite their differences, Mary, Jess, and Stephen are "stone" and "mortar hard" in an economy in which masculinity becomes synonymous with suffering and in which suffering, or "stone hard" toughness, functions as the sexual trope of female masculinity. "Stone butchness," as it is taken up in *SBB,* generally refers to the denial of sexual reciprocity for butches. The term emerges out of butch-femme cultures in the United States, and, while signifying any number of specific practices or strategies, the outcome is often the same: butches are perceived to be the ones denying themselves sexual pleasure. In other words, it can be argued that it is the figure of "stone butch masculinity" that, in many ways, marks the limits of and disrupts an easy and heteronormative reductive of butch-femme to heterosexuality. For stone eroticism and other-gendered exchanges of desire, the scene of heterosexuality is most certainly recalled but it is also most certainly displaced. Butch masculinity is the site of self-denial and sexual abnegation, whereas femme femininity is the site of erotic satisfaction. In other words, the butch denies his own pleasure while insisting upon sexually servicing the femme. *She* is the site of erotic control, not *he*. As Butler (1991, 25) describes it:

> A stone butch may well seek to constitute her lover as the exclusive site of erotic attention and pleasure. And yet, this "providing" butch who seems at first to replicate a certain husband-like role, can find herself [sic] caught up in a logic of inversion whereby that "providing-ness" turns to a self-sacrifice, which implicates her in the most ancient trap of feminine self-abnegation. She may well find herself in a situation of radical need, which is precisely what she sought to locate, find, and fulfill in her femme lover. In effect, the butch inverts into the femme or remains caught up in the specter of that inversion, or takes pleasure in it.

Precisely because of that inversion and its effect – masculinity's "radical need" – stone economies reference a very femme-centric organization of sexuality. Butler, however, does not specify the nature of this radical need. I suggest that, at least in the texts under consideration here, that radical need is the unsatiated and accumulating erotic anxiety of the masochistic subject. But it can also refer, as I argue in Chapter 2, to a theatre of transsubstantiation whose subjects understand themselves as overdetermined not only by onto-performative but also by corporeal failures. The "need," then, is for ontological re/cognition. In *The Well*, Stephen represented this theatre as the spectacle of Christ's suffering. The primary vehicle through which this non-visual subject could manifest itself to Stephen was an onto-performative disidentification with Christ. As I have argued, two imperatives overdetermine that disidentificatory articular practice – "Touch/See Me [the self between the visible body and the non-visible flesh]" or "Touch/See Me [in the wrong body] Not." I contend that female masculinity is framed or arrested in a passionate theatre of (trans-)substantiation, where the authenticity of the most intimately felt *self* could only become real (as a subject with substance, as a reality effect) through the recognition of the Other and a paradoxical and masochistic renunciation of the body in favour of the flesh. This penultimate and masochistic act of self-sacrifice is precisely what the signifier "stone" references; for subjects who experience themselves as wrongly corporealized (i.e., subjects like Stephen, Martin, and Jess, who understand themselves as wrongfully embodied) the sexual performative "Touch Me Not" materializes that which the sex/gender system has languaged out of existence and into No Man's Land: subjects who know they exist, yet who cannot materialize through "he" or "she" exclusively. In *SC*, Martin articulates the economy of No Man's Land through spatial metaphors of country; he does not return to England to complete the sex change. For him, it is completed in the metaphorical and sacred space between England (the old country) and the United States (the new). In the end, he finally locates on a farm very much like, but different from, the one on which he grew up in Swaithey, with a father(-figure) similar to but unlike Sonny. Jess, on the other hand, self-articulates from No Man's Land between genders by "unioning" and "labouring" for social justice. Neither character attempts to resolve the crisis of embodiment but both certainly remain haunted by its complex imperatives to self-articulation.

For each of my characters, and indeed for every FTM trans-sexual in any narrative I have read (and, in some cases, on the covers of those books as well), the most important imperative of materializing masculinity is a hard-looking flat chest. Mary describes her own breasts as white eggs, soft and porous, like abject embryonic fluid, "squashy" and parasitic; these breasts are quite different from the hardened mortar that is Martin: "She touched her breasts. The skin of them was very white, their texture indescribable, like no other part of her. They seemed like sacs enveloping the embryos of other things, as if something had laid two eggs under her skin and now these parasites were growing on her. She always touched them when she woke, hoping vainly to find them shrunk or burst or sliced away ... They were still there, hard yet squashy under her pyjamas" (112).

Above all else, a flat chest has become *the* visual signifier of maleness. Having a flat chest allows one to pass as a man on the street. The absence or presence of a penis, imagined or otherwise, has, in popular culture, been the signifier of gender; either you had one or you did not. In each of the texts under discussion that challenges that economy, either having or not having breasts has assumed that position and eclipsed the assumed presence of a penis. While packing or wearing strap-on dildoes, or stuffing one's crotch with a pair of socks to simulate a bulge, frequently accompanies a flat chest, removing or rendering breasts invisible seems to function in many performances of female masculinity as a rite of passage. The presumption of breasts circulates more thoroughly in popular culture than the penis because they are much more immediately visual and, therefore, far more "representable." Stephen Gordon agonizes over his chest in a mirror scene that many critics misread in order to assign the tag "female." The cover photograph of Frankie Hucklenbroich, author of *A Crystal Diary* (1997), shows the author wearing a man's jacket and black turtle-neck sweater, sitting in a chair with (quite large) breasts positioned under the flaps of the jacket, the side of one just barely visible. Jess Goldberg, like many other trans-sexual/trans-gendered subjects, saves money in order to begin sex reassignment transitions; in every case, the first intervention is always chest reconstruction. In the few extant FTM trans-sexual autobiographies – *A Self-Made Man: The Diary of a Man Born in a Woman's Body* (1996); *Emergence: A Transsexual Autobiography* (1977); *Dear Sir or Madam: The Autobiography of a Female-to-Male Transsexual* (1996); *What Took You So Long? A Girl's Journey to Manhood* (1995) – as well as in many drag king shows and other performances of female masculinity, taping, binding, or, for the trans-sexual autobiographies, surgical removal of breasts is the first step toward changing genders. It is a step that often precedes the use of male hormones.

Breasts mark their subjects as feminine: from their biological function to their fetishization in popular culture, breasts signify femininity. In popular culture, for instance, one does not need to go much further than the men's magazine *Esquire* for proof. "BREASTS! The Triumph of Cleavage Culture" screams the headline, while Pamela Anderson, *costumed* in a man's white T-shirt and man's briefs, stares aggressively into the camera, hands poised to lift the T-shirt and, presumably, expose her infamous breasts (February 1999). Inside, the article, "Breasts, Reassessed," is introduced with a digitally produced photograph of a naked man sleeping between a woman's breasts while the text tells us that "breasts have a potential for symbolic meaning unequaled by even the primary sexual body parts" (Udovitch 1999, 87). Breasts, in other words, function as a discourse of gender and are the "cultural artifact [of] the latter half of the twentieth-century."

> The flat-chested has its place in the fashion world ... but even within the slender subcategory of the supermodels, it is the curvier ... rather than the more willowy mannequins whose names you don't know, who usually have the mainstream appeal ... Barbie, Betty and Veronica, all still popular figures in the lives of little girls, have breasts that start at their shoulders and end at their rib cages, just above the waist. In fact, I would say that if there is one thing that feminism has had no impact on whatsoever, it is [female] body image. (87)

The article proceeds to taxonomize feminine subjectivity according to its breasts. There is the "dumb breast" (Marilyn Munroe); the "mean breast," best symbolized by Madonna's missile-shaped bras; the "power breasts" (Ally McBeal); and "breasts with agendas" ("bra-burners"). Above all, the article reassures us, "curves are, pound for pound, the best bargain" to be had (88). "Today's amazon is supposed to own her breasts, not cut them off or trade them in ... she is not oppressed by her breasts nor armed with them but empowered by them. Her femininity ... can't get there by following a straight line. She needs curves" (89).

Mark Simpson (1994) and Ann Bolin (1992) agree, exploring the failures and successes of both male and female body-builders, respectively, by examining how they manipulate breast tissue. In her study of female body builders, Bolin argues that notions of "fitness" are overshadowed by Western ideals of the feminine body as soft and curvaceous. These conflicting discourses constrain female body-builders and weight-lifters, who remain bound by beauty norms even as they denaturalize the female body. Despite the trend towards "jock chic" in mainstream culture, where athletic and muscular female bodies read against notions of frailty, female body-building remains saturated with contradiction. Bolin suggests that these contradictions affect even the judging of the sport to the degree that women who "look too much like men" can tame overdeveloped musculature with breast augmentation and hyper-femininity in hairstyles and haircolouring (blondeness remains the colour of choice), make-up, long fingernails, and so on.

Where female body-builders produce grotesque bodies that can signify masculinity (no breasts), male body-builders risk hyper-feminization, especially through steroid use and the over-development of pectoral muscles. Mark Simpson (1994) argues as much in one of his essays from *Male Impersonators,* appropriately entitled "Big Tits! Masochism and Transformation in Bodybuilding," where he interrogates male body-building as a site of paradoxical heterosexual reassurance but homoerotic enjoyment. Simpson argues that, while body-building involves the eroticization of masculinity, it does not automatically or logically lead to homosexuality; rather, Simpson argues, body-building, combined with steroid use, creates a site of hypermasculinity in which the exaggerated and anxious display of masculinity becomes its opposite. In other words, every time men try to grasp something consolingly, sturdily, essentially masculine, it all too easily transforms into its opposite (30). Steroid use in body-building, a measure used to combat the lack of physical "manliness," in effect promotes castration of the subject at precisely the same moment. Ironically, the unavoidable logic of steroid use builds up the male body only to simultaneously take the bodybuilder one step closer to its opposite. Simpson, quite by accident, locates one muscle-man's body as part of the grotesque when he argues that body-builders dramatize on their flesh the insecurity, the uncertainty, and the inevitable failures of hypermasculinity:[15] "Testosterone level[s] plummeted, sperm count went to zero and all the oestrogen [sic] in his body, which had been accruing for years, turned ... pecs into soft doughy breasts" (41).

For almost any subject who possesses them, breasts signify femininity; for these subjects of masculinity they signify mis(re)cognition, crisis, and disidentification. Like Martin, Jess relates to he/r breasts with profound confusion. Already feeling more appropriately gendered once s/he's taking testosterone, Jess describes he/r newly forming but now differently misrecognized body: "My beard grew in full of color: blond streaked with red and brown and white. In the open fields of life, my beard was a bush to hide behind. Almost no one seemed to recognize me anymore when I was out in public" (Feinberg 1993, 175). But as the hormones increasingly articulate Jess's body as masculine, they also increase the juxtaposition of that external impression of masculinity with Jess's breasts – a juxtaposition that becomes unbearable: "I hated my breasts more than ever. Binding them every day had flattened the muscles, and they hurt. But I had finally saved up two thousand dollars. I called the surgeon ... I told him I wanted to be flat-chested" (175).

Jess enters a hospital, has radical breast reduction surgery, and is released far too soon. Upon he/r return "home," a trope that, Prosser (1998, 179) has argued, organizes much of the novel, Jess comes face to face with the limitations of he/r strategies of containment. In other words, as I noted earlier, Jess sees he/r own stoneness functioning as a "home security system" that blocks unwanted and presumably unsafe intruders from gaining access to he/r, including he/rself. Repeatedly, Jess acknowledges that he/r always already overdetermined challenge was to learn to "be at home" in he/r body, regardless of its gender.[16] If Jess's body functions as a metaphorical home for he/r, then it also functions as one source of alienation. The result is that s/he he/rself has a difficult time arriving "home" after being away so long. "Home" is fetishized in this text and remains an impossibility. Hence, he/r attempt to come home after surgery does not succeed, as Prosser (1998, 184) suggests. Jess enters as a wounded intruder: "I had to walk a long way from the bus to my house. When I finally got home I put my key in the door, but I remembered the door needed to be pulled inward as the key was turned. When I finally pulled hard enough to turn the key, I knew I had hurt myself" (Feinberg 1993, 177). With a profound ambivalence and almost entire absence of affect, Jess names the stakes of living so profoundly alienated; that is, s/he articulates even further misrecognition and a renewed "non-person" status even after working to make he/r body "fit": "A dull pain throbbed in my chest. I stood up carefully. When I opened the closet door, I saw myself reflected in the full-length mirror mounted inside. I could tell from my beard growth I had slept for days. My chest was bandaged. There *it* was – the body I'd wanted. I wondered why it had to have been so hard" (177, emphasis added).

That Jess misrecognizes he/r own image even inside the "closet" compounds misrecognition upon misrecognition to expose the illusory status of "realness norms" both inside and outside that closet (Butler 1993, 130). *SBB* is, inevitably, a novel in which both identities and bodies are profoundly contingent and unstable. Jess's identity and body are constantly resignified and, like many subjects of masculinity, the boundaries of he/r masculinity are continuously policed against invasions of supposedly inauthentic forms of itself. While passing as Jesse, he rediscovers an old butch friend, Frankie, who is lovers with another butch, Johnny. Jesse responds with a kind of homophobia, arguing that, if the objects of Frankie's desire are not the right ones (i.e., femmes), then Frankie's masculinity is in jeopardy: "What makes you think you're still a butch?" Jess questions (207). But Jess he/rself has returned as Jesse, a *man:* "What makes *you* think you're still a butch," Frankie replies. All of the men in Feinberg's text – Jess, Jesse, Ben, Duffy, Al – function as particular instances of masculinity, each quite different from the other, all of which indict articulations of universal masculinity. *SBB* is profoundly troubled by questions of subjectivity relative to gender, supporting Butler's (1993, 128) assertion that gender performances are always already marked by invested misrecognitions as well as by an unstable coexistence between an efficacious insurrection and painful resubordination.

In *The Well*, Martin Hallam similarly misrecognizes Stephen (although for different reasons), even though the results are severely distressing for Stephen. Despite the alienation from, and often profound disidentifications with, their externalized self-representations, there exists in these subjects a further imperative of articulating masculinity – one that this category shares with, perhaps even foregrounds, male-embodied masculinity: the imperative NOT to be feminine or to be misread as female. Not only are breasts a signifier of such femininity but they also signify both the phallic gaze and the deployment of that gaze. In a phallic economy where the absence of breasts or, to write it otherwise, a lack of breasts, signifies phallic power, if a subject were to remove the signifier of objectification (i.e., breasts), then presumably that subject, in lacking that object, acquires phallic power.

In an economy where power is not synonymous with possessing a penis but with possessing the phallus, then transsexed or intersexed bodies – that is, bodies that *make the impression of a man* – challenge that economy without reinscribing a penis. Both Martin and Jess remove from themselves the objects of a male gaze – breasts – and with the help of testosterone pass as male; yet neither goes the full route of becoming masculine by adding a penis. Neither finds it necessary. Within a mamillian economy breasts function to invert lack; breasts become the signifiers of phallic power. If an empowered subject, one fully registering in the symbolic order, is masculine, and masculinity on a visual scale is epitomized by the absence of breasts, then the subjects of female masculinity are not, as Halberstam (1998a, 129) suggests, the subjects of a contradiction between a male subjectivity and a female body; rather, these are the subjects of a grotesque inversion of a phallic economy where subjects who lack the "pound(s) of flesh" that signify objectification purchase phallic power by losing breasts (Lacan, quoted in Silverman 1993, 183).

The perception of the existence or lack of breasts is, for the most part, dependent upon whether or not the body under discussion is clothed. Some might argue that the naked trans-gendered body could not exist, although such an argument – that such bodies might bear traces or scars of a former engendering that might render the current gender *inauthentic* – fails miserably when faced with the cover of Jason Cromwell's *Transmen and FTMs* (1999). The black-and-white photograph on the cover puts flesh on the argument I am making; it shows about ten or so men, several of whom are depicted without shirts, whose bodies fully read as male. In particular, one white man who stands facing the camera, his chest well developed and covered with a fine layer of chest hair, reveals no obvious scars. Loren Cameron's (1996) self-portraits and photographs in *Body Alchemy* similarly reveal reconstructed chests with few visible traces of medical interventions. These partially clothed bodies still read as masculine.

Several photographs of Cameron naked articulate masculinity paradoxically. Self-portraits, these images reveal a white man, bearded, with cropped hair, chiseled face, muscled legs, arms and chest muscular and well defined, tattooed, one hand squeezing the shutter-release bulb while the other balances a dumb-bell. Or they show the subject self-injecting what I presume to be testosterone or holding a surgeon's scalpel. All of these portraits fully reveal pubic hair yet, where one might expect to see a penis, one does not. Even with such an absence, the subject cannot read as anything other than masculine. The subject's well-developed and surgically reconstructed chest – without breasts – signifies what the lack of a penis fails to: the intersexed subject's masculinity worn like a second skin *as if it were* clothing.

"Isn't This Distance Also Real?"

Bakhtin's (1984) suggestion that one's self is enabled by one's disidentification with an Other without whom identification as self could not occur is worked into both of these texts with slightly different outcomes. In *SC*, when Mary attends Lindsey's wedding, she ironically mourns "this joining of the two sides – woman and man": "The bells of the church were pealing like mad, pealing for this joining of the two sides – woman and man. I thought, they're ringing like they ring at the end of all the wars. They think all the soldiers have come home. They don't know I'm still out there in the mud, in no-man's-land" (Tremain 1992, 168).

Mary and Martin are bound in a dialogic relation on either side of No Man's Land, where the one cannot exist without motioning to the other. To motion means to gesture to a person, to direct him or her to do something. But as a noun, it also references both movement (the changing of place or manner of moving the body, as in walking) and simulation of that motion or gesture (as in "going through the motions"). In the places where Mary exists, Martin is gestured to but cannot fully materialize. Once

Mary gives up going through the motions and changes places by leaving Swaithey for London, Martin emerges almost full time. The change in location mirrors Martin's repositioning: he is no longer inside, waiting to come out, but is worn on the outside instead.

Martin acts to materialize himself. He buys his first pair of jeans, never takes them off, and, in fact, bathes wearing them as if they were not only a second skin but the right skin. When Mary was a child, the girl's clothing she was often costumed in felt foreign and, as a kind of second skin, failed to do what that skin was supposed to do (i.e., to function as a boundary between inside and outside): "The heat and the smocking had made her chest itch so much she had scratched it raw and now little circles of blood were visible among the silky stitches" (9). That costume is violently rejected when Mary becomes an adult and moves to London. She throws her clothes out of the window of the rooms she rents to leave them lying on the ground like "suicided skirts" (178). While in London, Mary's name changes again and becomes Marty when he works for a poetry magazine called *Liberty*. Marty begins to develop a sense of belonging in space, which, in this novel, always functions as a trope of the body: "Martin developed a sense of 'becoming a part of' London, not just being 'in it'" (182). And Martin eventually finds a sympathetic physician who will assist Mary in initiating the acts that will result in the materialization of his body, an act that transmigrates Mary's body into Martin's body. "I had to move it," Mary decides, "or it would die right here [in Swaithey]" (173).

Martin's decision to materialize a male body occurs at the same time that his childhood sweetheart, Pearl, reaches adulthood. The fascination and love between Mary and Pearl began, at least for Mary, with Pearl's birth and are represented through an interesting simile: "Mary watched. There was something about Pearl that mesmerized her. It was as if Pearl were a lantern slide and Mary sitting on a chair in the dark" (10). A lantern slide is a slide used in very early types of slide projectors known as magic lanterns. The magic lantern was the pre-invention prototype of the slide projector, which positions the light source in front of the picture so that the image is formed by light reflected from the picture. In essence, the projector transfers images in an enlarged form onto a screen. The simile constructs Mary as the viewer of the image projected onto Pearl, suggesting that "Pearl," the white, translucent, rare gem, both refracts enough light to enable something else to project and is the slide upon which that image is formed.

Pearl functions as both the vehicle of Mary Martin's self-image, as the thing without which that image of Martin could not be formed, and as the epitome of white femininity. From her name, to her association with light, to her clothing (which is often white – "She gets into her white nightdress" [248]), to her career choice as a dental nurse complete with requisite white uniform and shoes, to her complete preoccupation with professional and personal cleanliness, Pearl functions as a trope of white emptiness and cleanliness. Not only is she always already shrouded in white, but Pearl also has the uncanny ability to whiten the world around her. On a train-ride home, Pearl looks out the window and even the previously green fields seem to transform themselves in her presence: "During her journey home, the sun went down and the green on the fields took on a peculiar whiteness, like frost" (271). Not only is her skin colour pale white but she seems to shimmer whiteness: "Pearl's swimming costume was turquoise, the colour of the water, and in the light of the baths her limbs looked shining white" (273). She visits Martin after his chest reconstruction surgery and tends to his postsurgical recovery. When Martin begins to emerge, Pearl mourns the loss of Mary: "I feel so sad," Pearl says, when Mary tells her about Martin, "It ... isn't that I'm disgusted. Not really. It's just that ... It was Mary I cared about. And you're killing her" (249). Pearl cannot love Martin the way she loved Mary and, eventually, she falls in love with Mary's brother, Timmy. This news, of course, is devastating for Martin, who had just returned home from the hospital where he had his breasts removed and chest reconstructed: "I deluded myself that my life as Martin, holding Pearl in my arms, was going to come one day. This was the name of my future, *Martin and Pearl, Estb. c. 1976.*" (311).

The date "1976" is a curious marker for *Martin and Pearl*. Martin's chest reconstruction surgery and Pearl's disclosure both occur in 1972. Martin's attempted rape of Pearl, an action that occurs on "the night of Pearl's secret," is not even recounted until chapter "1973," an action that ends with Pearl stained by Martin's phallic "fluids": "Using all my strength, I took her thin wrists in my hands and pinned them down behind her head ... I could feel my two triangles of wounds tearing and starting to bleed ... My blood came through the gauze and stained her" (311). Two important motifs emerge with this date: first, Mary's future as Martin is unknowable and unthinkable without Pearl. Her sense of herself, as Martin, does not exist without Pearl, an idealized white feminine subject who functions to reflect and to refract Martin. Recalling that there are no literal mirror scenes in *SC*, one is able to see that Pearl functions as Martin's metaphorical mirror, without which he fails to exist. Second, Pearl functions as a mirror that exists outside of linear time and that exists within traumatic, unconscious time as Mary. Even though Pearl refuses Martin's constructions of her ("All she kept saying was: 'I am not a thing. I am not a *thing*. I am not a *thing!*'" [312]), Pearl represents a temporal and geographical displacement for Martin. She is, up to this point, the space referenced by the title of the novel: his "sacred country," a future time and place from which he is now exiled. "Surgery alters time," Dr. Beales tells Martin just after he advises him to leave England because "there is nothing left in England that's precious to you any more ... Go and find something new" (317). That new, which is a new time, place, and, indeed, a new sacred country, is for Martin what it was for Stephen and Jess: an ontological space profoundly outside its originary temporal and geographical frames of reference. Like Sonny's, Martin's identification with British masculinity has failed, especially since "England" is slowly becoming a thing of the past, a shadowy simulacrum of its former glory. Even the land fails: "the land in England was turning against the farmer. It was so tired it refused to grow anything ... It had been on the side of the farmer for a thousand years and now it was on the side of ruin" (286). "England ... You mean to tell me England's still *there*?" says one American (304), less an observation and more an imperative echoed by Martin's arrival in Tennessee: "I no longer wait for time to pass ... The past is another country" (340).

If time is signified by space, then the space marked by "fem(me)ininity" exists in a curious relation to reading temporalities. It is almost impossible to read Leslie Feinberg's *SBB* and not see a similar, yet more productive, grafting of fem(me)ininity onto and out of female masculinity. If, in *The Well* and *SC*, fem(me)ininity becomes indistinguishable from femininity, then in *SBB* fem(me)ininity seems to be articulated in a time-space slippage and passes as radical lesbian feminism. One of the biggest heartbreaks that Jess must come to terms with in the novel is her relationship with Theresa. That *coming to terms* is announced in the beginning of the novel through the letter that sets the scene, as it were, for the dramas that unfold later. As Hemmings (1999) argues, the author of the letter acknowledges that Theresa, the former working-class femme to whom it is addressed, could be realized in any number of subjects and in any number of future class-based and sexual trajectories. She could be either "turning tricks," or "waiting tables," or "learning Word Perfect 5.1" (11). She could also be in a lesbian bar, "looking out of the corner" of her eye for the butchest woman in the room, or she could be with women who, unlike Jess and Mary, "only bleed monthly on their cycles" (11). Finally, the letter-writer acknowledges, Theresa could be passing as heterosexual but still working-class, "lying with an unemployed auto worker who is much more like me" (11).

As a slippery and indeterminate subject of either femininity or fem(me)ininity, Theresa leaves Jess when Jesse decides to pass as a man and Theresa refuses the non-consensual, implied heterosexuality that accompanies passing. In that moment in *SBB*, Theresa chooses the emerging lesbian-feminist separatist movement that provides a way for her to transcend her own past and the limitations of passing as heterosexual with Jess: "You were banished too," Jess writes, "to another land with your own sex" (11). In as much as Mary was invisible and unthinkable, banished to a space-off outside of the text, so, too, are Theresa and the other femmes "from the old days" who remain subject to a masculine gaze and definition. Clearly, and even though Feinberg can think fem(me)ininity in more complicated terms than Hall, femininity is still made visible in sexual terms only through the gaze, and then the presence, of a masculine subject, whether male or female. In other words, if the feminine woman is not heterosexual before returning the gaze, as Hemmings suggests, then neither is she lesbian (Hemmings 1999, 454). In narrative terms, this means that the femme is invisible as a queer sexual subject once she is out of the sight, or does not return the gaze, of the masculine woman (454). Theresa can be any or all of the Theresas named in the letter, especially when caught in Feinberg's gaze.

Extratextually, presuming such a place outside "text" is even possible, *SBB* has been slightly more productive. Less than two years after its publication, well-known lesbian poet Minnie Bruce Pratt (1995) published a collection of vignettes called *S/HE*. Pratt's book finally settled gossipy rumours that she and Leslie Feinberg had become lovers. What initially functioned as a network of information – that is, what was to become a very public love story with both authors undertaking book tours with the other and so on – eventually became a much larger incitement to reverse-discourse and to what I have been calling onto-performative and meta-rearticulations. In other words, the event of *SBB* has grafted that invisible subject of fem(me)ininity onto masculinity, from which fem(me) eventually separates.

S/HE is a collection of photo-poetic snapshots that is hailed by and writes back to *SBB*. Pratt writes about the ways in which she reads herself into *SBB* and, conversely, the way *SBB* is productive of her desire. Of a particularly memorable and public reading, where she heard Feinberg read excerpts from *SBB*, Pratt writes the following:

> Standing in the pit of the auditorium, you are someone I don't know yet, handsome in silky shirt and tie, hair clipped close almost as skin on your fine-boned head. You read a story about bar raids in the '50s, a dawn scene on the street between a butch just released from jail and the woman who has waited for her, who now smooths her shirt and mourns the bloodstains that will never wash out. As you read, I am the woman who touches the shirt, startled to be so translated to a place I think I've never been ... In the dim light of the auditorium, you see me standing in your past. (65)

Acknowledging that she is not a "femme from the old days," Pratt resists and repudiates Feinberg's misreading of her in letters, "to write to correct you, to explain about my lesbian-feminist coming-out" (65). Nevertheless, Pratt remains hailed and *S/HE* becomes one of the first texts to delineate fem(me)ininity outside of a masculine gaze.[17]

Curiously, this particular scenario from *SBB* is referenced repeatedly, where a woman or femme, depending on who is telling the story, waits for the butch who has just been released from jail and whose shirt is covered with bloodstains. In Jess's letter at the beginning of *SBB* she writes: "I remember when we got outside to the parking lot you stopped and put your hands on my shoulders and avoided my eyes. You gently rubbed the bloody places on my shirt and said, 'I'll never get these stains out.' Damn anyone who thinks that means you were relegated in life to worrying about my ring-around-the-collar" (Feinberg 1993, 10). Like Mary in *The Well*, who similarly undertook the task of mending Stephen's clothing (one of the primary signifiers of masculinity), Theresa (in *SBB*) and Pratt (reading herself into the scene) seem to organize their desire around masculinity's most visible sign – clothing. What makes this particular realization of fem(me)ininity slightly different is its ironic relation to the narratives of femininity. "Ring around the collar" is a phrase from a television commercial that sold a stain-removal product and whose narrative spun around the neurosis of a white, middle-class suburban housewife who worried constantly about the obviousness of sweat stains on her husband's white work-shirts. Of course, the stain on the butch's white shirt is a bloodstain, left there after yet another brutal beating, and it signifies daily and unavoidable trauma. The femme's ironic resignification of this popular advertising jingo both queers and eroticizes gender in the face of a daily onslaught of hostilities. It also witnesses female masculinity's vulnerabilities in a context where, as I have suggested already, such vulnerabilities appear in what Biddy Martin (1996, 41) calls a mediated form that carefully orchestrates and limits the conditions for contact.

> You ran a bath for me with sweet-smelling bubbles. You laid out a fresh pair of white BVD's and a T-shirt for me and left me alone to wash off the first layer of shame. I remember, it was always the same. I would put on the briefs, and then I'd just get the T-shirt over my head and you would find some reason to come into the bathroom, to get something or put something away. In a glance, you would memorize the wounds on my body like a road map. (Feinberg 1993, 9)

If gender is, as Butler (1991, 25) suggests, the repeated stylization of the body, then "heterogendered" desire is a fairly precise and culturally prescribed stylization and eroticization of psychological processes (Martin 1996, 42). In all of the texts under consideration here, masculinity is represented as a woundedness where it manages the presentation of that vulnerability without being reduced to it and, ultimately, controls it by orchestrating and limiting the terms of contact and attachment. Fem(me)ininity, at least as it is imagined by a masculine gaze, is represented as possessing a stoic and quiet strength that tends and witnesses those wounds. As Biddy Martin suggests, it is masculinity's greatest triumph to prevail over those same vulnerabilities and dependencies:

> Like the Lost Boys, the wounded [butch] is inhibited from making it completely alone; he expresses a need and a longing, a loss that primarily ... the girls ... can help heal, by sympathizing, admiring, and worrying. [His] wound accounts for his dependence on others without jeopardizing his capacity for independence and heroics. To survive and flourish, he must, after all, return to the game and prevail – prevail not only over his opponents but also over his own vulnerabilities and his dependence on others. (40)

Indeed, this may well be the case of that which is excluded or which cannot appear in gender identifications, signified in *SBB* by the bracketed and feminizing "e" on Jesse when Jess is passing as male, returning to constitute desire. Or, to phrase this as does Butler (1991, 25): "That which is excluded for a given gender presentation to 'succeed' may be precisely what is played out sexually." In this case, what returns are masculine dependencies and fem(me) sexual power.

> Later, in bed, you held me gently, caressing me everywhere, the tenderest touches reserved for the places I was hurt ... You didn't flirt with me right away, knowing I wasn't confident enough to feel sexy. But slowly you coaxed my pride back out again by showing me how much you wanted me. You knew it would take you weeks again to melt the stone ... Only you could melt this stone. (Feinberg 1993, 9-11)

If Halberstam (1998a, 2) is correct in arguing that the best way to discern masculinity is by analyzing it at a distance from the body authorized to perform it (the discursively produced male body), then the subjects of female masculinity remain bound by the same contradictions as does male-embodied masculinity. There is a contradiction that functions to constitute the male subject, and that is the imperative to *not be the feminine* (the object of desire) but, rather, to successfully *identify with the masculine,* which, because of a profound ambivalence, is not fully possible either. The problem is that, in order to differentiate themselves from, and even overthrow, the father, men of any gender must find a way to become different men from those in the generation before them. But in all of these novels, fathers, including the aristocratic father of *The Well* (Philip), have a way of destroying themselves (Sonny) or being destroyed by social conditions (Jess's father). Thus, it seems that asserting power over the father becomes a productive impossibility. Martin ultimately fails to accomplish this assertion but also decides not to return to England for complete sex reassignment surgery. Like Stephen, he refuses the *command* from medical and psychiatric discourse to fully align power, heteronormativity, and anatomy. Unlike Stephen, Martin makes the No Man's Land between genders qua countries his own "sacred" country:

> Sterns sends me a command. He says: "It's time to come home. It's time to go on with your life." He believes I should have what he calls "reconstructive surgery." He thinks I am one of the few female-to-male transsexuals for whom the creation of a penis is of critical importance. This penis [would be] real flesh, my flesh, moved and sculpted ... Sterns believes that I will never be happy until I am capable of [being a woman's lover] ... He thinks this is what I keep dreaming about ... I tell Sterns in a letter that I have no desire to return to England. (Tremain 1992, 352-3)

What Martin keeps dreaming about is revealed in the novel's ending. Where Jess's and Stephen's birth parents fall out of the picture, Martin's mother remains an integral part of the text and, indeed, of Martin. In fact, her first words to Martin end the text: "Tomorrow was the word I kept using. I'd say: 'Tomorrow, I will do something about Mary'" (362). Estelle decides to write a message on a home-made greeting card, although we do not know for sure that she actually sends it. The act of writing the card is a complex one for Estelle, who similarly fails to find an adequate language with which to speak but who nevertheless names Martin in a second-person, epistolary speech act:

> It is easier to write a greetings card in the mind than it is to actually write it. The message in the mind can always be altered. It can go through any number of invisible revisions. It could be metaphorical or fantastical ... The act of writing it has changed it. It isn't really what you meant to say. It isn't even a greeting. I stare at it. I read it again and again and again, until the words have no meaning at all: "Dear Martin, Please forgive me. I hope you can. From your mother, Estelle." ... At least the writing is quite neat. That's something. It doesn't look as though it's been written by a mad person but only by a woman with no imagination. (362-3)

But words do have meaning, especially the word "Martin." While Estelle does write the word "Martin," the world of Martin does not supersede the reality of Mary in the same way that, in *SBB,* Al superseded the world of "Allison." The supposedly real and self-evident world continues to be privileged over the supposedly non-visible, and Estelle, whose name means "guiding star," fails to reconcile with Martin.

Where Martin's "No" fates him to almost complete social isolation, Jess's failure to fully become a man eventually acts as a catalyst for sociality. Jess's ultimate rejection of the categorical imperatives of masculinity does not end the novel. In a moment of profound crisis, in which s/he could no longer see he/rself in a mirror, s/he remembers both he/rself, but also Stephen, in the mirror, "the child who couldn't be catalogued ... I saw her standing in front of her own mirror, in her father's suit" (Feinberg 1993, 222). Those necessary and, I argue, productive conceptual failures, the inability to be catalogued or languaged, would be undermined if Jess continued he/r transition into manhood. Jess does not return to an originary beginning. S/he he/rself realizes that s/he, in fact, could not "go home. I wasn't traveling backward. I was hurtling forward toward a destination I couldn't see" (223). That destination is in a queer New York that emerges post-lesbian-feminism – a time and place unimaginable to Jess, one both outside the novel's frame of reference and still strangely anticipated by its metatextual ending: "Was it my imagination or were a few of the young women butch, a few femme?" It is precisely this butch-femme community that appeared during the late 1980s and early 1990s that was to call *SBB* their own.

Even though Jess remains a figure out of time, s/he eventually works to find friends and employment in New York. He/r community is built around Ruth, a *male-to-femme* trans-sexual woman, while s/he also finds employment as a typesetter. Jess is able to work with Ruth to resolve questions that remain inarticulate. Where once Jess was unable to find he/r way into language and representation ("There's things that happened to me because I'm a he-she that I've never talked about ... I've never had the words ... I needed my own words" [275]), s/he is able to now find a way to re-present he/rself and he/r past. Where Jess lived in a world where he/r identity existed outside of language and text, he/r work as a typesetter, setting type in relief and in the proper order for printing, provides for he/r entry into the symbolic order. Just as Jess lived on the boundaries that regulate normative gender identities and function as their inverse opposite, so s/he now works at night setting in relief the code that made printed language possible: "At night I lived inside the coding strings, my face illuminated by the ghostly light of the terminal. The code phrases became my poetry. The curves of type against space sang to me: the melody meant everything, the words meant very little" (263). Jess *labours* to manifest histories – the very ones that produce he/r – to materialize that which functions as a necessary Other to heteronormative cultures: "At work, when everyone else is at lunch, I've been typesetting all the history that I've found, trying to make it look as important as it feels to me. That is what I want to leave behind" (271).

Jess is able to take the inverted and abject shadows of the world and reveal them as an important part of the machineries that allow the so-called "real" to function as the real. One of the most profound scenes in the novel occurs when Jess visits Butch Al in a mental asylum. The shadows compete with the supposedly "real" when Jess manipulates the master's tools by passing as "Allison's nephew" to call Al back for one last good-bye (Lorde 1984, 122). Both of these worlds compete in this scene for dominance, even as Allison eclipses Butch Al:

> Al was locked up in a fortress ... "Al," I said softly. I looked around, but no one was paying any attention to us ... "Al, it's me, Jess. Maybe you don't recognize me, but maybe if you looked at me you would." Al didn't move ... I put my hand ever so gently on Al's arm and looked long and hard at her profile. (Feinberg 1993, 287)

In that moment, Allison continues to eclipse Al just as the real eclipsed the shadow, and as Martin continues to be *disappeared* by Mary in *SC*. An old *woman*, not butch Al, sits tied to a hospital chair and Jess(e) almost completely gives up on seeing he/r mentor Al.

> "I'm sorry," I said, "forgive me, Al. This was selfish. I didn't realize until just now ... Go back to wherever you go. I'm sorry." (288)

But in that moment, Butch Al reappears out of Allison's body.

> "It's OK, kid," a familiar old friend's voice said. "It's alright." I looked up and saw Butch Al smiling at me. The tears streamed down my face. She wiped them with one hand ... "You look nice," she said. "Can anybody else see you, or just me?" "I'm real, but only you can see me." Al nodded and turned back to the window. "We're from the old days." An emotional storm cloud passed over her face. "Leave the old days alone. Don't bring me back, I'm dead." ... "Al," I said, but her spirit had left like the wind slamming a door shut. "Al?" [But] she's gone. (288)

In a dream that turns Plato's allegory of the cave inside out by suggesting that the world outside the cave is only "real" if its inverted and necessary Other is not, Jess rearticulates the terms of the shadowy and supposedly "un-real" world around he/r relative to the world that s/he and Al were necessary to but from which they were excluded.[18]

> There were people all around who were different like me. We could all see our reflections in the faces of those who sat in this circle ... One of the oldest in the circle caught my eyes ... She held up an object. I understood I was supposed to accept the realness of this object. I looked more closely. It was the ring that the Dineh women gifted me with as an infant ... She

> pointed to the circle the ring cast on the ground. I nodded, acknowledging that the shadow was as real as the ring. She smiled and waved her hand in the space between the ring and its shadow. *Isn't this distance also real?* She indicated our circle. I looked at the faces around me. I followed the shadow of her hand against the wall of the hut, seeing for the first time the shadows surrounding us ... *Aren't these connected, she asked wordlessly?* (300-1)

Jess's letter to Theresa, which prefaces the novel but which is actually written at its end, marks the emergence of a different time and place, one whose frame of reference is both remembered and memorialized by Feinberg's novel. The irony of the reception of *SBB* is that it also helped to reanimate butch-femme cultures as it looped back through these archives. Curiously, though, Jess functions, in the end, as both subjected to and alienated by that same world. Late in the novel, Jess emerges from a subway entrance to hear a gay and lesbian demonstration. S/he eventually speaks at that rally, which, as many trans-sexual theorists document and which Jess alludes to, both welcomes and excludes subjects such as he/r. The irony of Jess's impromptu speech at the rally is that s/he still must articulate (i.e., language he/rself) *out* of the binds of even queer misreadings in order to be intelligible: "The woman who was chairing looked at me. 'Did you want to speak?' I nodded, dizzy with anxiety. 'C'mon up, brother,' she urged me." Jess begins he/r speech with yet another in a long series of onto-performative articulations, only this one functions as a repudiation first: "I'm not a gay man" (296). Those misreadings are the beginnings of new disidentifications, articulations, alliances.

> "My name's Beatrice. I really like what you said." I shook her hand and found her power in the sureness of her grip. "You been out a long time, huh?" she asked me. I didn't know if she meant how long I'd been gay or how long I'd stood and watched the gay movement from the outside. Both were true. (297)

Like *The Well*, both *SC* and *SBB* remain bound by their discursive frames of reference and dialogic articulations. They are constituted, however, at least to a certain extent, by a collapse of the temporal and geographical moments out of which their subjects emerge. While it might be excessive to say that each narrative marks the end of history, it is entirely possible that they both mark the end of historical time as their subjects experience it. Each of these subjects by necessity disarticulates and rearticulates the terms of its own unthinkability, unlearning the supposedly self-evident certainties of the genders overdetermined by the sex/gender system and replacing them with what that system needs to repudiate in order to function. Martin and Jess both accomplish what was unthinkable for Stephen Gordon as he stood in front of his mirror attempting to language himself out of the shadows and into existence. Martin and Jess both refuse the impossibilities of supposedly self-evident certainties. All through *SC* Walter, who, like Mary, similarly escapes Swaithey to transform himself into something new – a country music star – puns on the instabilities and multiple meanings associated with the word "country." Referencing both nation and a particular genre of American rural song, Walter's world of country music mirrors Mary Martin's quest not only to escape but also to contest the limitations of a language that claims she cannot exist. "Country" music becomes a metaphor for the process of self-invention, the limitations of which Martin unthinks. As Martin prepares to leave the past (England) for what he hopes will be his utopic and imaginary sacred country (Tennessee, United States of America), he reunites with Walter, who gives him the names of friendly places in Nashville: "You go in there and hang around. People are kinder there," Walter tells Martin. When Martin asks why, Walter responds that it is because "they are country people." "Swaithey people are 'country people'," responds Martin, confused about what exactly it is that Walter references by the term "country." Walter explains to Martin that he means "country" to signify not only a geographical entity but also a lifestyle and identity (country-and-western music people). Walter maps both of these meanings – that is, country-and-music culture and England as the old past country – onto regimes of knowledge, a re-charting that allows Martin to hope that his arrival in Nashville will articulate new possibilities: "It's not the same. Swaithey people think they know things. They think they've got everything mapped out. Country Music isn't about knowing things, it's about knowing nothing and discovering everything for the first time" (Tremain 1992, 267).

By the end of the novel, Martin's refusal of complete reassignment surgery allows him to remap gender, starting with his own intersexed status (neither one gender nor the other but both) from an imaginary No Man's Land. Whereas *SBB* ends with Jess "unioning" not necessarily with transgender activists but, rather, with Duffy in order to work as a union organizer in the city (Feinberg 1993, 299), *SC* returns Martin to an almost isolated life on a small Tennessee work farm. *The Well* and *SBB* end with different visions of community, each doing different kinds of cultural work. In Hall's (1928) text the vision is one in which Stephen, as both invert and artist, imagines his prophetic role as authorized by "the quick, the dead, and the yet unborn ... [S]he could see their marred and reproachful faces with the haunted, melancholy eyes of the invert – eyes that had looked too long on a world that lacked all pity and all understanding"

(436). Stephen emerges from his vision with his purpose as artist clearly defined: "there was only one voice, one demand; her own voice into which those millions had entered ... 'Give us also the right to our existence!'" (437). Similarly, Jess writes he/r letter to Theresa and sends it to the Lesbian Herstory Archive in New York City, established by Joan Nestle, whose own writings helped to theorize and authenticate butch-femme sexual cultures. *SBB* also ends with Jess working as a union organizer to ally with union men and women in a class-based infrastructure to "labour" across differences within class. Duffy, Jess's long-time union organizer, narrates his own violent experiences with a communist panic, similar to the moral panic against which Jess fought: "'Got red-baited out of the bindery where we used to work,' Duffy explained. 'I got kind of burned out, drank too much. Then I quit drinking and got that job organizing, and I'm still working for the same union'" (Feinberg 1993, 298).

If *SBB* ends with the image of a union across differences as a solution to a communist panic, then *SC* ends with an entirely different kind of union. I have said that *SC* ends with Martin living an "almost" isolated life on a farm in a wishful nowhere found in Tennessee in order to foreground my own ideological occlusions when reading this text. In an earlier draft of this chapter, I had misread where Martin actually lives. If being "Mary" means living in an alien body complete with the two white egg-like substances on her chest, then to be Martin means not only to no longer have breasts but also to (metaphorically) change colour; that is, gender changes, at least those that transform "Mary" into "Martin," are racialized in this text. While living in Tennessee, Martin becomes a labourer on the farm of an old white judge, Judge Riveaux, at a place that reminds Martin of his father's farm in Swaithey: "There's no garden, just as there was no real garden at Swaithey" (Tremain 1992, 348). Martin agrees to work for Judge Riveaux alongside his other farm labourers, a black couple (Jeremiah and Beulah) and their two children. What's significant about this family is that Jeremiah (a name that seems dramatically out of place in the 1970s in Tennessee) becomes Martin's immediate boss. Seeming as if they have just stepped out of a Faulkner novel, Jeremiah and Beulah speak in a broken English while working beside Martin: "An' she' right. I got some reasons. One reason I got is her [Beulah]. An' Mrs Riveaux, Miz Judge, she always did every way treat me fair" (351). Jeremiah and Beulah have become a kind of substitute family for Martin as he begins and ends his days working as if he were a black labourer/servant on the estate of a white patriarch in the southern United States. For Martin, the United States becomes a utopic, imaginary, and sacred country of rebirth.

The subjects of female masculinity articulate self/selves as that which exists in that gap between the body and the flesh, in the space between the real and the shadow. These formerly impossible but new subjects are no longer marked by Stephen's long scar across his forehead but, instead, are a new gender marked by sacred scars across their chests. These are the telling and productive failures of female masculinity, where butches and FTMs function in a "country" where all men fail but where only a few are man enough to enjoy it.

4
Boys Do Cry: Hilary Swank and the Politics of a Pronoun

Boys Don't Cry and Bodies in Crisis

In his review of *Boys Don't Cry*, J. Hoberman (n.d.) writes:

> Coproduced by the tireless Christine Vachon, *Boys Don't Cry* has a family resemblance to *I Shot Andy Warhol*, which she produced in 1996 [both produced by the production company Killer Films]. Like the Warhol film, *Boys Don't Cry* is a polished first feature, ripped from the headlines and constructed around a stellar stunt performance. More crucially, both movies are intelligently glamorous evocations of sexual insurrection. But where Valerie Solanas the antiheroine of *I Shot Andy Warhol* was her own ideologue, the surreal being at the heart of *Boys Don't Cry* left no text ... (n.p.)

The understated but very successful film by first-time director and Columbia University film student Kimberly Peirce won not only critical acclaim but also mass media attention when its lead actress, Hilary Swank, won an Academy Award and became "a household name ... and the toast of the town as one of the most acclaimed actresses of the year" (Hollywood.com web site). On the night of the 2000 Academy Awards female masculinity; the events in Falls City, Nebraska, on 31 December 1993; and the dynamic duo of Swank and Peirce took centre stage. "We have arrived!" was the banner e-mail on one trans-gender/trans-sexual listserv the next morning.

Such an arrival makes Hoberman's assertion that "the surreal being at the heart of this film left no text behind" even more ironic. Disregarding the adjective "surreal" as text, it is obvious that there is not an absence of text about this being but, rather, a wild proliferation of discourse, an excess of texts – in fact, so many competing, contradictory, and sometimes acrimonious texts that they confound even my attempts to avoid those discourses by, at least temporarily, not naming this subject. To name this subject is to hail it into subjectivity and discourse; but naming can also threaten closure and summary. To refer to our subject as "he, Brandon Teena," is to surely evoke one text – Brandon as a boy, as a heterosexual boy – an assignation dramatically different from "she, Teena Brandon," lesbian passing as a boy; or "s/he, Teena Brandon," butch dyke; or "he, Billy Teena," the "trailer-park Romeo," all actual names that this subject used at different times in his and/or her young life. As I explained in my introductory chapter, these are precisely the same knowledge-producing and discursive operations that invest subjectivities with contradictory currency.

In her acceptance speech at the Academy Awards, Hilary Swank made an important intervention/interruption in this scenario by eulogizing the political text she thinks our subject left behind: "And last, but certainly not least, I want to thank Brandon Teena for being such an inspiration to us all. His legacy lives on through our movie to remind us to always be ourselves, to follow our hearts, to not conform. I pray for the day when we not only accept our differences, but we actually celebrate our diversity." Swank was, of course, acknowledging the price Brandon paid for bequeathing that legacy. By the end of the week immediately following the Academy Awards, Swank was sharply criticized by Brandon's mother for using male pronouns to refer to Brandon. Swank quickly responded to her criticism by issuing a public apology to Brandon's family for supposedly "misrepresenting" him by using a masculine pronoun (beatboxbetty, n.d.).

Similarly, Peirce, as filmmaker, is not without controversy; currently her work is drawing legal protests both from the people whose lives and real names she uses in the film and from Aphrodite Jones (1996), a journalist who wrote a nonfiction book about Brandon's life and death and who claims she owns the "life rights" of the major characters in the narrative. Jones *owns* the legal right to tell the working-class stories of the Brandon family, the Tisdel[1] sisters, and the other major players in the story of Brandon's life and death. If Jones does not get paid first, no one can be paid, including the actors in *Boys Don't Cry* (hereafter *BDC*) but also, for instance, the Tisdel sisters, who signed story rights over to Jones. Despite the class-based gaze of this story evident in descriptors like "Romeo and Juliet in a trailer-park," the ownership of these "life stories" inflects this situation with class politics right from the start (Ebert 1999, n.p.). While Jones's book was the first, she paid for her rights in an economy where it seemed no one would be concerned about what happened in Falls City, where these working-class lives are measured in dollar-values all the time. The former sentiment proved wrong, but the latter remains profoundly and ironically accurate.

One of these characters who no longer owns the right to her own story is Lana Tisdel, Brandon's lover, who has also filed suit against Peirce. Her chief complaints about Peirce's movie are that it puts her at the scene of the murders and shows her doing little to help afterwards; Tisdel also claims that the final love scene in the film between Lana and Brandon is a fiction that implies that she (Lana) is a lesbian, something she continues to deny (Beaird n.d., n.p.). I return to a discussion of Lana later in this chapter; at this point, however, I want to flag the differences between Lana Tisdel as a character in the film and Lana Tisdel as the actual off-screen person who was Brandon's lover. Peirce's film follows unwittingly in the same footsteps as Feinberg's and Hall's novels in that readings of their work suffer from a blurring of reality and fiction (in so far as these can be separated). While almost all of *Masculinities without Men?* has explored prose narrative, I am drawn to Peirce's film because it shares tropes, codes, discourses, and voices with the three prose narratives; more important, it works those codes and tropes through the same discourses of race, class, and gender – a reorganization that foregrounds the function of the gaze in mediating ideologies, subjectivities, and narratives.

Confusions over Brandon emerge at two other places. A recent *A&E American Justice* mini-documentary interviewed one member of the jury that convicted Tom Nissen and John Lotter for murdering Brandon. This person talked about the profound confusions caused by the lack of a stable referent. To be specific, that juror discussed the ways that the shifting pronouns in the courtroom almost resulted in a "hung jury." Some people referred to Teena, some to Brandon, others talked about the deceased as a "he," some as a "she." Many times the jury had to stop the proceedings to ask for clarification about who was actually referenced by the pronouns. In *BDC*, this kind of heteroglossia plays out in different ways. In an early scene in the film, for example, Brandon, who is already passing as male, defends a potential love interest against the unwanted advances of a very large man in a bar. Seconds before the man throws the first punch at Brandon, he yells, "You got to be kidding, you little fag!" The confused epithet marks Brandon as a site where queer identities, unbeknownst to the characters in the narrative, come full circle to a dialogic heterosexuality; it also marks Brandon's success at creating a verisimilitude of soft heterosexual masculinity, an identity overdetermined as failed masculinity.

The destabilized and destabilizing pronoun referents of any conversation about Brandon reveal the complexities of the texts that he left behind and the challenges that those texts create for the relationships between language, subjectivities, and bodies. As border wars, they demonstrate the overdetermined link between narrative and truth. Numerous filmmakers are seeking to present different versions of Brandon's narrative. These versions compete not only for ownership of the dead but also for the means of reproducing the so-called truth about Brandon. The filmmakers of *The Brandon Teena Story* fight with Kimberly Peirce in the pages of the gay magazine *The Advocate* over who has told the "real" story of Brandon (Muska and Olafsdottir n.d.). Susan Muska and Greta Olafsdottir claim that *BDC* lacks a moral point of view and a political critique of what happened to Brandon. As it turns out, Muska and Olafsdottir themselves had optioned and sold the rights to their documentary to Hollywood producer Don Murphy, a project also eclipsed by Peirce's film; apparently they are not pleased with the success of *BDC* (Glitz n.d., n.p.).

The recent disputes over Brandon Teena's textuality allow me to return to the argument I outlined in my introduction. Both Brandon and Peirce's film are situated discursively within No Man's Land, where "authentic" masculinity is under dispute and where the supposedly self-evident relation between male subjectivity, physicality, and power is contested. In this chapter I want to do a number of things. First, I want to reiterate my argument that, in the No Man's Land between lesbian masculinity, trans-sexual masculinity, and (for lack of a better term, where that "lack" is significant) "male masculinity," subjects only temporarily secure meaning by evoking and then repudiating one of the others. Second, I want to recall that three people were killed in that farmhouse on 31 December 1993: Candace, Brandon, and Phillip DeVine, a young black man who was a lover of Lana Tisdel's sister, Leslie. Phillip's death is not depicted in *BDC*. It is important to theorize this racial occlusion and to secure it within the operations of white supremacy. Finally, I want to return briefly to the question that haunts this entire project – that is, the ways in which masculinity is imbricated with femininity and, in the case of female masculinity, with femme. My argument remains simple: that to name the film's subjects, like any of the subjects in the texts under discussion, with even the smallest and apparently most self-evident signifier(s) available in language (i.e., with a pronoun[s]) is to overdetermine that subject as text, as subjectivity, in discourse.

Operations of language both rely on but resist, claim but refuse, subjectivity at the moment of its most profound but most productive derisions – something that began with late nineteenth-century sexology. Hoberman's (n.d.) assertion notwithstanding, Brandon functions as a metatext, always already overdetermined as text but, at the same time, putting that text into crisis. To frame this axiom slightly differently: the utterance of a pronoun can be likened to *parole,* which simultaneously references *langue,* that supposedly transcendental ground that secures the meaning of the *parole* in the body. Once named, each pronoun as signifier (i.e., "he, Brandon Teena" or "she, Teena Brandon") does at least two kinds of cultural work: each functions as the fruition and limit of the discourses underwriting the sex/gender system. But each utterance also functions to radically interrupt those discourses – an interruption that signals the entry into the mainstream of subcultural identities and categories. This entrance is marked by a non-linear temporality (Foucault reminds us that "discourse is not life; its time is not yours" [quoted in Butler 1993, 223]) and by a parasitic deconstructive series of operations that illustrate Bakhtin's (1984, 202-3) assertion that, "when one finds a word, one finds it already inhabited ... every thought, feeling and experience must be refracted through the medium of someone else's discourse, someone else's style, someone else's manner [so much so that] almost no word is without its intense sideward glance at someone else's." While that occupation of language in No Man's Land proved fatal for Brandon, it provides important texts to both *think and unthink*.

But let me "up the anti" on these discursive battles (de Lauretis 1990, 255). If, in No Man's Land, we can no longer use the body as a foundational guarantor of gender, and if we can no longer measure the former by the latter (or vice versa), then what secures the other performances of gender that are the secondary effects of that supposed foundation – identities such as lesbian, butch, femme, heterosexual? What is it that might distinguish lesbian from woman, trans-sexual masculinity from butch masculinity, trans-sexual man from bio-boy, lesbian femininity from heterosexual femininity? Performances of masculinity, female and otherwise, in *BDC* foreground its many registers. Recall that Sedgwick (1995) names these registers threshold effects, places where incremental movement along one dimension (say, for instance, Brandon as a butch lesbian) suddenly appears as a variable on an entirely different dimension (Brandon as a heterosexual boy). In terms of gender, Sedgwick advises, it is sometimes necessary to cross over the threshold of one thing (lesbian masculinity), or flip its switch from on to off, in order to register on another scale completely (heterosexual masculinity). In her performance of female masculinity in *BDC*, Swank accomplishes "realness effects" akin to those of the drag kings who create an illusion, or simulacrum, of a reality that is better or more real than the so-called original. Part of the "surprise" of her performance is that it accomplishes this without the "layering" that often helps drag kings to achieve verisimilitude. Unlike many, but not all, drag kings, Swank seems to identify as female and feminine; she had to find her way onto a map of masculinity,[2] and then enter a portal to female masculinity, and then "switch off" in order to register as simply masculine. In other words, to roughly rearticulate Sedgwick, the rheostat that might adjust the seamless gradations from femininity to female masculinity to, in this case, heterosexual masculinity ("man") seemingly had to be interrupted by the on/off switch of woman first, lesbian second (18).

If, as I have been arguing, the body is not the stabilizer of gender, then what is? Butler, Sedgwick, S. Hall, Bakhtin, and many others might agree that one of the most frequently used stabilizers of gender is discourse and, specifically, narrative. Subjects either recognize or misrecognize themselves in femininities and masculinities that constitute us and that we, in turn, rearticulate (Sedgwick 1995, 19). In an undergraduate English course entitled "Recent Women's Fiction," and in which I taught *SC*, I posed two questions to my students: (1) "Would I be able to recognize myself if I were not my gender?" and (2) "How do you know you are your gender?" One of the more interesting answers was: "identity is like an image of yourself that you want to move towards. This is what I was thinking about in class when you asked, 'How do any of you know you are your gender?' My immediate response was, well I know I'm a girl cause I know that I want to be a girl, and it's a constant working towards that image of what I want to be, while recognizing it as a desire, not a stable core." In *BDC* Brandon recognizes himself as boy through a negation: "I'm not a dyke," which also means, "I'm not a woman." As we proceed to watch him watch himself in mirrors, comb his hair in a more masculine way, bind his breasts and stuff his pants with a pair of socks, we read him moving towards an image he has of himself. Not only does a dynamic of self-recognition or misrecognition articulate the meeting place of discourse, subjectivity, and physicality, but that dynamic is only knowable as and through those articulations. One of the heady pleasures of *BDC* lies in watching Brandon elaborate that fantasy of himself as a boy; that pleasure is equalled later by devastation as the camera's gaze is complicit with the shattering of that fantasy.

One of the most telling and non-verbal articulations in *BDC* occurs in and around the stylization and recognition of Brandon's hair as masculine. The necessity of a masculine hair-cut resonates from the opening words of the movie to the final murder scene; in many ways, the style of Brandon's hair constructs part of the newly emerging cultural identity of "boy." While there tends to be a somewhat disturbing uniformity amongst the subjects of femininity in the film (Lana's mother, Kate, Candace, and Lana), masculinity ranges from the stereotypical constructions of working-class men as drunken truckers; to rough, violent "rednecks" like Nissen, Lotter, and the boys who chase Brandon through the trailer park yelling "dyke" and "faggot"; to inept law enforcement officers (Sheriff Laux); to Brandon, the teenage, non-phallic, sweet, good-looking, charming young boy with small hands, good hair, a tidy appearance – one who, above all, treats women with respect. Swank's portrayal of Brandon both relies on and queers the new teenage "boy," the "not-male" pin-up, whose appeal is similar to that of Leonardo DiCaprio or the proliferating boy-bands. These teen idols and objects of teenage girl(-power) fandom and consumption are sexualized through a feminizing gaze to safely threaten with the qualities they lack: phallic power (Studlar and Sandler 1999, 9).

In *BDC* we first encounter Brandon as a voice saying "shorter" at the beginning of the film. When the credits stop rolling, we realize that Brandon is instructing his cousin to cut his hair even shorter. As he looks into the mirror, he continues to style his hair until he is satisfied that it looks convincingly masculine. The scene then cuts to a roller rink where Brandon, who will eventually introduce himself as Billy, is to meet a young girl named Nicole. Brandon is wearing a curious outfit as he approaches the rink doors – a western shirt and a very large cowboy hat that his cousin eventually pulls off his head. Brandon attempts to pass as a country-and-western cowboy,[3] the likes of which we have seen already in *Sacred Country,* when Walter transforms himself into a country singer. As "Billy" walks towards Nicole, who is standing with a group of her girlfriends talking about the qualities that make up her "dream" boy, we overhear her conversation: "Yeah, that's okay," she says, "as long as he's sweet and has good hair, that's important."

Throughout the film we see Brandon repeatedly looking at himself in mirrors, continually combing and recombing his hair into a more masculine style in order to achieve "good hair." Brandon's sense of himself as an object of (adolescent) desire is evident in these looking relations, where the camera feminizes him as a subject of non-phallic masculinity through its gaze as we watch him watching himself be watched (Berger 1972, 46). But Brandon also possesses a masculine gaze himself. He seduces Lana by watching her sing karaoke (a country song that later plays after the murder scene just before the closing credits) and then by chasing her around the yard of her mother's house as he takes Polaroid pictures of her. The film's gaze also focuses exclusively on Lana's face and breasts during their first sex scene to show the effects of the very thing Brandon is not supposed to possess – phallic power. During that scene we see Brandon have oral sex with Lana but we also see him reach into his pants just before the camera cuts to Lana's face while he presumably enters her with a penis/dildo. These contradictory-looking relations further the gender instabilities already present in both the film and Brandon's identity. In the end, after the rape has occurred in Falls City and Brandon has been outed, it is his hairstyle that most disturbs Lana, even after she has made love to him. Lana and Brandon are planning to leave Falls City; Lana is packing her things and Brandon sneaks in through her bedroom window to help her pack. He attempts to kiss her and Lana turns away, asking, "Did you do something to your hair?" Brandon answers, "I don't know ... but I'll try to put it back," and proceeds to correct his hair in the mirror. Hairstyles in this film, especially Brandon's, function to demarcate the space of boy relative to other masculinities.

Such gender instabilities are further evident in two dialogic utterances in the film: "I'm not a dyke" and "I have a sexual identity crisis." These function as double-voicing articulations, sites where stabilizing (centripetal, moving towards centre) and destabilizing (centrifugal, out from centre) conceptualizing impulses collide. These utterances substantiate Foucault's (1985) assertion that language as discourse is productive, and Bakhtin's

(1981) primary axiom that the utterance always evokes its present, past, and possible future contexts. Butler (1991, 18) performs the productivity of language in the forceful but almost annoying disavowal for which she is most famous: "Who or what is it that is out, made manifest and fully disclosed, when and if I reveal myself as lesbian ... To claim that this is what I am is to suggest a provisional totalization of this 'I' ... such a statement presupposes that the I exceeds its determination, and even produces that very excess in and by the act which seeks to exhaust the semantic field of that 'I.'" Butler's remarks allow that the constitutive nature of the word signifies multiple meanings and traces of its past usages, refuting yet affirming those echoes, traces, and reverberations as it inevitably relies on them. If language is the space of confrontation of differently oriented accents, then by rearticulating and "re-languaging," subjects reconfigure both the social context in which speech occurs and themselves. To repeat: these transformations are what constitute language as dialogic.

The contestation and rearticulation of gender variant subjectivities in language – intersexual individuals; non-operative, pre-operative and post-operative FTM and MTF trans-sexuals; trans-gendered people – which exist outside of a supposedly referential epistemology and linguistic system, function as touchstones for what can be (somewhat reductively) identified as the noisy and dialogic condition, if not crisis, of language and bodies in postmodernity. As I explained in Chapter 1, that crisis of language is particularly evident in the deployment of gendered pronouns. In *Masculinities without Men?* I have used pronouns strategically in order to identify tactical rearticulations of counter-discursive subjectivities and practices that have produced new social formations. In other words, if subjects are in dialogue with discourse and speak it as often as they are spoken by it, then the processes of "self-articulation," which have been the object of this book and of Peirce's film, are themselves already – indeed, always already – metadiscursive. If, as Stuart Hall (1996, 141) suggests, those articulations produce arbitrary unities out of contradictory elements, then the linkages between those unities can be broken. Hall's theory of articulation seeks to break the links between concepts that are the residue of opinion and custom.

Throughout *Masculinities without Men?* I argue that theorizing articulations and disarticulations leads inevitably to the question of how the event of *BDC* occurred when it did. How is it that this film and its narrative are intelligible at all? What are the discursive and articular relations between Brandon's deferral, "I'm not a dyke," and his confession to Sheriff Laux that he has a "sexual identity crisis"? Does one of these utterances secure the other? And how can that summary be secured, especially in No Man's Land? Are butch and female-to-male trans-sexuality as much at odds with each other in No Man's Land as is trans-sexual boy with bio-boy? Does "butch" capitalize on both the failed successes of "lesbian," which itself disavowed and repudiated masculinity so thoroughly as to constitute it as an absence that became a successful presence?

Barbara Johnson (1987, 16) anticipated such paradoxical questions when she wrote on the failure of success:

> If the deconstructive impulse [of female masculinity or queer theory or trans-sexual theory or performativity] is to retain its vital and subversive edge, we must become ignorant of it again and again. It is only by forgetting what we know how to do, by setting aside the thoughts that have most changed us, that those thoughts and that knowledge can go on doing what a surprise encounter with otherness should do, that is, lay bare some hint of an ignorance one never knew one had.

BDC performs the imperative, both pedagogical and political, of reading for productive ignorance and surprise, of reading for both the radical instabilities and yet political imperatives of the body and, in this case, its death, as an object of ignorance. With regard to my use of the term "ignorance" I refer again to Johnson, who argues that to read for ignorance means to read to un-know, "to become conscious of the fact that what one thinks is knowledge is really an array of received ideas, prejudices and opinions – a way of not knowing that one does not know. Thus, the question is not of how to transmit but of how to suspend knowledge" (84-5). *BDC* shows us that these identities do not pre-exist knowledge and truth regimes but, rather, are occlusions that are also co-extensive and simultaneous with, and as, their means of articulation.

To articulate or attempt to know the subjects at the heart of *BDC* – that is, subjects who are off the gender map – is to theorize how they are mostly dysfunctional elements of the sex/gender systems and knowledge regimes. However, it also means to read not what appears in or as a representation but, rather, to read for the space-off, for the blind spots of those representations. Recall that, in Chapter 3, I argued that Martin Hallam's masculinist homosocial country in *The Well* is situated in the space-off; there I borrowed from Teresa de Lauretis (1987), who poses a problem that is central to my work: how does one discern subjectivity in representational practices that always already occlude that which cannot be discerned? To frame this in de Lauretis's terms: "Most of the available theories of reading, writing, sexuality, ideology, or any other cultural production are built on ... narratives of gender ... bound by the heterosexual contract" (25). The solution de Lauretis suggests is to read them "elsewhere": "That elsewhere is not some mythic distant past or some utopian future history: it is the elsewhere of discourse here and now, the blind spots, or the space-off, of its representations. I think of it as spaces in the margins of hegemonic discourses, social spaces carved in the interstices of institutions and in the chinks and cracks of the power-knowledge apparati" (25). That space-off, or elsewhere, is the productive place within representation, especially in dialogic image-making, that is not visible in the frame but inferable from what the frame can register (26). As Peirce puts it in *BDC*, Brandon dies in Falls City, a town that Brandon's cousin tells us "isn't even on a map." Brandon dies in the space-off of American class geography, and, while Peirce puts Brandon on the map by introducing this new subject into the field of vision of American popular culture, the costs of cartographic intelligibility are high.

Throughout *Masculinities without Men?* I suggest that Rose Tremain and Leslie Feinberg complete an articulation that Radclyffe Hall begins but is not able to fully realize. When Stephen is at the mirror he is unable to articulate what is outside the frame of that mirror – his body from the waist down. A crisis over how to represent the invert, and as what, has figured as the crisis in each text, from Stephen's scene at the mirror (which fails to show his body) to Rivkele's epistemological crisis in *The God of Vengeance* (when she does not know if she is still a virgin after having had sex with a woman). Bourdet also grapples with this crisis in *The Captive,* in which Mme D'Aiguines, the invert seductress, never appears. The invert is relegated to the space-off, a place of productive possibility, where the fantasy of embodiment can be embellished. Because the invert's body is not representable in language, it remains imaginable in that space just outside the frame. Feinberg attempts to refocus the reader's gaze from that space-off to the field of vision but is unsuccessful as Jess repeatedly obsesses over her/his identity while looking into mirrors. Of all the authors under discussion, Tremain is the least anxious about Martin's body and its representability as imaginary. Recall that *Sacred Country* has no mirror scenes; in a sense, the narrative functions as a metaphorical mirror. The novel ends with Martin living and working in an imaginary Tennessee, where the reader can discern the shape of his imaginary identity more fully. After Martin's resounding "No" to Dr. Stern's suggestion that he complete his identity with a surgically created penis, the question of Martin's masculinity rarely surfaces again.

The space of identity is one site where power/knowledge regimes *work*. As such, it can also be a site of "un-knowing" – a site not of the absence of knowledge but of contradictory and unstable ambiguities that render knowledge regimes dysfunctional. The subjects of these spaces cite and articulate authoritative sex/gender discourses to enable, at the same time, resistant counter-citational disarticulations. To create "something new," as Gerald Hannon (1998) discovered when he attended the "Crossing Borders" trans-convention and reported on his experiences for *NOW Magazine,* an identity or a gender supposedly not thinkable inside the sex/gender system evokes but simultaneously repudiates – "grafts" – that new identity (trans-gender boy) onto identities (butch non-phallic masculinity and heterosexual boy) that are thinkable. The effect is to resignify what that gender looks like and, indeed, how it dys-"articulates" them as subjects similar, but ultimately not reducible, to it. Peirce makes Brandon intelligible by having him performatively cite authoritative discourses ("I'm not a dyke") to enable an articulation (Brandon as a man and boy) that severely in-site(s) and destabilizes masculinity, showing it as a category in crisis. However, as I discuss in Chapter 5, when she depicts Brandon's exposure with such verisimilitude, Peirce also forces this subject back into an economy where the penis is the ground of identity.

But Brandon also articulates himself through another utterance in the film, confirming Stuart Hall's (1981, 235) assertion that "almost every fixed inventory will betray us." This citation also signals the ambivalences at the core of those performatives. After the rape scene Brandon is interviewed by Sheriff Laux, who repudiates and reiterates the violence of the rape by blaming Brandon and berating him with questions about his gender. Brandon knows that he will not be taken seriously if he cannot make himself intelligible. This ritual accounting, like the many that take place outside of the cinema, is where the production of the unsymbolizable, the unspeakable, and the unintelligible is most articulated with, and as, social abjection. At this point, Brandon says, "I have a sexual identity crisis," drawing on the clinical language and taxonomies of psychiatry to give an accounting of himself as abject. This scene is handled with great skill by Peirce for Sheriff Laux is not depicted without his own share of abjection. Yet, at the same time, Brandon's articulations are precisely the stakes to be won or lost. Once again, clinical assessment provides intelligibility, definition, and an alibi. That alibi reworks emotional and conceptual contradictions in order to clear a space of recognition and to enable articulation. Hence the importance of this film and its mainstream recognition, or misrecognition, is the double-stake of containment and resistance that it makes inevitable. To recall Stuart Hall: popular culture is more than just one of the sites where that ambivalent struggle for and against definition is engaged; it is, in fact, the very thing to be won or lost in that struggle (1981, 259). In many ways, the fact of the movie's popularity suggests Brandon's admittedly contingent "success" in that moment.[4]

Thinking Whiteness

More troubling are two other articulations that also occur in the film. In December 1993 three people were murdered in that Nebraska farmhouse: Brandon, Candace (or Lisa), and Phillip DeVine, a young black man who was dating Lana's older sister, Leslie, and was, like Brandon, staying at Candace's. Peirce's version of these events only depicts the deaths of

Candace and Brandon. Peirce's occlusion of Phillip's death is a troubled whitewashing of the events. If, as I suggested earlier, gender functions as a threshold effect where movement along one axis can suddenly register on another, and that, in order to read for masculinity, we have to shut off the switch of femininity, then to read for race, and for whiteness as a race, the opposite is true. When reading whiteness as a race it is necessary to flip the switch from off to on, to invert a racializing gaze – to invert what is normally hypervisible (people of colour) in order to read for what is everywhere but invisible, that is, whiteness.

As a racialized identity, whiteness operates best when it cloaks itself to function not as a particular race but as *the* human race, as universal humankind. White supremacy allows whiteness to remain unmarked; it works by cloaking itself as the universal and the norm around which all other races, especially those marked by colour, supposedly circulate and define. On the one hand, white domination is reproduced by the way that white subjects colonize the definitions of normal. In this regard, Brandon's death stands in as a tragedy that can signify many other tragedies, including, apparently, Phillip's. To have depicted Phillip's death in *BDC* would require an explanation of the perceived intrusion of race into a film about gender and trans-sexuality. On the other hand, if the invisibility of whiteness colonizes the definitions of other norms, then it also marks itself as a category so that the representational power of whiteness comes precisely from its belief in itself as being so thoroughly everywhere and everything that it fails to visually register at all: hence, the assertion that this film is not about race but about gender. Yet, if the house in which the murders occurred is figured as a discursive and oppositional site, then Phillip's death was as much the effect of masculine rage as Brandon's was the effect of white rage. If Peirce chose to read through one lens at time, which she clearly did, then it possibly makes sense not to show Phillip's death. But a multi-accentuated dialogic lens that can read for complexity will show that the subjects of that site – a white working-class single mother, a black man dating a white woman, and a white trans-sexual man dating a white working-class girl – are all, at one time or another, Others necessary to a white masculinity that responds with rage to these dysfunctional realignments of power. The fact that Phillip's death is not depicted can only be read as yet another articulation of white supremacy where one identity (gender) trumps another (race) to leave whiteness invisible and naturalized.

Peirce's occlusions in the production of the film are entirely different from the kind of white class-based identities – that is, "white trash" identities – visible within the film's narrative. The term "white trash" refers to a hybrid intertwining of racial and class identities and foregrounds the contradictory and conflicting relations of power between those two sites. As Wray and Newitz (1997, 4) argue, white trash is a complex cultural category that refers both to actually existing white people living in (often rural) poverty but that also designates a set of stereotypes and myths about poor whites. The expression functions to identify that which seems unnameable: a race (white) that is used to code an economics (class) coupled with an insult that signifies excess (trash). Race functions, then, to explain that which is much harder to discern – class (8).

If race vis-à-vis Phillip's death lurks in the space-off of this film, then the symbolic location inside the film functions as a geographic and class space-off where white trash is the form of whiteness that is most visible. The class-based culture of Falls City naturalizes class differences. Most of the interior scenes in *BDC* take place either inside bars or in Lana's mother's house. The first time we meet Lana we see her in a bar, drinking, unable to stand on her own without the help of her friends. Candace works in the bar and both girls seem to spend leisure time drinking and singing karaoke. Lana's dream is to become a famous karaoke singer. Later in the film the girls find employment in the canning factory, working the night shift and, on their days off, drinking. The viewer's first encounter with Lana's mother shows her passed out from too much alcohol. To be working-class, according to this film, means to spend a great deal of time consuming alcohol. That leisure-time activity seems to commence with the onset of adolescence.

White masculinity in the text does not fare any better. Annalee Newitz (1997) argues that whiteness often emerges as a distinct racial identity when it can be identified as somehow primitive or inhuman. To see a white as a white rather than as just "another person" that white needs to be marked out as different from those whites who observe her/him (134). Newitz cites, for example, *Hillybillyland*, the study of representations of "mountain people" in Hollywood film, to argue that the figure of a white trash man is a spectacle not just because he is poor but also because he is sometimes monstrously so. Almost without exception, the men in *BDC* seem monstrously inhuman. Lotter explodes into homicidal rage seemingly over nothing; Nissen lifts his pant leg to reveal self-inflicted scars from knife games that he and Lotter play. The men who are stock features in the bars of the film either aggressively harass the girls or start bar brawls. None of them is employed; most seem single or otherwise unattached; and Nissen and Lotter seem savagely white. After being accused of raping Brandon, John Lotter replies: "If I wanted to rape someone, I have Mallory" – a female friend. The only working-class men who have jobs in *BDC* are the law enforcement officers, Sheriff Laux in particular; his treatment of Brandon easily situates him as savage and excessively brutal. The working-class whites in this film are racialized and demeaned because they fit all too easily into the primitive/civilized binary as nihilistic primitives (134).

5
Postscript: Notes Towards a Radical (Re)Thinking of the Politics of Gender

In *BDC*, Lana is depicted as young white trash but she is also depicted as a subject of fem(me)ininity; moreover, the film's fictionalized post-rape love scene between Lana and Brandon reconfigures Lana as a lesbian. Despite Lana Tisdel's objections, in the two love scenes between Brandon and Lana in the film, both subjects *become* their gender rather than *transcend* it. Through these dialogic sex scenes, *BDC* severs the overdetermined linkage between queerness and masculinity by bringing fem(me)ininity into focus. The result is that Brandon's identity as a trans-sexual boy is not completely stable in the film; indeed, his proximity to Lana overdetermines how we might read him. But the camera is also complicit in de- and re-constructing Brandon's identity and works against the dialogism of these scenes to contain how he should be viewed.

The first love scene between Lana and Brandon shows him operating with the very thing he is supposed to lack – that is, phallic power. Brandon and Lana have sex for the first time outside, at night, on a blanket, in the shadow of the lights from the factory. The sex scene is choreographed around Lana's pleasure so that the camera focuses on her face from above. Lana's (not Brandon's) top and bra are off, and, as I have already suggested, the camera lingers on her face while Brandon performs oral sex. When we see Brandon again, he is still fully clothed and remains dressed even when he enters Lana with what is presumably a dildo. Curiously, the camera quickly flashes down Brandon's shirt, again from what we are to perceive as Lana's viewpoint, to reveal very slight cleavage. Lana seems, from this point on, to have an idea that Brandon's body is female, even though she later runs her hand over the bulge in his pants. Her narration to Candace and Kate about the event tells a different story, however, one that reveals Lana's participation in the adolescent fantasy that Brandon builds and which she shares: "Afterward, we took our clothes off and went swimming," she tells them, infusing the narrative and its setting with a kind of pastoral and adolescent innocence.

If (Mary) Martin Ward's is not, in a productive way, a body that mattered, then Brandon's matters a great deal. Admittedly, given the visual nature of the film genre, it is much more difficult to de-emphasize the body. But where Stephen Gordon's and Jess Goldberg's identities are caught in the gaze of identity knowledge regimes as they are reflected in the mirrors into which each looks, Tremain writes as if Martin's penis is a non-issue, not-knowable, and, therefore, outside of economies that invest it with a particular kind of currency. It is as if Tremain replies to Brent Ledger's anxieties about trans-sexuality masculinity as depicted in the documentary *You Don't Know Dick*; Tremain's reply might be that, yes, what you cannot see, you cannot know. As I have argued already, the economy that defines Martin thrives on his epistemological "un-representability." The size, shape, and look of his (imaginary or otherwise) penis does not matter for, in the end, Tremain situates him outside that phallic economy fully passing as male (albeit in a somewhat unrealistic rural, poor space-off very different from the one in which Brandon lived). *BDC*, on the other hand, shows the very painful way that knowledge regimes are authenticated as Brandon's phallic power is exposed and refuted. The film confirms paradoxical subject positions, especially in the disrobing scene. The fantasy of gender that Brandon builds and that Lana eventually desires and shares is enabled, but that same fantasy is violently shattered when Lana and the viewer are forced to witness Brandon's body. Brandon's penis, both the simulacra that he uses with Lana and the presumed one that emerges when he is passing, "works," as he says in the film, but is revealed and therefore "known" and "re-cognized" as fantasy.

The second sex scene occurs much later in *BDC* after Brandon has been exposed and raped. Brandon's fantasy of his boy body is traumatically violated in the same way as is Mary Martin's fantasy when her father violently cuts away the binder that concealed her breasts. Nissen and Lotter corner Brandon in the bathroom and tear his pants off. When Lana is forced to look at Brandon with his pants pulled down and no penis in sight, the film action stops to show what Brandon sees as he looks away from Lana. The film shows another Brandon, not harmed, standing behind Candace and Kate. This second Brandon is wearing a blue shirt and is shown as if in a mirror (in the same way we see Stephen) from the waist up. The camera then cuts to the second Brandon's gaze and shows us what he sees – that is, the first Brandon with his pants down and his arms being held by Nissen and Lotter. The second Brandon is unable to bear what he sees (i.e., himself being exposed), and he simply walks away. In this intense moment, the dialogic split in Brandon between the imposed and (en)forced reality of his body competes and wins over the fantasy of his identity as a boy. From this moment on, his lack of penis and his rape overdetermine him as female, allowing the viewer, like the other characters in the film, to read him this way. The second sex scene attempts to assuage that violation but the events of the narrative refuse that assuagement.

After Brandon has been exposed and raped, Lana visits him in the middle of the night in the shed near Candace's house, where he now is staying. Brandon moves to rest his head on her breasts while Lana asks him, "what were you like before all this? I mean, were you like me, a girl girl?" Brandon answers, "Yeah, like a long time ago and then I guess I was just like a boy girl, and then I was just a jerk." Lana's hands continue to tenderly caress Brandon's hair and face as he confesses that many of the things he had told Lana were lies. Lana leans in and kisses Brandon, then they move as if to have sex. Lana then hesitates and says, "I don't know if I'm gonna know how to do it." Brandon replies: "I'm sure you'll figure it out."

At this point the camera moves behind Brandon's back and Lana takes Brandon's shirt off, with his back facing the camera. We only see his back, while Lana looks at his body. This love scene is less an attempt to reassert Brandon as female and more an attempt to construct Lana as femme. The direct suggestion of the film is that this time Lana makes love to Brandon, even though, as Lana takes his shirt off, the camera does not show his chest: that is only available for Lana's pleasure. What the viewer sees is Lana looking, touching Brandon's head and back with very fem(me)inine hands, decorated with rings, long nails, and bright red nail polish. Brandon as a "boy" is gone, that identity departing during the exposure scene in which Brandon looks at a version of himself leaving. But Brandon as a "trans-gender boy" nevertheless remains, Brandon still signifying both masculinity and a kind of vulnerability and woundedness that requires that Lana take care of him both emotionally and sexually. Lana nurses him back into a version of himself in the same way that Theresa nurses Jess in *SBB*. Once again, in a film made at the very end of the twentieth century, female masculinity seems synonymous with woundedness; fem(me)ininity is reconstructed as sexually powerful, nurturing, and aggressive. The "surprise" of Peirce's film is that it unwittingly brings fem(me)ininity into focus and transforms a previously unreadable image into one that is, at least contingently, visible.

This reconstruction is made possible partly because of the last twenty years of writing that has emerged out of lesbian butch-femme cultures. One of the reasons for the border war between butch and FTM transsexuality is that, within the twentieth century, lesbianism has been articulated with masculinity vis-à-vis gender inversion. What we are beginning to see now is resistance to that articulation by those occluded from it; that is, by femme lesbians. In interview after interview, Kimberly Peirce repeats over and over again that she was drawn to this story because she "fell in love with a girl who was living in a trailer park, who didn't have much money, who didn't have any role models, and yet who successfully transformed herself into a fantasy of a boy" (Glitz n.d., n.p.) In attempting to remain true to the precision of those desires, Peirce argues that the film is "an emotional artefact" of the love between Brandon and Lana. While the film is being hailed as the arrival of FTM trans-sexuality in mainstream culture, I read it as an attempt to queer Lana in order to render her more an artefact of the filmmaker's investments. Peirce herself sums up the noisy dialogism in No Man's Land between lesbian masculinity, trans-sexual masculinity, and popular constructions of masculinity as follows: "In addition to representing a queer archetype, Brandon actually embodied many traits of the traditional Hollywood hero. He had the innocence and tenderness of Montgomery Clift in *Red River* or a young Henry Fonda, the naive determination of Jimmy Stewart. He was a rebellious outsider like James Dean, a shy, courtly gentleman around women like Gary Cooper ... Bringing Brandon to Hollywood was like bringing him home" (n.p.).

Peirce locates Brandon within a very particular Hollywood tradition of masculinity. That reading of Brandon is curious, given that it situates him always already within the realm of fictionalized but also vulnerable masculinities. Such fictionalizations of so-called reality suggest that *BDC* suffers from identity confusion as a film; it is not a documentary, yet Peirce claims to have been true to other emotional relationships between Lana and Brandon. Tisdel's lawsuit betrays her own anxiety and frustration over the film's verisimilitude, claiming that Peirce misrepresented basic facts. But Peirce relied on many textual accounts of Brandon's death in the media, many of them sensational, to graft this hybrid film narrative from those accounts and her own interviews with the main characters in the story. As an example of a trans- or even inter-generic text, *BDC* is the product of both a formal and an epistemological grafting, with one text being a hybrid of another; a new form or entity is produced from a meeting point of two things, with the new entity not being reducible to either. Peirce, Swank, and Chloë Sevigny (the actor who plays Lana) graft a seemingly new Brandon and Lana from the textual accounts of their lives, each produced from but not reducible to the media representations. Each is a "trans" form from the other – that is, a hybrid form that does not transcend the so-called original but, rather, hails from and moves between its parts.

Brandon's life, not at all unlike Stephen's, Jess's, and Martin's, is text; each is knowable only in relation to each other as texts, in conversation with a history of discourses, textual practices, and their many articulations. Trans-subjectivity emerges in the contradictions, lacunae, and space-offs of discursive formations – in the No Man's Land between genders and pronouns; between narratives, discourses, and ideologies; and, indeed, in conversations between texts and their readers. What is produced in that elsewhere is the impossible: bodies that defy matter.

Notes

Introduction: The New Men of 1998

1 My work here inevitably raises questions about femme subjectivity that are beyond its scope. I do not attempt to answer those questions but, instead, bracket them as important touchstones for future research. That said, later chapters do suggest that female masculinity often needs to bracket femininity in order to foreground masculinity, something that has particularly disturbing and misogynist implications for fem(me)ininity.

2 I write "trans-sexual" and "trans-gender" for several reasons. As I explain later in this chapter, the suffix "trans" is often used to suggest that its subjects, those referenced by either the term "sexual" or the term "gender," somehow "transcend" gender by "exploding" the binary gender system. These subjects do transcend the discourses of the sex/gender system that ground all meanings of gender in the appropriately sexed body. However, to say that these subjects "transcend" gender seems to suggest that they do not find themselves articulated by gender. They most certainly do embody and perform gender difference. But the body that houses that performance is a "transnatural" body produced with the help of science, endocrinology, surgeries, and so on (Doan 1994, 152). Thus, I write "trans-sexual" and "trans-gender" with hyphens in order to defamiliarize the way that these terms manipulate and produce gender difference by deploying what I call an alibi of gender essence – an alibi provided by the sexologists and clinical psychiatry that authorizes interventions if the correct narrative is present. Again, these discourses do not transcend gender but, rather, are productive of subjectivities that are rewritten/rearticulated by those same subjects. I hyphenate in order to foreground these productive but troubling relations between bodies, subjectivity, discourse, temporalities, and languages that, albeit perhaps only contingently, eventually produce something resembling (trans-)gendered subjects.

3 Kimberly Peirce's film, *Boys Don't Cry* (1999), dramatizes Brandon's rape and murder in Falls City, Nebraska. Curiously, Peirce does not include DeVine's murder in her film at all, an omission that, while likely not intended as a racist exclusion, can only function as such given its reception within economies of white supremacy. I theorize this racial occlusion more fully in my postscript.

4 When I use the term "class" I refer less to a particular structure or economic group than to one particular *effect* of an economic matrix or social formation; that is, I am not so interested in defining what class *is* as I am in looking at how it functions. For my purposes here, it functions as a relation of and to power – not only to a means of production but also to the means of "re-production"; that is, modes of self-representation. Brandon's rape and murder not only deny him the right to self-define within his own short life but also deny his self-definition as a man to survive him. It is crucial at this point to reiterate that not only does no one axiom of identity – race, class, gender, or sexuality – exist prior to the other but also that each is only realized through the other.

5 By "discourse" I mean both speech and language as signifying systems. These sign systems are produced and manipulated in and through history, popular culture, print-based media and fictions, institutions and their effective practices, everyday talk, narrative,

community-based or social infrastructures like newsmagazines and so on, which all claim some truth value.

Chapter 1: Alibis of Essence and Enemies Within

1 The nineteenth-century homosexual became a personage, a past, a case history, and a childhood, in addition to being a type of life, a life form, and a morphology, with an indiscreet anatomy and possibly mysterious physiology. Nothing that went into his total composition was unaffected by his sexuality. It was everywhere in him: at the root of all his actions because it was their insidious and indefinitely active principle; written immodestly on his face and body because it was a secret that always gave itself a way. It was consubstantial with him, less as a habitual sin than as a singular nature ... Homosexuality appeared as one of the forms of sexuality when it was transformed from the practice of sodomy onto a kind of interior androgyny, a hermaphroditism of the soul. The sodomite had been a temporary aberration; the homosexual was now a species. (Foucault 1978, 43)

Foucault is, of course, writing about "the homosexual" as male, but his argument does not preclude the possibility of reading what the earlier sexologists identified as the "female invert," the subject of Hall's novel and *Masculinities without Men?,* into this oft-quoted passage.

2 It is possible to trace in passages like these Foucault's account of the "perpetual spirals of power and pleasure":

> Imbedded in bodies, becoming deeply characteristic of individuals, the oddities of sex relied on a technology of health and pathology. And conversely, since sexuality was a medical and medicalizable object, one had to try and detect it ... in the depths of the organism, or on the surface of the skin, or among all the signs of behavior. The power which thus took charge of sexuality set about contacting bodies, caressing them with its eyes, intensifying areas, electrifying surfaces, dramatizing troubled moments. It wrapped the sexual body in its embrace ... Power operated as a mechanism of attraction; it drew out those particularities over which it kept watch. Pleasure spread to the power that harried it; power anchored the pleasure it uncovered. (Foucault 1978, 44-5)

Both Foucault's prose and the strangely clinical, but equally evocative, tone of these passages from *Sex Variants* continue to perform the spirals of power and pleasure in each successive and always already voyeuristic rereading.

3 Mackenzie's novel is a satirical parody of female homosociality and of the tensions between "female friendship" and "inversion." Like many parodic or satirical novels, the specificity of the form is often missed.

4 *Regiment of Women* was first published by Heinemann Books in 1917, while *Dusty Answer* was first published by Henry Holt and Company in 1927. Radclyffe Hall was familiar with all of these novels (Baker 1985).

5 I use the masculine pronoun when referring to Stephen. My reading of *The Well of Loneliness* is grounded in a recognition of the limitations of pronouns to refer to genders outside of the sex/gender system. At the same time, linguistic, grammatical, and discursive markers of subjectivity such as "he" or "she" are the primary means through which subjects are "languaged" or "discoursed" into being in the first place (S. Hall 1997, 143). Thus, while neither "he" nor "she" is entirely accurate, Radclyffe Hall chose "she" to make Stephen intelligible. My "discourse" is happening in an entirely different historical moment, one that affords me the opportunity of arguing that "he" comes far closer to describing Stephen than does "she."

6 Urania Manuscripts was a very small non-affiliated organization in Los Angeles, California, that, in honour of Ulrichs's life work, translated and published many of his very early works as well as the works of others. Each text, annotated and translated from the German by Michael A. Lombardi, was inscribed with the following: "In Honor of the 153rd Birthday Anniversary of Karl Heinrich Ulrichs." And Ulrichs is clearly constructed as a hero of the early twentieth-century German, and now American, "gay rights" movement.

7 Terry 1999; Doan and Bland 1998; Duggan 1992; Weeks 1981.

8 Stuart Hall suggests that, since the nineteenth century, science has been functioning the way religion and anthropology used to, as "knowledge soothers used to make people sleep better in their beds" (*Race: The Floating Signifier,* video).

9 All references can be located in *The Director of Public Prosecutions* v. *Jonathan Cape and Leopold Hill,* 9 and 16 November 1928. All transcripts are part of the Henry Lovat Dickson Collection, National Archives of Canada, Ottawa.

10 While what follows is an analysis of the continued production of Britishness at the end of the First World War, I am also suggesting that this moment was one in which whiteness and Britishness were synonymous. Considerations of race, ethnicity, nation, and culture must acknowledge that, while these are unique and distinct analytical categories, at certain moments in history they are folded into each other. While this chapter recognizes the analytical and epistemological differences between them, its work necessitates an understanding of how race has been constructed as – and, indeed, articulated through – discourses of citizenry as nation, as empire, as sexuality.

11 Radclyffe Hall kept few personal journals, but Diana Souhami's (1998, 171) new biography of Hall suggests that she identified with Oscar Wilde and his refusal of public shaming: "A generation after Wilde her cause was to rid lesbianism of the stigma of moral degradation. In her book she articulated a female homosexual identity. That, she knew, would incur the scrutiny of the law."

12 Newspapers covering the trial both in 1918, and then again in 1951 (when the scandal was revived), refused to print the word "clitoris," substituting a dash instead.

13 Allyson Booth's (1996) *Postcards from the Trenches: Negotiating the Space between Modernism and the First World War* documents and analyzes the rhetoric that Britain used to represent and justify its entry into the war and the ways in which that discourse not only personifies but also genders and sexualizes Germany, Belgium, and England: "The country of Belgium (personified as a woman) was described as having been raped by the country of Germany (personified as a psychopath) because of the ways in which her boundaries had been involuntarily violated by him" (71). See also Raitt and Tate's (1997) *Women's Fiction and the Great War*; Fussell's (1975) *The Great War and Modern Memory*; and Hynes's (1990) *A War Imagined: The First World War and English Culture.* Hoare (1997, 42-4) documents the ways in which the signifier "Germany" also articulated "deviant" desires: "In 1908, the Eulenburg scandal rocked Germany, involving Kaiser Wilhelm and his intimate friends, known to their enemies as the Knights of the Round Table or the Camarilla." Prince Philip von Eulenburg was an intimate friend of the Kaiser's, and in 1907 the two were accused of being lovers. A series of very public trials ensued, at which Magnus Hirschfeld testified. And, as "Oscar" came to signify "sodomite" in Britain, so "Eulenburg" came to signify it in Berlin. Hoare suggests that the phrase "Do you speak German?" functioned as a queer code in Paris for a short time after the scandal in Berlin, which was known as "Sodom-on-Spree."

14 Interestingly, "to render" means not only to "give in return" or to "give back" but also "to reproduce, portray, give representation or performance or effect of," the latter definition being the one that gave the term its currency within early modernist poetics. I am certainly evoking those definitions; however, it is the meaning "to produce for inspection" that best serves my purposes here. As I argue in Chapter 2, Hall constructs *The Well*'s protagonist out of the discourses on masculinity available to her at that time – discourses produced and reified in and around the Pemberton Billing trial and policed by the judicial gaze: heteronormativity, British aristocracy, and British nationalism. Stephen fails, as it were, because those discourses require that this masculine subject be housed in a male body.

Chapter 2: Passionate Fictions

1 During the writing of this book, an event occurred that suggests that only *now* has the discursive and constructionist turn finally been taken. On Wednesday, 24 March 1999, the director of civil status in Montreal agreed to allow a female-to-male trans-sexual (FTM) to change his gender legally from female to male, even though he had not undergone genital surgery (*Globe and Mail,* 15 March 1999, A11).

2 A *Bildungsroman* is a novel that follows the development of the hero from childhood into adulthood, usually highlighting a troubled quest for identity. When the novel describes the formation of a young artist, as does *The Well of Loneliness*, then it is called a *Kunstleroman*.

3 "We need no longer go to history to trace the knowledge of human nature in all its stages and periods. Why? Because now the great map of mankind is unrolled all at once and there's no state or gradation of barbarism and no mode of refinement which we do not have at the same instant under our view." From a letter written by Edmund Burke in 1777. Stuart Hall (1996b) refers to this quote in the video *Race: The Floating Signifier* to discuss the cultural functions of science in identifying and quantifying the supposedly natural ontological differences between races. The scientific gaze produced a similar taxonomy of human sexual deviancy – a taxonomy that, as I argued in Chapter 1, Radclyffe Hall rearticulates through Stephen Gordon in *The Well* and that the twentieth-century writers I discuss in Chapter 3 also find themselves both inside and outside at the same moment.

4 As Oscar Wilde, Pemberton, Billing, and an entire canon of English writers made very clear, "sometimes [trans-sexual men] do like [trans-sexual men]" (Woolf 1928, 81).

5 David and Jonathan are the biblical archetypes of inseparable male friends. David was a harp-player for Jonathan's father, Saul, who envied David his prowess after the latter killed Goliath. A friendship grew between David and Jonathan, and, on several occasions, Jonathan secretly agreed to help David flee from Saul against Saul's orders. Jonathan was later killed in battle, and Saul committed suicide. David lamented the death of both father and son but separately mourned Jonathan's death, claiming their friendship "surpassed the love of women" (2 Samuel 1).

6 I am reformulating what has become known in legal circles as the "homosexual panic" defence, which allows a person accused of anti-gay violence to argue that his responsibility for the crime was diminished by a pathological psychological condition brought on by an unwanted sexual advance by another man. I am using the phrase "femaled panic" to describe a different kind of response by a female-embodied man who has wrongfully been read and treated as female (as has Stephen by Martin).

7 What Stephen could not have known is that it is conceivable to read his intense attraction to Martin as sexual but as "homosexual" rather than as "heterosexual"; that is, where the DSM-4 necessitated that female-to-male trans-sexuals be heterosexually oriented post-surgery (i.e., be heterosexual men), many pre- and post-operative FTMs understand themselves as homosexual (attracted to men, trans-sexual or otherwise). As suggested by the cover of Jason Cromwell's (1999) *Transmen and FTMs: Identities, Bodies, Genders and Sexualities* (a series of photographs of trans-sexual men – some without shirts, revealing surgically reconstructed chests – erotically embracing each other), many trans-sexual men want to be in sexual relationships with other men but only as men, not as women. Thus, when Stephen longs for Martin to "treat her as a man," he is attempting to formulate his inarticulate homosexual attraction to Martin (Hall 1928, 100-1).

8 Lynda Hart (1998) has formulated an interesting distinction between the "body" and the "flesh" – a distinction that I presume here. She argues that both are illusions, that is, both are cultural and phantasmic constructs. However, she argues that the function of the body as an invention of reality is to keep us anchored in the world we have constructed as real. "The 'body' of my [book] title might be understood as the cultural constructions, the architectures, the fixed, stable sites that we know are inventions of reality, but that we disavow as such in order to survive the disequilibrium of our desires for the 'real' of our fantasies" (10). The flesh, on the other hand, "is a place toward which we reach that always exceeds our grasp, that indeed *must* elude us for it is the site beyond (or before) the 'body' that permits us to continue *making* reality even as our desire disavows it" (10). In other words, the flesh is that phantasmic object of our desires, our own longings for and resistances to merging the distinctions between the real and the phantasmic. Desire, she argues finally, takes place between the body and the flesh. I posit a similar distinction between these two sites and argue that, for many of my subjects, the gap between the body and the flesh is constitutive of a complex and gendered corporeality.

9 Stephen's choice of heroes is interesting as both are remembered for their leadership and courage. William Tell was a Swiss legendary hero who symbolized the struggle for political and individual freedom. The actual existence of Tell is disputed. However, according to popular legend, he was a late thirteenth- and early fourteenth-century peasant who defied Austrian authority, was forced to shoot an apple from his son's head, was arrested for threatening the governor's life, saved the governor's life en route to prison, escaped, and ultimately killed the governor in an ambush. These events, together with the others, supposedly motivated the people to rise up against Austrian tyrannical rule.

Horatio Nelson was a British naval commander in the wars with Revolutionary and Napoleonic France, and he won a number of crucial victories. As a military leader Nelson was worshipped by officers and sailors alike, and he was instrumental in helping to break the unimaginative strategic and tactical doctrines of the British navy. Upon his death England gave him a majestic funeral in St. Paul's Cathedral, and his popularity as his "country's hope in battle" was recorded and countless monuments, streets, and inns were named after him. He is often remembered in history books as the one who introduced, as normal practice, a new personal quality of leadership in which subordinates were treated as human beings. One of his most famous battle calls mirrors a call that Stephen also hears when England enters the First World War but is prevented from completely fulfilling: "England expects that every man will do his duty" (Lloyd 1973).

10 This particular formation, which combines femme and femininity so as to manifest the relation and yet the *différance* of these two subjects, comes from Duggan and McHugh (1996).

11 The term "naturalized" to describe an effect of engendering was suggested to me in conversation with Anna Camilleri, whom I thank. While usually referring to a performative moment in which an immigrant is conferred with Canadian (or indeed any national) citizenship, I use it here to reference a performative reading practice that infers a body type based on a (mis-)reading of a gender performance – one that is assumed to have emerged naturally out of that body.

12 It is important to reiterate here that the subjects that I refer to as intersexed are different from those who find themselves subjected to and by medical discourses that have assigned them, often non-consensually, that identity. The subjects under discussion in this work *choose*, however complicated that choice might be, to surgically and hormonally realign bodies and subjectivities; one of the limitations facing FTM trans-sexuals is the inadequacies of the surgeries. While medical technologies have perfected surgeries that can transform male bodies into non-procreative but fully functioning female bodies, the equivalent surgeries (those that can transform female bodies into fully functioning male bodies) do not yet exist. Thus, the result, not the intention, is often intersexed bodies that pass as male when clothed and/or naked from the waist up but not from the waist down. As Prosser (1998), Devor (1997), and others have argued, the so-called fact of being an FTM trans-sexual often means living more permanently with an indeterminate body, a body that is neither male nor female. These medical failures flag the temporal relations of sex reassignment surgeries and draw our attention to a problematic temporal relation between gendering onto-performative speech acts – "I am a boy" or "I am a girl" – and the eventual corporeal embodiment that is often, but not always, the effect of these utterances. I theorize this temporal relation more fully in Chapter 3.

13 What is especially ironic about Prosser's insistence on labelling *The Well* is that many FTM trans-sexual autobiographical narratives invoke Hall's novel only to establish their own, and trans-sexuality's, essential difference from the subject of Hall's text. For instance, in the first known FTM trans-sexual autobiography, *Emergence: A Transsexual Autobiography*, Mario Martino (then still Marie) recalls buying a copy of *The Well of Loneliness* hoping to help his female partner come to terms with their situation. It did not work, and Martino explains why:

> [It was] about the love relationship between two women, it was so honestly and beautifully written that Becky felt she could accept their liaison. "Does everyone feel this way, Marie?" "Heavens, no! Besides, Becky, *you and I are not lesbians*. We

relate as man to woman, woman to man." ... I could never fit the mold of woman. (Martino 1977, 132, emphasis in original)

Chapter 3: Impressions of the Man

1 I will not attempt a definition of what may or may not constitute a "lesbian" or "butch" or "trans-sexual" text; I attempt instead to provide a genealogy of a specific reading practice as well as of a relation. I am not so much interested in what a "lesbian" or "butch" or "trans-sexual" text is but, rather, in what it allows a reader to do. Since this narrative serves to frame a number of the issues that are taken up in further detail later in the chapter, I let the terms stand (albeit within quotation marks), in part to problematize them and also to keep them from running away with themselves.

2 Both *Lesbian/Woman* and *Sappho Was a Right-On Woman* were published by what we now call "mainstream" publishers (Bantam, and Stein and Day, respectively). Perhaps this is not surprising, given the lack of alternative publishers in the 1970s; however, it still strikes me as a curious fact, perhaps noteworthy with regard to the intended audience of such texts. While they are clearly addressed to "lesbian" readers, they both read as though intended for non-lesbian readers as well.

3 What is perhaps even more noteworthy for my purposes here is the role of the "author" in those practices. In "What Is an Author?" Foucault (1977c, 123) argues that the author's name cannot be understood simply as an element of speech; rather, its presence is functional in that it serves as a means of classification, allowing a number of texts to be grouped together and establishing relationships of homogeneity, filiation, reciprocal explanation, authentification, or common utilization among them. Furthermore, the author, or what Foucault comes to call the "author-function," functions as a discursive practice in and of itself: "In this sense, the function of an author is to characterize the existence, circulation, and operation of certain discourses within a society" (124).

4 Numbers vary dramatically. Wagner (1982, 214) herself reports: "The demand in Canada for the services of the children seemed unlimited; in the years before the First World War up to 30,000 applications had been received annually ... The movement had so grown in size and complexity that it was practically impossible for an objective assessment to be carried out."

5 By this I mean temporally, both behind in place and later in time but also in pursuit (or quest) of.

6 While Stephen is perfectly logical as "he" or "him," Jess seems less so. As the novel itself suggests, Jess makes sense only outside of these categories. While it is possible to use the newly invented non-gendered pronouns "ze" and "hir," I find them too awkward for this project. Thus, I have chosen "s/he" and "he/r" to, in essence, perform the impossibilities of the split and differently gendered subject who remains both bound by, but strangely and grotesquely outside of, the sex/gender system.

7 *OUTLAW*. Alisa Lebow with Leslie Feinberg, US, video, 26 minutes, 1994 (WMM).

8 While seeming to share many features, the differences between these trans-narratives, the *Bildungsroman,* and the coming-out narrative warrant brief mention. The *Bildungsroman*, as a fairly conventionalized form for coming-of-age stories, tends to present that "coming-into-age" within a linear notion of time and a construction of subjectivity as, for the most part, quite stable. The coming-out narrative, as a similarly conventionalized form, also tends to reproduce those conservative features of the realist *Bildungsroman*, only it foregrounds the "self," "body," and "age" of that coming-into against the teleological backdrop of sexual identity. The narratives under discussion here problematize these constructions of "self" and "body" relative to "time" and the supposed self-evidence of that body's gender. In other words, the "place" of the trans-narrative – the not-yet-materialized body outside of conventional temporal frameworks – is quite different from the place of the non-trans *Bildungsroman* and coming-out narrative.

9 Mary Martin's name changes constantly in *SC*: "Mary" exists where "Martin" does not yet, and, in the end, when "Martin" finally exists, "Mary" does no longer. Thus the main character of Tremain's novel is known either as "Mary," or "Martin," or, occasionally, as "Marty." "Mary Martin" exists in this text only in relation to her grandfather, Cord, who,

after Mary first tells him that she is, in fact, Martin, actually calls her "Mary Martin." Cord is recognizing Martin's struggle to self-define, but he is also evoking the American singer and actress, Mary Martin, best known for her singing roles in musicals but also for her work in the title role of J.M. Barrie's children's play *Peter Pan*. Barrie's play first opened, starring Mary Martin as Peter Pan, on 24 October 1954 at the Winter Garden Theatre in London. The play celebrates the adventures of a little boy who refuses to grow up and, like Mary Martin, travels to a utopic "Never Never Land" and becomes a legend. More recently, the pejorative "Peter Pan Syndrome" has been coined to describe men who refuse to mature and accept the responsibilities associated with adult masculinity (see Kiley 1983).

10 King George the Sixth died on 6 February 1952 and was buried on 15 February. It is fitting that this novel opens with his passing, as *SC* is as much about the changing identity of England as it is about changing genders. It opens with the passing of the king responsible for accelerating the evolution of the British Empire into the Commonwealth of Nations and the postwar transformation of Great Britain into a welfare state, and it ends in 1980, just after the election of Margaret Thatcher. It is all the more appropriate that this novel, which is so much about silences that articulate and communicate more than language (which always fails), opens with the death of George, for he had a severe speech impediment.

11 The *Oxford English Dictionary* definitions of "silence" mark the limits of these functions: "1. abstinence from speech or noise, being silent, the fact of not mentioning a thing; 2. absence of sound, stillness; without speech or other sound; 3. oblivion, state of not being mentioned; 4. make silent by force, superior argument."

12 I am relying on multiple meanings of the word "union": like his father, Jess becomes actively involved in his trade union; Jess's unioning, however, also functions as a trope whereby those marked by difference and oppression can work across those differences. I also use the noun "union" to reference a larger entity resulting from combining, but not assimilating, parts of constitutive elements, especially that nexus of discourses that work together to articulate subjectivity: class, race, gender, and sexuality. American history is filled with loud and often violent ironies relative to its ideological and political investments in unions, especially noticeable in and around fantasies of national citizenry, enfranchisement, the "American Dream," and "equality." These historical and contemporary ironies are manifested in both identity politics, with its focus on "common ground," and in the fantasies of sexual and racial assimilation.

13 Bindings are made from either long strips of cotton, wide tensor bandages, or medical abdominal binders worn across the chest to flatten the breasts and create the illusion of flat-chestedness.

14 The images used to characterize this toughness – mortar, granite, even stone – are all materials commonly perceived as white and are associated with whiteness.

15 The figure that Simpson goes on to describe has made several appearances in popular film recently, the most memorable as Bob in *Fight Club* (1998). Bob is a former weight lifter, whose previously overdeveloped pectoral muscles have fallen. Bob signifies doubly in the film as (1) both a grotesque and feminized man, upon whose bosom the main character weeps while in a men's self-help group, and (2) as a grotesque butch, a quasi-man who is quickly killed off once he becomes part of Tyler's masculinist/masochistic and fascistic anti-corporate underground. Even in death, Bob's grotesque body continues to signify femininity as he becomes the violated and idealized mother.

16 It is overdetermined because, as Jess later determines, s/he cannot be at home in he/r body until it is no longer indicted by the question, "Is it a man's or woman's?"

17 Other texts that articulate femme outside of or challenge a masculine gaze include the film *Bound* (1996); Joan Nestle's (1998) new collection of essays entitled *A Fragile Union,* in which she discloses that her new lover is femme; poetry, short fiction, and performance pieces by Toronto artist Anna Camilleri, formerly of Vancouver's performance troupe Taste This, whose collection *Boys Like Her* (1998) explores fem(me)ininity and female masculinity without radical othering; and, most recently, award-winning short filmmaker Machiko Saito's *PreMenstrual Spotting* (1997) and *15 Minutes of Femme TV*

(1998). Camilleri's "Super Hero" and Saito's work are particularly noteworthy as they both not only articulate fem(me)ininity outside of masculine gaze but also aggressively challenge and assault that gaze so much that the viewer has little choice but to either endure shattering, violent images, or look away. Sadly, all of these works, which are equally referenced by the term "trans gendered" (no hyphen to suggest that they defamiliarize and rearticulate work that I have reconfigured as "trans-gendered") are beyond the scope of this work. None the less, they constitute an important and emergent rearticulation of fem(me)ininity beyond the limits and control of masculinity.

18 The validity of those shadows is anticipated by *SBB*'s front-cover image, which shows Leslie Feinberg in negative; that is, the cover photograph on the back shows a flat-chested Feinberg standing at a podium while the front cover appears to be a negative of a close-up photograph of Feinberg. The photographs, relative to each other, show that a photograph (as representation, as text) cannot materialize without the negative.

Chapter 4: Boys Do Cry

1 To avoid confusion between "Lana Tisdel," the character in *Boys Don't Cry,* and Lana Tisdel, the actual person, I use "Lana" when referring to the character and "Tisdel" when referring to the figure upon whom "Lana" is loosely based.

2 Again, one of the things that marks Swank's performance of masculinity as realistic but that confuses "Hilary" and "Brandon" in the service of an anti-transphobic and anti-homophobic agenda is the, by now, well-known fact that she prepared for the role by "actually" passing as a boy in her personal life. Interviews with Swank always focus on how she borrowed her husband's clothing and accompanied him to social events as "Hilary's brother." Swank also talks about losing weight to make her body seem more boyish, but she also recalls how difficult it was to find a hair stylist who would cut her apparently long hair into a boyish style, something that a number simply refused to do ("Beat").

3 The cowboy image surrounds Brandon. Local Falls City and Lincoln newspapers reported that Brandon was buried in "men's clothing, wearing her [sic] favorite cowboy shirt and black cowboy hat." The next day a relative of Brandon's insisted that the papers print a retraction stating that Brandon was buried in "a black and white striped shirt purchased in the women's section of a local store" (Minkowitz 1994, 24). Again, such proliferating and competing narratives remind us that definitions and self-definitions are not secondary to discourse and power; they are, as Stuart Hall (1981, 239) suggests, the sites where this struggle is engaged. They are, in fact, the stakes to be won or lost in that struggle.

4 That success was compromised by the most recent legal decision on Brandon's case. In a truly bizarre ruling, on 6 December 1999 Nebraska District Judge Orville Coady ruled that Richardson County authorities were 14 percent responsible for Brandon's wrongful death by passing on certain information to Nissen and Lotter and by not arresting them. Brandon's mother, JoAnn Brandon, had sought $350,000 in a wrongful death suit against the Richardson County officials, charging that then Richardson County sheriff Charles Laux had allowed the two men who raped Brandon on 25 December 1993 to remain at large and to go on to kill Brandon, along with his two friends, on 31 December. The suit also charges Laux with deliberately inflicting emotional distress on Brandon while interviewing him when he reported the rape. Judge Coady awarded $86,224 in damages and found Lotter and Nissen 85 percent liable for Brandon's death. Coady also ordered Laux to apologize to Brandon's family, "her" friends, and to his own community for continually referring to Brandon as an "it." Brandon's "forced confession" functioned to pathologize him in front of an expert who had already done so. Brandon did this in order to report the crime committed against him and to be taken and treated seriously. In many ways Brandon was unable to do successfully what the subjects of *The Well of Loneliness, Stone Butch Blues,* and *Sacred Country* could do, that is, to find a way to rearticulate himself using the same discourses that had articulated him as a subject in the first place. While Feinberg, Hall, and Tremain all allow their characters to work within and then transform the discourses that have produced them, Peirce does not. Brandon was,

and remains, permanently fixed and languaged by those discourses. He is so permanently fixed that Nebraska District Judge Orville Coady divided up responsibility for his death as follows: Nissen and Lotter were 85 percent responsible, County Sheriff Laux was 14 percent responsible, and Brandon himself was 1 percent responsible (FTM International Newsletter 19).

References

Abbott, Sidney, and Barbara Love. 1972. *Sappho Was a Right-On Woman: A Liberated View of Lesbianism*. New York: Stein and Day.

Adams, Rachel. 2000. "Masculinity without Men." *GLQ: A Journal of Lesbian and Gay Studies* 6, 3: 467-78.

Allen, Clifford. M.D. 1950. "The Personality of Radclyffe Hall." *International Journal of Sexology* 4, 2: 95-8.

Althusser, Louis. 1971. "Ideology and Ideological State Apparatuses." Trans. Ben Brewster. *Lenin and Philosophy and Other Essays*, 170-86. New York and London: Monthly Review Press.

Anderson, Benedict. 1983. *Imagined Communities: Reflections on the Origin and Spread of Nationalism*. London: Verso.

Asch, Sholem. 1972 [1923]. *The God of Vengeance: The Great Jewish Plays*, ed. Joseph C. Landis. New York: Horizon Press.

Austin, J.L. 1975. *How to Do Things with Words*. Oxford: Clarendon Press.

Bagnell, Kenneth. 1980. *The Little Immigrants: The Orphans Who Came to Canada*. Toronto: Macmillan of Canada.

Baker, Michael. 1985. *Our Three Selves: The Life of Radclyffe Hall*. London: Hamish Hamilton.

Bakhtin, Mikhail. 1968. *Rabelais and His World*. London: MIT Press.

–. 1981. "Discourse in the Novel." In *The Dialogic Imagination*, 259-422. London: University of Texas Press.

–. 1984. "Discourse in Dostoevsky." In *Problems of Dostoevsky's Poetics*, 181-269. Manchester: Manchester University Press.

–. 1986. *Speech Genres and Other Late Essays*. London: University of Texas Press.

Bakhtin, Mikhail, and P. Medvedev. 1978. *The Formal Method in Literary Scholarship*. London: Johns Hopkins University Press.

Baldwin, James. 1985. *The Price of the Ticket: Collected Nonfiction, 1948-1985*. New York: St. Martin's Press.

Barnes, Djuna. 1928. *Ladies Almanac*. New York: Cutting Edge.

–. 1979 [1949]. *Nightwood*. London: Faber and Faber.

Barthes, Roland. 1993. *Mythologies*. Trans. Annette Lavers. London: Vintage.

Baudrillard, Jean. 1995. *Simulacra and Simulation*. Trans. Sheila Glaser. Ann Arbor: University of Michigan Press.

Beaird, Joe. N.d. "Film about Famed Murder Sparks Controversy and Lawsuits." APB Celebrity News. <http://www.APBnews.com> (accessed 1 November 1999).

beatboxbetty. N.d. "Interview with Hilary Swank." <http://www.beatboxbetty.com> (accessed 2000).

Bederman, Gail. 1995. *Manliness and Civilization: A Cultural History of Gender and Race in the United States, 1880-1917*. Chicago: University of Chicago Press.

Bennett, Arnold. 1928. "Review." *Evening Standard,* 9 August: n.p.
Benjamin, Walter. 1992. *Charles Baudelaire: A Lyric Poet in the Era of High Capitalism.* London and New York: Verso.
Berger, John. 1972. *Ways of Seeing.* London: Penguin Books.
Bersani, Leo. 1995. "Loving Men." In *Constructing Masculinity,* ed. Maurice Berger, Brian Wallis, and Simon Watson, 116-23. New York and London: Routledge.
Bly, Robert. 1990. *Iron John.* Reading, MA: Addison-Wesley.
Bolin, Anne. 1992. "Vandalized Vanity: Feminine Physiques Betrayed and Portrayed." In *Tattoo, Torture, Mutilation, and Adornment: The Denaturalization of the Body in Culture and Text,* ed. Frances E. Mascia-Lees and Patricia Sharpe, 79-99. New York: State University of New York Press.
Booth, Allyson. 1996. *Postcards from the Trenches: Negotiating the Space between Modernism and the First World War.* New York: Oxford University Press.
Bornstein, Kate. 1993. "Life's a Butch: Leslie Feinberg from Behind the Stone Wall." *Lambda Book Report.* 3 May: 28.
Bourdet, Edouard. 1926. *The Captive.* Trans. Arthur Hornblow Jr. New York: Brentano's.
Boutilier, Nancy. 1995. "Breaking the Rarified Air of Freedom." *Lambda Book Report: A Review of Contemporary Gay and Lesbian Literature* 4, 8: 6-7.
"Brandon Teena Update." 2000. *FTM International Newsletter* 46: 19.
Breen, Margaret Soenser. 1997. "Narrative Inversion: The Biblical Heritage of *The Well of Loneliness* and *Desert of the Heart.*" In *Reclaiming the Sacred: The Bible in Gay and Lesbian Culture,* ed. Raymond-Jean Frontain, 187-206. New York: Haworth.
Brittain, Vera. 1968. *Radclyffe Hall: A Case of Obscenity?* London: Femina Books Ltd.
Britzman, P. Deborah. 1989. *Lost Subjects, Contested Objects: Toward a Psychoanalytic Inquiry of Learning.* Albany: SUNY Press.
Butler, Judith. 1990. *Gender Trouble: Feminism and the Subversion of Identity.* New York and London: Routledge, Chapman and Hall.
–. 1991. "Imitation and Gender Insubordination." In *Inside/Out: Lesbian Theories, Gay Theories,* ed. Diana Fuss, 1-31. New York: Routledge.
–. 1993. *Bodies That Matter: On the Discursive Limits of "Sex."* New York and London: Routledge.
–. 1997a. "Melancholy Gender/Refused Identification." In *The Psychic Life of Power,* 132-66. Stanford: Stanford University Press.
–. 1997b. *Excitable Speech: A Politics of the Performative.* New York: Routledge.
Cameron, Loren. 1996. *Body Alchemy: Transsexual Portraits.* Pittsburgh: Cleis Press.
Carlson, Christy. 2000. "After Modernism: Feminist Readings of Modern Women Writers." PhD diss., York University.
Castle, Terry. 1996. *Noel Coward and Radclyffe Hall: Kindred Spirits.* New York: Columbia University Press.
Chauncey, George. 1989. "Christian Brotherhood or Sexual Perversion? Homosexual Identities and the Construction of Sexual Boundaries in the World War I Era." In *Hidden from History: Reclaiming the Gay and Lesbian Past,* ed. Martin Duberman, Martha Vicinus, and George Chauncey Jr., 294-317. New York: Meridian Books.
Collins, Jim. 1989. *Uncommon Cultures: Popular Culture and Post-Modernism.* New York and London: Routledge, Chapman and Hall.
Cromwell, Jason. 1999. *Transmen and FTMs: Identities, Bodies, Genders, and Sexualities.* Chicago: University of Chicago Press.
Curtin, Kaier. 1987. *"We Can Always Call Them Bulgarians": The Emergence of Lesbians and Gays on the American Stage.* Boston: Alyson Publications.
Dane, Clemence. 1936. *Regiment of Women.* London: Heinemann Books.
David, Hugh. 1997. *On Queer Street.* London: HarperCollins.
de Lauretis, Teresa. 1987. "The Technology of Gender." In *Technologies of Gender: Essays on Theory, Film, and Fiction,* 1-30. Bloomington and Indianapolis: Indiana University Press.
–. 1990. "Upping the Anti (sic) in Feminist Theory." In *Conflicts in Feminism,* ed. Marianne Hirsch and Evelyn Fox Keller, 255-70. New York and London: Routledge, Chapman and Hall.

–. 1993. "Sexual Indifference and Lesbian Representation." In *The Lesbian and Gay Studies Reader*, ed. Henry Abelove, Michèle Aina Barale, and David M. Halperin, 141-58. New York: Routledge.

Devor, Holly. 1997. *FTM: Female-to-Male Transsexuals in Society*. Bloomington: Indiana University Press.

Diagnostic and Statistical Manual of Mental Disorders, 4th ed. 1994. Washington, DC: American Psychiatric Association.

Doan, Laura. 1994. "Jeanette Winterson's Sexing the Postmodern." In *The Lesbian Postmodern*, edited by Laura Doan, 137-55. New York: Columbia University Press.

–. 1998. "'Acts of Female Indecency': Sexology's Intervention in Legislating Lesbianism." In *Sexology in Culture: Labelling Bodies and Desires*, ed. Laura Doan and Lucy Bland, 199-213. Chicago: Chicago University Press.

Doan, Laura, and Lucy Bland, eds. 1998. *Sexology Uncensored: The Documents of Sexual Science*. Chicago: Chicago University Press.

Douglas, James. 1928. "A Book That Must Be Suppressed." *Sunday Express*, 19 August, n.p.

Douris, Athena. 1998. "The Well of Genderlessness." *Girlfriends: Culture Politics Sexuality* 5, 4: 18.

DuBois, W.E.B. 1990. *The Souls of Black Folk*. New York: Vintage Books.

Duggan, Lisa. 1992. "The Trials of Alice Mitchell: Sensationalism, Sexology and the Lesbian Subject in Turn-of-the-Century America." PhD diss., University of Pennsylvania.

Duggan, Lisa, and Kathleen McHugh. 1996. "A Fem(me)inist Manifesto." *Women and Performance: A Journal of Feminist Theory* 8: 2.

Dyer, Richard. 1988. "White." *Screen* 29, 4: 44-64.

Ebert, Roger. 1999. *Chicago Sun-Times* (Film column), 15 September, n.p.

Ellis, Havelock. 1926 [1893]. *Man and Woman: A Study of Human Secondary Sexual Characteristics*. 6th ed. London: A. and C. Black.

–. 1929. "Sexual Inversion in Women." In *Studies in the Psychology of Sex*. Vol. 2: *Sexual Inversion*, 3rd ed., 195-263. Philadelphia: F.A. Davis Company.

–. 1967. *My Life*. London: Neville Spearman.

Faderman, Lillian. 1981. *Surpassing the Love of Men: Romantic Friendship and Love between Women from the Renaissance to the Present*. New York: Morrow Quill Paperbacks.

–. 1991. *Odd Girls and Twilight Lovers: A History of Lesbian Life in Twentieth-Century America*. New York: Penguin Books.

Fanon, Franz. 1967. *Black Skin, White Masks*. Trans. Charles Lam Markmann. New York: Grove Press.

Faulkner, William. 1984. *The Sound and the Fury*. New York: Random House.

Fausto-Sterling, Anne. 1995. "How to Build a Man." In *Constructing Masculinity*, ed. Maurice Berger, Brian Wallis, and Simon Watson, 127-34. New York: Routledge.

Feinberg, Leslie. 1993. *Stone Butch Blues: A Novel*. Ithaca, NY: Firebrand Books.

–. 1998. *Trans Liberation: Beyond Pink or Blue*. Boston: Beacon Press.

Felman, Shoshana. 1987. *Jacques Lacan and the Adventure of Insight: Psychoanalysis in Contemporary Culture*. Cambridge, MA: Harvard University Press.

–. 1993. *What Does a Woman Want?* Baltimore: John Hopkins University Press.

Foucault, Michel. 1972. *The Archaeology of Knowledge and The Discourse on Language*. Trans. A.M. Sheridan Smith. New York: Pantheon.

–. 1977a. *Language, Counter-Memory, Practice: Selected Essays and Interviews by Michel Foucault*, ed. Donald F. Bouchard, 139-64. Ithaca, NY: Cornell University Press.

–. 1977b. *Discipline and Punish: The Birth of the Prison*. Trans. Alan Sheridan. New York: Vintage Books.

–. 1977c. "What Is an Author?" In *Language, Counter-Memory, Practice: Selected Essays and Interviews by Michel Foucault*, ed. Donald F. Bouchard, 113-38. Ithaca, NY: Cornell University Press.

–. 1977d. "Intellectuals and Power." In *Language, Counter-Memory, Practice: Selected Essays and Interviews by Michel Foucault*, ed. Donald F. Bouchard, 205-17. Ithaca, NY: Cornell University Press.

–. 1978. *The History of Sexuality.* Vol. 1: *An Introduction.* Trans. Robert Hurley. New York: Random House.

–. 1980. "Truth and Power." In *Power/Knowledge: Selected Interviews and Other Writings, 1972-1977 by Michel Foucault,* ed. Colin Gordon, 109-33. New York: Pantheon Books.

–. 1981. "Omnes et Singulatim: Toward a Criticism of 'Political Reason.'" In *The Tanner Lectures on Human Value,* ed. S.M. McMurrin, 223-54. Vol. 2. Cambridge: Cambridge University Press.

–. 1985. *The History of Sexuality.* Vol. 2: *The Use of Pleasure.* Trans. Robert Hurley. New York: Random House.

–. 1991. "The Ethic of Care for the Self as a Practice of Freedom." In *The Final Foucault.* Trans. J.D. Hauthier, ed. James Bernauer and David Rasmussen, 1-20. Cambridge, MA: MIT Press.

Freud, Sigmund. 1960 [1905]. *The Standard Edition of the Complete Psychological Works of Sigmund Freud,* trans. and ed. James Strachey, 135-72. Vol. 7: *Three Essays on the Theory of Sexuality.* London: Hogarth.

–. 1984. "The Economic Problem of Masochism." In *On Metapsychology: The Theory of Psychoanalysis,* trans. and ed. James Strachey. Vol. 2. New York: Penguin Books.

Fussell, Paul. 1975. *The Great War and Modern Memory.* Oxford: Oxford University Press.

Gilbert, Sandra M., and Susan Gubar. 1988. *No Man's Land: The Place of the Woman Writer in the Twentieth Century.* Vol. 1: *The War of the Words.* New Haven and London: Yale University Press.

Ginsberg, Elaine K., ed. 1996. *Passing and the Fictions of Identity.* Durham, NC: Duke University Press.

Glitz, Michael. N.d. "Brandon Goes to Hollywood." *The Advocate.* <http://www.theadvocate.com> (accessed 28 March 2000).

Graff, E.J. 1993. "Delusions of Gender: *Sacred Country* and *Stone Butch Blues.*" *The Women's Review of Books* 10, 10-11: 25-6.

Halberstam, Judith. 1998a. *Female Masculinity.* Durham: Duke University Press.

–. 1998b. "Transgender Butch: Butch/FTM Border Wars and the Masculine Continuum." *GLQ: A Journal of Lesbian and Gay Studies. The Transgender Issue* 4, 2: 287-310.

Halberstam, Judith, and C. Jacob Hale. 1998. "Butch/FTM Border Wars: A Note on Collaboration." *GLQ: A Journal of Lesbian and Gay Studies. The Transgender Issue* 4, 2: 283-5.

Hall, Radclyffe. 1928. *The Well of Loneliness.* New York: Avon Books.

–. 1929. *Unlit Lamp.* New York: J. Cape and H. Smith.

Hall, Stuart. 1996a. "On Postmodernism and Articulation." In *Stuart Hall: Critical Dialogues in Cultural Studies,* ed. David Morley and Kuan-Hsing Chen, 131-50. London and New York: Routledge.

–. 1996b. "For Allon White: Metaphors of Transformation." In *Stuart Hall: Critical Dialogues in Cultural Studies,* ed. David Morley and Kuan-Hsing Chen, 287-305. London and New York: Routledge.

–. 1997. *Representation: Cultural Representations and Signifying Practices.* London: Sage.

–. 1981. "Notes on Deconstructing 'The Popular.'" In *People's History and Socialist Theory,* ed. Raphael Samuel, 227-40. London: Routledge and Kegan Paul.

Hannon, Gerald. 1998. "Dicking over Genitals." *NOW Magazine* 2-8 April: 18-21.

Hart, Lynda. 1994. *Fatal Women: Lesbian Sexuality and the Mark of Aggression.* Princeton, New Jersey: Princeton University Press.

–. 1998. *Between the Body and the Flesh: Performing Sadomasochism.* New York: Columbia University Press.

Hellman, Lillian. 1942. *The Children's Hour: Four Plays.* New York: Modern Library.

Hemingway, Ernest. 1969. *A Farewell to Arms.* New York: Scribner's.

–. 1970. *The Sun Also Rises.* New York: Scribner's.

Hemming, Clare. 1999. "Out of Sight, Out of Mind? Theorizing Femme Narrative." *Sexualities* 2, 4: 387-96.

Hennegan, Alison. 1982. "Introduction." In *The Well of Loneliness* by Radclyffe Hall, xiv-xv. London: Virago.

Henry, George W. 1948. *Sex Variants: A Study of Homosexual Patterns*. Committee for the Study of Sex Variants, Inc. New York: P.B. Hoeber.
Henson, Leslie J. 1997. "Articulate Silence(s): Femme Subjectivity and Class Relations in *The Well of Loneliness*." In *Femme: Feminists, Lesbians and Bad Girls*, ed. Laura Harris and Elizabeth Crocker, 61-7. New York and London: Routledge.
Hewitt, Paul, with Jane Warren. 1996. *A Self-Made Man: The Diary of a Man Born in a Woman's Body*. London: Headline Book Publishing.
Hill, Darryl B. 2002. "Female Masculinity." Book reviews. *The Journal of Men's Studies* 10 (Winter), 2: 237.
Hoare, Philip. 1997. *Oscar Wilde's Last Stand: Decadence, Conspiracy, and the Most Outrageous Trial of the Century*. New York: Arcade Publishing.
Hoberman, J. N.d. "Oscars!" *Village Voice* <http://www.villagevoice.com/issues/9939/hoberman.php> (accessed December 1999).
Holmes, Morgan. 1995. "Queer Cut Bodies: Intersexuality and Homophobia in Medical Practice." Paper presented at Queer Frontiers: The Fifth Annual National Lesbian, Gay, and Bisexual Graduate Student Conference. University of Southern California, 23-6 March.
Hooke, S.H. 1929. "A Biological Sin." *The Canadian Forum: A Monthly Journal of Literature and Public Affairs* 9, 103: 243-4.
Hucklenbroich, Frankie. 1997. *A Crystal Diary*. Ithaca, NY: Firebrand Books.
Hurston, Zora Neale. 1978. *Their Eyes Were Watching God*. Urbana, IL: University of Illinois Press.
Hutcheon, Linda. 1988. *The Poetics of Postmodernism: History, Theory, Fiction*. New York: Routledge, Chapman and Hall.
Hynes, Samuel Lynn. 1990. *A War Imagined: The First World War and English Culture*. London: Bodley Head.
Johnson, Barbara. 1987. *A World of Difference*. Baltimore: Johns Hopkins University Press.
Jones, Aphrodite. 1996. *All She Ever Wanted*. New York: Pocket Books.
Kaplan, E. Ann. 1997. *Looking for the Other: Feminism, Film, and the Imperial Gaze*. New York and London: Routledge.
Katz, Jonathan Ned. 1995. *The Invention of Heterosexuality*. New York: Penguin Books.
Kessler, Suzanne. 1998. *Lessons from the Intersexed*. New Brunswick, NJ: Rutgers University Press.
Kettle, Michael. 1977. *Salome's Last Veil*. London: Hart-Davis.
Kiley, Dan. 1983. *The Peter Pan Syndrome: Men Who Have Never Grown Up*. New York: Dodd, Mead.
Kimmel, Michael S., and Michael Kaufman. 1995. "Weekend Warriors: The New Men's Movement." In *The Politics of Manhood*, ed. Michael S. Kimmel, 15-43. Philadelphia: Temple University Press.
Klaich, Dolores. 1974. *Woman Plus Woman: Attitudes Toward Lesbianism*. New York: Simon and Schuster.
Krafft-Ebing, Richard von. 1965 [1839]. *Psychopathia Sexualis: A Medico-Forensic Study*. New York: Stein and Day Publishers.
Lacan, Jacques. 1991. "Courtly Love as Anamorphosis." In *The Seminar of Jacques Lacan*, ed. Jacques-Alain Miller. Book 7: *The Ethics of Psychoanalysis, 1959-1960*, trans. Dennis Porter, 131-54. New York: W.W. Norton.
Laclau, Ernesto. 1977. *Politics and Ideology in Marxist Theory*. London: Verso.
Larsen, Nella. 1986. *Passing*. New Brunswick, NJ: Rutgers University Press.
Ledger, Brent. 1998. "Getting to Know Dick: Transsexuals are Guardians of Gender Status Quo." *Xtra!* 357: 37.
Lee, Gretchen. 1998. "Pink and Blue: Interview with Leslie Feinberg." *Curve* 8, 5: 31.
Lehmann, Rosamond. 1927. *Dusty Answer*. New York: H. Holt.
Lloyd, Christopher. 1973. *Nelson and Sea Power*. London: English Universities Press.
McClintock, Anne. 1993. "Maid to Order: Commercial S/M and Gender Power." In *Dirty Looks: Women, Pornography, Power*, ed. Pamela Church Gibson and Roma Gibson, 207-31. London: BPI Publishing.

–. 1995. *Imperial Leather: Race, Gender and Sexuality in the Colonial Contest*. New York: Routledge.

MacDonald, Ann-Marie. 1996. *Fall on Your Knees*. Toronto: Vintage Canada.

Mackenzie, Compton. 1928. *Extraordinary Women: Theme and Variation*. London: M. Secker.

McLaren, Angus. 1997. *The Trials of Masculinity: Policing Sexual Boundaries, 1870-1930*. Chicago: The University of Chicago Press.

MacPike, Loralee. 1994. "A Geography of Radclyffe Hall's Lesbian Country." *Historical Reflections/Réflexions Historiques* 20, 2: 217-42.

Madden, Ed. 1997. "The Well of Loneliness, or the Gospel According to Radclyffe Hall." In *Reclaiming the Sacred: The Bible in Gay and Lesbian Culture*, ed. Raymond-Jean Frontain, 163-85. New York, NY: Haworth.

Martin, Biddy. 1996. *Femininity Played Straight: The Significance of Being Lesbian*. New York and London: Routledge.

Martin, Del, and Phyllis Lyon. 1972. *Lesbian/Woman*. San Francisco: Glide Publications.

Martino, Mario, with Harriett. 1977. *Emergence: A Transsexual Autobiography*. New York: Crown Publishers.

Marx, Karl. 1977. "The Eighteenth Brumaire of Louis Bonaparte." In *Karl Marx: Selected Writings*, ed. David McLellan, 300-25. Oxford: Oxford University Press.

Mercer, Kobena. 1994. *Welcome to the Jungle: New Positions in Black Cultural Studies*. New York: Routledge.

Minkowitz, Donna. 1994. "Love Hurts." *Village Voice*, 19 April: 24-30.

Mosse, George L. 1985. *Nationalism and Sexuality: Respectability and Abnormal Sexuality in Modern Europe*. New York: Howard Fertig.

Muñoz. José Esteban. 1999. *Disidentifications: Queers of Color and the Performance of Politics*. Minneapolis: University of Minnesota Press.

Munt, Sally, ed. 1998. *Butch/Femme: Inside Lesbian Gender*. London: Cassell.

Muska, Susan, and Greta Olafsdottir. N.d. "Reel Nebraska." *The Advocate*. <http://www.theadvocate.com> (accessed 28 March 2000).

Nestle, Joan. 1987. *A Restricted Country: Essays and Short Stories*. Ithaca, NY: Firebrand Books.

–. 1998. *A Fragile Union: New and Selected Writings*. San Francisco: Cleis Press.

Newitz, Annalee. 1997. "White Savagery and Humiliation, or A New Racial Consciousness in the Media." In *White Trash: Race and Class in America*, ed. Matt Wray and Annalee Newitz, 131-54. New York and London: Routledge.

Newton, Esther. 1989. "The Mythic Mannish Lesbian: Radclyffe Hall and the New Woman." In *Hidden from History: Reclaiming the Gay and Lesbian Past*, ed. Martin Duberman, Martha Vicinus, and George Chauncey Jr. , 281-93. New York: Penguin Books.

Noble, Jean, and Leslie Taylor. 1994. "History Take Note. I Did Not Stand Alone! An Interview with Leslie Feinberg." *Icon Magazine* April: 14.

"NYC." N.d. Amazon Books. Customer review of *Stone Butch Blues*. <www.amazon.com> (accessed August 2000).

Parker, Andrew, Mary Russo, Doris Sommer, and Patricia Yaeger, eds. 1992. *Nationalisms and Sexualities*. New York: Routledge.

Phelan, Peggy. 1997. *Mourning Sex: Performing Public Memories*. London and New York: Routledge.

Pratt, Minnie Bruce. 1995. *S/HE*. Ithaca, NY: Firebrand Books.

Prosser, Jay. 1998. *Second Skins: The Body Narratives of Transsexuality*. New York: Columbia University Press.

Racevskis, Karlis. 1991. "Michel Foucault, Rameau's Nephew, and the Question of Identity." In *The Final Foucault*, ed. James Bernauer and David Rasmussen, 21-33. Cambridge: MIT Press.

Radicalesbians. 1972. "The Woman-Identified Woman." In *Out of the Closets: Voices of Gay Liberation*, ed. Karla Jay and Allen Young, 172-77. New York: New York University Press.

Raitt, Suzanne, and Trudi Tate, eds. 1997. *Women's Fiction and the Great War*. Oxford: Clarendon Press.

Rees, Mark. 1996. *Dear Sir or Madam: The Autobiography of a Female-to-Male Transsexual.* London: Cassell.
Reik, Theodore. 1941. *Masochism in Modern Man.* Trans. Margaret H. Beigel and Gertrud M. Kurth. New York: Farrar, Straus and Company.
Rich, Adrienne. 1983. "Compulsory Heterosexuality and Lesbian Existence." In *The Signs Reader: Women, Gender, and Scholarship,* ed. Elizabeth Abel and Emily K. Abel, 139-68. Chicago: University of Chicago Press.
Robinson, Amy. 1994. "It Takes One to Know One." *Critical Inquiry* 20: 715-36.
Rubin, Gayle. 1975. "The Traffic in Women: Notes on the 'Political Economy' of Sex." In *Toward an Anthropology of Women,* ed. Rayna R. Reiter, 157-210. New York: Monthly Review.
–. 1984. "Thinking Sex: Notes for a Radical Theory of the Politics of Sexuality." In *Pleasure and Danger: Exploring Female Sexuality,* ed. Carole Vance, 267-319. Boston: Routledge.
–. 1992. "Of Catamites and Kings: Reflections on Butch, Gender, and Boundaries." In *The Persistent Desire: A Femme-Butch Reader,* ed. Joan Nestle, 466-82. Boston: Alyson Publications.
–. 1994. "Sexual Traffic." *Differences: A Journal of Feminist Cultural Studies. More Gender Trouble: Feminism Meets Queer Theory* 6, 2-3: 62-99
Ruehl, Sonja. 1982. "Inverts and Experts: Radclyffe Hall and the Lesbian Identity." In *Feminism, Culture and Politics,* ed. Rosalind Brunt and Caroline Rowan, 15-36. London: Lawrence and Wishart.
Rule, Jane. 1975. *Lesbian Images.* New York: Pocket Books.
Russo, Mary J. 1995. *The Female Grotesque: Risk, Excess, and Modernity.* New York: Routledge.
Saussure, Ferdinand de. 1983. *Course in General Linguistics,* ed. Charles Bally and Albert Sechehaye with the collaboration of Albert Riedlinger, trans. Roy Harris. London: Duckworth.
Savran, David. 1998. *Taking It Like a Man: White Masculinity, Masochism and Contemporary American Culture.* Princeton: Princeton University Press.
Scarry, Elaine. 1985. *The Body in Pain: The Making and Unmaking of the World.* Oxford: Oxford University Press.
Sedgwick, Eve Kosofsky. 1985. *Between Men: English Literature and Male Homosocial Desire.* New York: Columbia University Press.
–. 1990. *Epistemology of the Closet.* Berkeley and Los Angeles: University of California Press.
–. 1992. "Nationalisms and Sexualities in the Age of Wilde." In *Nationalisms and Sexualities,* ed. Andrew Parker, Mary Russo, Doris Sommer, and Patricia Yaeger, 235-45. New York: Routledge.
–. 1993. "Queer Performativity: Henry James's *The Art of the Novel.*" *GLQ: A Journal of Lesbian and Gay Studies* 1, 1: 1-16.
–. 1995. "Gosh, Boy George, You Must Be Awfully Secure in Your Masculinity!" In *Constructing Masculinity,* ed. Maurice Berger, Brian Wallis, and Simon Watson, 11-20. New York and London: Routledge.
Silverman, Kaja. 1993. "Masochism and Male Subjectivity." In *Male Trouble,* ed. Constance Penley and Sharon Willis, 33-64. Minneapolis: University of Minnesota Press.
Simpson, Mark. 1994. *Male Impersonators: Men Performing Masculinity.* New York and London: Routledge.
Skinner, Shelly. 1994. "The House in Order: Lesbian Identity and *The Well of Loneliness.*" *Women's Studies* 23, 1: 19-33.
Slack, Jennifer Daryl. 1996. "The Theory and Method of Articulation in Cultural Studies." In *Stuart Hall: Critical Dialogues in Cultural Studies,* ed. David Morley and Kuan-Hsing Chen, 112-27. London and New York: Routledge.
Smith-Rosenberg, Carroll. 1975. "The Female World of Love and Ritual: Relations between Women in Nineteenth Century America." *Signs* 1, 1: 1-30.

Souhami, Diana. 1998. *The Trials of Radclyffe Hall*. London: Weidenfeld and Nicolson.
Stallybrass, Peter, and Allon White. 1986. *The Politics and Poetics of Transgression*. Ithaca, NY: Cornell University Press.
Stam, Robert. 1989. *Subversive Pleasures: Bakhtin, Cultural Criticism, and Film*. Baltimore: Johns Hopkins University Press.
Stimpson, Catharine R. 1989. "Zero Degree Deviancy: The Lesbian Novel in English." In *Where the Meanings Are: Feminism and Cultural Spaces,* 97-100. New York and London: Routledge.
Stoler, Anne Laura. 1995. *Race and the Education of Desire: Foucault's History of Sexuality and the Colonial Order of Things*. Durham and London: Duke University Press.
Stowe, David W. 1996. "Uncoloured People: The Rise of Whiteness Studies." *Lingua Franca* September/October: 71-77.
Stryker, Susan. 1998. "The Transgender Issue: An Introduction." *GLQ: A Journal of Lesbian and Gay Studies* 4, 2: 145-58.
Studlar, Kevin S., and Gaylyn Sandler. 1999. "Introduction: The Seductive Waters of James Cameron's Film Phenomenon." In *Titanic: Anatomy of a Blockbuster*, ed. Kevin S. Studlar and Gaylyn Sandler, 1-13. New Jersey: Rutgers University Press.
Taste This (Anna Camilleri, Ivan E. Coyote, Zoë Eakle, Lyndell Montgomery). 1998. *Boys Like Her: Transfictions*. Vancouver: Press Gang Publishers.
Terry, Jennifer. 1991. "Theorizing Deviant Historiography." In *Differences: A Journal of Feminist Cultural Studies. Queer Theory: Lesbian and Gay Sexualities* (guest ed. Teresa de Lauretis) 3, 2: 55-74.
–. 1999. *An American Obsession: Science, Medicine, and Homosexuality in Modern Society*. Chicago: University of Chicago Press.
Thomas, Calvin. 1996. *Male Matters: Masculinity, Anxiety, and the Male Body on the Line*. Urbana and Chicago: University of Illinois Press.
Thompson, Raymond, with Kitty Sewell. 1995. *What Took You So Long? A Girl's Journey to Manhood*. London: Penguin.
Tremain, Rose. 1992. *Sacred Country*. London: Hodder and Stoughton.
Udovitch, Mim. 1999. "Breasts Reassessed." *Esquire* 131, 2: 82-9.
Ulrichs, Karl Heinrich. 1977 [1868]. *Raging Sword: The Riddle of Nature and of Uranian Love*, trans. Michael A. Lombardi. Los Angeles, CA: Urania Manuscripts.
Volcano, Del LaGrace. N.d. "Gender Terrorist." Unpublished manifesto. Available at <http://www.disgrace.dircon.co.uk/page1.html>.
Wagner, Gillian. 1979. *Barnardo*. London: Eyre and Spottiswoode Publishers.
–. 1982. *Children of the Empire*. London: Weidenfeld and Nicolson.
Weed, Elizabeth, ed. 1989. *Coming To Terms: Feminism, Theory, Politics*. New York: Routledge, Chapman and Hall.
Weeks, Jeffrey. 1981. *Sex, Politics and Society: The Regulation of Sexuality Since 1800*. London and New York: Longman.
Weeks, Jeffrey, and Sheila Rowbotham. 1977. *Socialism and the New Left: The Personal and Sexual Politics of Edward Carpenter and Havelock Ellis*. London: Pluto Press.
West, Cornel. 1993. *Race Matters*. Boston: Beacon Press.
Whitlock, Gillian. 1987. "Everything Is Out of Place: Radclyffe Hall and the Lesbian Literary Tradition." *Feminist Studies* 13, 3 (Fall): 555-82.
Woolf, Virginia. 1928. *A Room of One's Own*. London: Penguin Books.
–. 1942. *Orlando*. London: Hogarth Press.
Wray, Matt, and Annalee Newitz, eds. 1997. *White Trash: Race and Class in America*. New York and London: Routledge.
Žižek, Slavoj. 1994. "Courtly Love, or, Woman as Thing." In *The Metastases of Enjoyment: Six Essays on Woman and Causality*, 89-112. London: Verso.

Jurisprudence

People v. *Friede et al.* 21 February 1929. *Censorship Landmarks*. Edward de Grazia. New York: R.R. Bowkes Co., 1969. 78-9.

The Director of Public Prosecutions v. Jonathan Cape and Leopold Hill. 9 and 16 November 1928. All transcripts are part of the Henry Lovat Dickson Collection, National Archives of Canada, Ottawa.

Film and Video

Boys Don't Cry. [videorecording] Dir. Kimberly Peirce. Beverly Hills, CA: Twentieth Century Fox Home Entertainment, USA, 1999.

The Brandon Teena Story. [videorecording] Dir. Susan Muska and Greta Olafsdottir. New York: Zeitgeist Films, USA, 1998.

15 Minutes of Femme TV. [short film] Dir. Machiko Saito. USA, 1998.

The Life and Death of Teena Brandon. [videorecording] A & E American Justice. New York: A & E Television Networks, 1996.

OUTLAW. [videorecording] Dir. Alisa Lebow with Leslie Feinberg. USA, 1994.

PreMenstrual Spotting. [short film] Dir. Machiko Saito. USA, 1997.

Race: The Floating Signifier. [videorecording] By Stuart Hall. Dir. Sut Jhally. Northampton, MA: Media Education Foundation, 1996.

You Don't Know Dick: Courageous Hearts of Transsexual Men. [videorecording] Dir. Candace Schermerhorn, Bestor Cram. Berkeley, CA: University of California Extension, Center for Media and Independent Learning, USA, 1997.

Index